Prelude to the Enlightenment
French Literature, 1690-1740

The Sentimental Revolution: French Writers of 1690-1740
University of Washington Press, 1966

Illustration taken from the 1783 Hôtel Serpente edition of *Mémoires et aventures d'un homme de qualité* by Abbé Prévost.

Prelude to the Enlightenment

French Literature, 1690-1740

By Geoffroy Atkinson
and Abraham C. Keller

London
GEORGE ALLEN & UNWIN LTD
RUSKIN HOUSE • MUSEUM STREET

PRINTED IN GREAT BRITAIN
in 11pt Baskerville type
by Billing & Sons Limited
Guildford and London

Preface

THIS is the third volume of a study of the period from 1690 to 1740 in French history and literature. In the present volume, as in the two that preceded, numerous passages are quoted from documents written by members of the middle class, as well as by members of the petty nobility who had been reduced to poverty and disappointed by changing times. Many of those quoted were second-rate authors, and few had any intention of writing either history or literature.

The first volume, dealing with an aesthetic subject, was written in French and published in Europe.[1] Admiration for the beauties of natural scenery and the yearning for a simple and virtuous life far from crowded and sordid cities, if not altogether absent, had been rarely confessed in the works of French authors of the Classical age. They were, however, increasingly expressed after 1690. Though Jean-Jacques Rousseau's writings on these subjects far surpass in eloquence those of his predecessors, it is important to recognize that the works of these lesser authors constituted part of Rousseau's literary background and therefore represent one phase of the sentimental movement. From the scores of passages in the first volume of this study, it becomes clear that the genius of Jean-Jacques Rousseau did not invent the appreciation of nature in eighteenth-century French literature, in the sense that Alexander Graham Bell invented the telephone. Moreover, French readers would probably not have welcomed Rousseau's writings in the 1750s and 1760s without the preparation of the public during the preceding half century, often by mediocre writers. Those earlier writers, now justly forgotten by the general public, deserve some attention from those of us who try to appreciate the period of the Enlightenment in all its fullness and variety.[2]

[1] Geoffroy Atkinson, *Le Sentiment de la nature et le retour à la vie simple* (*1690–1740*), Société de Publications romanes et françaises, Vol. LXVI (Geneva: E. Droz; Paris: Librairie Minard, 1960).

[2] 'Il est dorénavant impossible d'affirmer que le dix-huitième siècle fut plus raisonnable en son début, plus sentimental en sa fin,' writes M. Roger Laufer

In a second volume,[3] written in English, certain far-reaching changes in the literature and life of France in the half century after 1690 were studied, as these appeared in some hundreds of periodicals, novels, plays, sermons, diaries, letters, and descriptions of other lands and peoples. Two 'new' features of the writing at this period were particularly striking in the passages cited in that second volume: (1) Heartfelt pity for contemporaries, for the poor, and for children, as well as self-pity, which had rarely been expressed by good French authors of the seventeenth century, was increasingly evident in writings after 1690; in the preceding period, writers who confessed their personal feelings were generally unwelcome on the literary scene. (2) Moral judgments by self-respecting commoners were more and more frequent after 1690. These writers, no longer ashamed of their opinions, sometimes openly objected to being looked down upon by noblemen who were their social 'betters' but who flouted the principles of middle-class morality.

There is little doubt that, during the period we are discussing, there was a significant growth in the reading public. As compared to the relative homogeneity of the preceding era (though that homogeneity has certainly been exaggerated), there was a wider and more varied public, with a greater diversity of tastes. Above all, we must not, because we are approaching the 'Enlightenment', picture millions of intellectual Frenchmen eagerly awaiting the writings of the men who – as we now know – were about to work changes in the course of history: the Voltaires, Montesquieus, and Diderots. Rather, the volume and variety of books published offer such obvious evidence of growing diversity that we have not deemed it necessary to assemble statistics (thus leaving the way open for some needy graduate student); and everything we learn about the social development of the time makes this broadening appear unmistakable. Middle-class

---

(*Style rococo, style des 'lumières'* [Paris: José Corti, 1963], p. 8), citing Atkinson's *Le sentiment de la nature.*

[3] Atkinson, *The Sentimental Revolution: French Writers of 1690–1740* (Seattle: University of Washington Press, 1965).

authors were writing, quite consciously, for the enjoyment of their fellow commoners, often with open or tacit disregard of the approved values of traditional aristocratic society.

It is a noteworthy feature of eighteenth-century French society that, in spite of a deeply established class system, intellectuals as a group straddled the classes. Not only were they, as individuals, at least as likely to come from peasant or working-class families as to be of noble birth, a fact which made them a heterogeneous and rather democratic group, but they experienced a degree of mobility and acceptance which was unique in the time. This acceptance may have been due to a desperate need which the ruling society felt for intellectuals,[4] or it may represent, more broadly, part of the collapse of the social system. The first alternative would attribute a certain amount of conscious and voluntary effort to the nobility; the second would make the process rather a historical necessity. In either case, the fact that the intellectuals were honoured without regard to their class origins must be likened to, and to a certain extent associated with, the eventual success of the bourgeoisie in penetrating the social structure, for of all the bourgeois the intellectuals were, with perhaps only the richest financiers, those who found acceptance by the aristocracy.[5]

Socially, the history of eighteenth-century France was very much taken up with the efforts of the middle classes to break down the barriers and restrictions which the monarchy and the nobility had erected against them. Some of these were tangible: one had to be a noble to attain high office in the Church or a commission in the army, for example; others were in the realm of attitude and public regard and were often more painful than actual exclusion, especially for men who had all the money they wanted or could use. But the long battle against the seventeenth-century attitude (as seen in

[4] 'They gained respect because they fulfilled a social need that had, perhaps, not been felt so acutely since the intellectual upheaval of the Renaissance period: a need for the clarification and reinterpretation of social values, and for concrete commentary on "social problems".' Elinor G. Barber, *The Bourgeoisie in 18th Century France* (Princeton, N.J.: Princeton University Press, 1955), pp. 130–31. (This is by far the most valuable study of the subject that I know of.)

[5] *Ibid.*, pp. 20–21.

the writings of La Bruyère and others) which considered the financial occupations demeaning showed important signs of being won by the middle of the eighteenth century – well before the Revolution itself, when the bourgeoisie displaced the nobility as the class whose values were to govern society. The bourgeoisie did not, of course, deliberately seek to make a social revolution; in many ways it was a conservative class, and it accepted the social pattern as a whole. But its interests demanded certain changes – and in large part the intellectual and social history of the eighteenth century, including much of the literature we have perused, reflects that need.

If we try to establish the identity of the 'middle class' or 'bourgeoisie', we shall have no easy time, unless we content ourselves with 'commoners', or, all who were not of the hereditary titled nobility. The upper limit of the bourgeoisie is fairly clear at the point of title, for, though even here some confusion arises from the fact that frequently in French history titles (and therefore nobility) could be bought, yet by and large a man with a title conferred by the monarch was a noble, whether that title was conferred last year for a price or handed down from time immemorial. The lower limits of the bourgeoisie were much more nebulous, the social status of a peasant or craftsman as against an independent merchant, and especially that of a man who started as the one and ended as the other, being open to question. Mobility, of course, was easier from the lower to the middle classes than from the middle to the upper, chiefly because status was not as crucial an issue; but within the mass of commoners hierarchy of many kinds existed, and we shall find snobbishness among commoners to be a not infrequent phenomenon.

The over-all campaign of the middle classes centred on raising the social status of trade, a campaign in which they were severely hampered by their own considerable acceptance of the aristocratic prejudices, in sharp contrast to the attitude of the bourgeois of England and America.[6] In this campaign,

___

[6] See *ibid.* pp. 62–65. Barber quotes Duclos to the effect that in France 'there are few rich people who at times do not feel humiliated at being considered nothing but wealthy' (*ibid.*, p. 57). Similarly, Lacroix: 'The royal decree, due to Colbert (1669), declaring trade and nobility to be compatible, had remained a dead letter. Nor had the edicts which authorized the nobles to take part in

literature played a major role, for the theatre and novels, written largely by middle-class authors for bourgeois audiences, helped significantly to establish everyday life and family problems of non-noble persons as worthy of attention, sympathy, and tears, and in the long run it became possible to affect the attitudes which governed the minds of men. In part because the regressive society of the age of Louis XIV ceased to hold together politically and economically, in part because the moral licence which characterized the last years of Louis XIV's reign and the period of the Regency naturally encouraged irreverent thoughts, there was a general receptiveness which militated in favour of new standards.[7]

Sentimental authors not only wrote about 'Love', but praised *doing good* as a virtue quite distinct from what had long been thought of as 'Christian charity'. Quarrels over matters of doctrine, which had raged in the seventeenth century among Jesuits, Jansenists, and Quietists, were gradually replaced after 1715 in the minds of many by the secular notion of benevolent action, not only as a social duty but as a personal pleasure. Thus, while the intellectual *philosophes* were tearing down traditional doctrines by logic and wit, sentimental authors appear to have reasserted the fundamental moral principles of the New Testament which had always been taught by parents to their children. That sentimental authors showed this positive attitude did not imply that they were necessarily more 'religious' than the *philosophes*; it did indicate the importance of pity in their emotions, and their lack of a

---

wholesale commerce without forfeiting their dignity been of any more effect. The magistracy looked down upon commerce even more than did the nobility, and those traders, who were ashamed of their calling, dubbed themselves financiers. . . . Nothing could eradicate this prejudice. . . . It was in vain that the economists and philosophers, who had so much influence over men's ideas and actions in the eighteenth century, recommended trade to the poorer classes of the nobility. . . . They made few converts.' Paul Lacroix, *France in the Eighteenth Centry : Its Institutions, Customs and Costumes* (1876) (New York: F. Ungar, 1963), pp. 224–25.

[7] One historian has it that 'public opinion first assumed a definite shape in France at the beginning of the eighteenth century', which, though perhaps a slightly overdramatic formulation, may not be far from the truth. See Louis Ducros, *French Society in the Eighteenth Century*, trans. W. de Geyer (London: G. Bell and Sons, 1926), p. 313.

fashionable appreciation of wit, when applied to what middle-class men thought to be serious subjects.

In this volume, as in the two which preceded, tendencies in the society of the period 1690–1740 will be examined, again primarily through contemporary writing. The quotations assembled will bear upon personal emotions, literary attitudes, and several aspects of the way in which men looked at the world around them. It is perhaps worth repeating our view that the quotations, and not our comments, are the meat of this book. It is through them that we can hope to learn how men felt and thought and how the world appeared to them.[8]

Professor Geoffroy Atkinson gathered the illustrative material for this volume before his death and prepared drafts for a Preface and Introduction, as well as tentative outlines and comments. Besides making considerable changes in these, I have (1) selected the quotations (those which I thought most interesting and illustrative) and translated and arranged them; (2) written most of the connective material and the Conclusion, for both of which – though I hope they remain faithful to the aims of Professor Atkinson – I assume full responsibility; (3) checked and completed bibliographical and textual details; and (4) prepared an Index covering both the quotations and the commentary, in order to make the book as usable as possible. These matters, which would have gone smoothly and fast in the golden hands of Geoffroy Atkinson, took long in mine.

I should add that, because of Atkinson's love of original editions, much of his work was with rare books available only in a few libraries. For the convenience of readers who might want to examine the quotations in context, I have transferred the references to modern editions where I knew such to exist.

In working on this book I found Professor Atkinson's views and approach congenial, as indeed I had in conversations with him generally during his lifetime. Obviously he, as well as any of our readers, might have chosen arrangements of the

[8] I am hopeful that the context provided for quotations from unknown or little-known authors will be sufficient for the reader. To have expanded the context greatly would have made this volume excessively bulky and would, in my judgment, have been contrary to Atkinson's conception of the work.

material different from mine, or handled the commentary differently. Beyond these considerations, however, I am convinced that the literature itself contains great interest and variety and even a certain fascination.

ABRAHAM C. KELLER
Tours, France
September, 1970

Contents

Introduction

THE fifty years from 1690 to 1740 are generally known to have led to the full flowering of what is called the Enlightenment in France, with Bayle, Fontenelle, Montesquieu, and Voltaire leading the attack upon tradition. Studies by Gustave Lanson, Daniel Mornet, Paul Hazard, René Pintard, and others have investigated that attack, and especially the development of rationalism, which was one of its principal ingredients. But there can be no doubt that, although some people were reading rationalistic arguments in the half century which concerns us here, many others were not greatly interested. It seems quite unlikely that those who sought relaxation in books were interested in rationalistic attacks upon tradition; lists of books for sale show fairy tales, accounts of travel, and mediocre sentimental novels in large number. Probably a majority of readers were not inclined by education or temperament to read books of a metaphysical, theological, or scientific character. In addition to those who enjoyed fairy tales and heart-rending novels of love or incredible adventure, considerable segments of the reading public were consuming witty poems, plays, and tales on subjects far from either the rationalistic or the deeply sentimental; the plays of Marivaux, which gave the word '*marivaudage*' to the French language, presented light-hearted and brilliant conversation on the subject of love. Within the traditional forms, classical tragedy was transformed at the hands of Voltaire, in whose plays, written in verse and more or less 'according to the rules', the pathetic took the place of the *tragic*, a concept which both he and the audiences of the 1730s had apparently ceased to understand. Moreover, the strict literary canons of the preceding classical period in literature had not extended to all genres. Concerning novels, especially, no rules had ever been formulated, and the great increase in the number of novels is one of the outstanding features of the early eighteenth century.

The famines of 1694, 1709, and 1725, the loss of one million in the population of the kingdom between 1685 and 1720, the

B

visible decline of French power in Europe, and serious inter-
ruptions of foreign trade made a deep impression, particularly
upon middle-class authors, a number of whom were already
living from hand to mouth. By the year 1740 not only had the
composition of the public in Paris changed; many earlier
judgments and attitudes had also changed considerably. On
the intellectual and rationalistic side, the activities of French
Protestants, whose periodicals in Holland had begun to be
published soon after 1685 and continued to be brought into
France in ever larger numbers, certainly had great influence
in France, as they did in England and Switzerland. On the
sentimental side, the plague that afflicted thousands in Mar-
seilles not long after the death of Louis XIV and the sealing
off of the South of France by military forces to stop the spread
of the terrifying disease, caused the circulation of many
pathetic reports of families divided without word of one
another. Events of another sort afflicted Frenchmen of all
groups and classes during the Regency: a dozen successive
devaluations of the currency within a few years and the
financial cataclysm of the failure of Law's Bank and the
Mississippi scheme upset many notions of long standing and
inflamed the passions even of solid citizens, as financial panics
and inflation have always done.

The psychological reactions of the public of eighteenth-
century France were, of course, quite varied, even within the
same social group. For instance, the Duc de Saint-Simon, a
particularly rugged reactionary, seems to have been annoyed
by the famine of 1694 only because he found it difficult to
supply his military command with fodder for horses. He took
no other notice of that catastrophe in his much-reprinted
Mémoires! On the other hand, at least one family of great
antiquity was directly afflicted. The grandson of that great
lady of French letters, Mme de Sévigné, underwent extreme
hardship and was persuaded by his parents in 1695 to marry
the daughter of a banker 'sprung from nothing', in order to
're-gild the escutcheon of his family'. It is easy to understand
that the psychological sequel was more than a little un-
satisfactory, to both the young nobleman and his wife.

Those critical of economic and political administration in

with favour by the authorities. But a comedy that appeared in 1709, just two years after Vauban's *Projet*, was welcomed by the public because it pilloried a servant who had become exceedingly rich thanks to his position as tax-farmer. *Turcaret*, by Lesage, is a bitter commentary upon the scandalous rise of rascally, low-born men of keen wits to positions of power and influence in society. The punishment of a character like Turcaret by other characters of the play was very different indeed from what the public of Molière had enjoyed forty years earlier, when attending *L'Avare*. Lesage's audience, and people who read the printed play, roundly hated men like Turcaret, whom they recognized on the street and whose power they feared, whereas the disapproval and laughter of Molière's audience had had a universal, not a topical, ring. Lesage was appealing to an angry passion of his contemporaries, not to the reasonable judgment of an audience that laughed at ridiculous exaggeration.

So far we have been dealing with rather well-known authors, and to some extent their works help us trace the social revolution which took place following the Golden Age of French letters. To those who know only the famous authors, it might seem that there was a sudden and jolting change from one period to the next. But this is not the case, as we shall observe in the chapters that follow. Indeed, such sudden changes have probably never occurred in literature. On the contrary, intellectual and social changes in a nation appear to be expressed slowly in the works of secondary authors whose attitudes are finally expressed with lasting art by those whom we know, centuries later, as 'great authors'.

In attempting to judge the emotions of a period in the past, there is, of course, great danger in supposing that people then felt as we would feel if we were suddenly thrust back into their environment. A great deal of fallacious criticism has been based on such subjective judgment – for example, the tearful romantic writing about such a poet as François Villon. The only sure defence against such errors lies in the reading of many contemporary documents that show how large numbers of people did in fact see and judge their own environment. Such extended reading obviously involves going through a great deal of second-rate prose and verse, much of which is distinctly less beautiful than it is revealing.

One of the most striking observations to be made in reading large quantities of second-rate works of 1690–1740 is that, as in the period from 1830 to 1850, and again in the twentieth century, there was a great increase in the vocabulary that was considered acceptable in works of imagination. Among the minor writers of the half century to be studied here, the limited vocabulary of the 'high writing' of the seventeenth century gives way to a much wider and freer use of language. Realism in the novel and in prose dramas is brought about largely by this means. Sentimental writing is also made more deeply emotional by the use of words describing common things, seen every day by the reader. And it is perhaps not mere accident that, during this same period, when middle-class preoccupations with money, weather, and the out-of-doors became important features of serious prose, scientific observation also entered significantly into literature. Some of our text will be concerned with these matters.

In concluding this introduction, it seems fitting to quote Mme de Staël. 'It seems to me,' she wrote, 'that the intellectual, moral and political factors that change the spirit of literature have not been sufficiently analysed.'[1] If this study can even slightly reduce the applicability of this statement to the period 1690–1740 in France, something will have been accomplished.

---

[1] *De la littérature*, **Discours** préliminaire.

PART I

The Emotional Revolution

CHAPTER I

Personal Emotions

LIKE any other substantial period in European history, the years from 1690 to 1740 contained many diverse movements and tendencies. A few of these pointed the way to the Enlightenment or to Romanticism, but most, as might be expected, led to dead ends and are of interest simply as characteristic of this period. No attempt will be made here to establish any unity of the literature and thought in these early decades of the eighteenth century, for such attempts often succeed only if ideas and emotions expressed by secondary writers are disregarded or minimized.

This book will, we hope, present a fair sampling of the literature of the time. Our period is not very exciting by the excellence of its literary output, for we are beyond the great writers of the Classical age and have not yet reached the major production of the eighteenth century, though we do embrace the young Voltaire and most of Prévost and Marivaux. Inevitably we will be most tempted by material that anticipates the famous books or movements of the eighteenth century, but to give the reader a picture of what was being published and read there will be a fair amount of the useless, or dead-end, stuff. Much of this second-rate literature is dull for a modern reader; there is, therefore, good practical reason for giving attention to the writings that can be associated with something significant in the future; a large dose of the merely representative material, low in both historical and aesthetic interest, could easily prove fatal to any but the most sturdy (or unbalanced) intellectual constitution.

SENSIBILITÉ

In the realm of personal emotions, there is no doubt that our period is marked, more than anything else, by the growth of *sensibilité*. To use a dictionary definition, *sensibilité* is the capacity of being moved to compassion, pity, or tenderness – a capacity that ought not to change, or grow, from one age to another. However, the social acceptability of being moved and the self-consciousness of the individual in the face of emotion, which have also come to be embraced in the meaning of *sensibilité*, are conditioned by society to a considerable extent, and here our period saw an immense growth. Overt expression of emotion, an awareness that it was proper and even necessary to react strongly, and indeed a certain pride in being emotionally stirred, are visible on every hand in the writings of this period and represent a real transformation in values. Men and women weep and faint so readily and are so attached to their show of feelings as a mark of their humanity that they can easily be mistaken for extreme romantics of the nineteenth century.

Native tradition offered the French writers of our period less than they could find abroad to exalt *sensibilité*. The expression of emotion tended, in seventeenth-century France, to be considered destructive, and though historians of French literature have often gone too far in making restraint character-istic of the literature of the age of Louis XIV, restraint may at least be said to have been more honorable than its opposite. Mme de Sévigné's frequent irrationality, as seen in the quota-tion to follow, was, like her whole tendency to abandon herself to emotion, not typical of the Classical age. This phase of eighteenth-century literature, therefore, was not a continuation of a dominant trend of the preceding period, but rather an intensification of what had been an undercurrent, an under-current that derived considerable momentum from literary influences from Italy and England and from new conditions in France. One of these conditions was undoubtedly the growing power and influence of men of the lower and middle classes who had become rich. The tastes of these men, and of their women, embraced sentimentality to a degree which would surely have been exceptional and unacceptable among the ruling groups of the Classical age.

The following quotations will give the reader some idea of

the role of *sensibilité* in the writings of our period. They are prefaced, as it were, by two seventeenth-century statements, and they include just enough to suggest the influence from both north and south, of which we will see more later.

Mme de Sévigné wrote to her daughter, on February 25, 1671: 'Good Lord, how I long to receive news of you and how very dear you are to me! It seems to me that I do injustice to my feelings, trying to explain them with words: it would be necessary to see how I feel toward you in my heart.'[1]

Saint-Evremond wrote as follows to the Maréchal de Grammont, in 1665: 'Ill fortune is not content to bring us mishaps: it makes us more sensitive to every kind of wound; and nature, which ought to resist it, is in collusion with it, lending us more tender feelings so as to suffer from the blows which it inflicts.'[2]

The general attitudes which were to dominate our period were well expressed by the Reverend Father Bernard Lamy in a book of 1676 which continued to be reissued and read for several decades: 'When we feel no passion, we are unable to act, and nothing shakes us from indifference but the jolt of some emotion. One may say that passions are the essence of the soul's action. . . .'[3]

Here was an ancient doctrine, repeated by the Church fathers since St Augustine, which none of the major authors of the late seventeenth century would have disputed. It was accepted alike by tragic poets, comic and satirical writers, Christian philosophers, and novelists like Mme de La Fayette and Fénelon. But in the early eighteenth century, with the

[1] 'Mon Dieu, que j'ai envie de savoir de vos nouvelles, et que vous m'êtes chère! Il me semble que je fais tort à mes sentiments de vouloir les expliquer avec des paroles : il faudroit voir ce qui se passe dans mon cœur sur votre sujet.' Mme de Sévigné, *Lettres* (3 vols; Paris : Gallimard-Pléiade, 1953–57), I, 208.

[2] 'La mauvaise fortune ne se contente pas de nous apporter des malheurs : elle nous rend plus délicats à être blessés de toutes choses ; et la nature, qui devrait lui résister, est d'intelligence avec elle, nous prêtant un sentiment plus tendre pour souffrir tous les maux qu'elle fait.' Charles de Saint-Evremond, 'Lettre à M. le Maréchal de Grammont' (1665), in *Œuvres* (7 vols ; London, 1725), III, 218.

[3] 'Pendant que nous sommes sans passions, nous sommes sans action, et rien ne nous fait sortir de l'indifference que le branle de quelque affection. On peut dire que les passions sont le ressort de l'ame. . . .' R.P. Bernard Lamy, 'Discours . . . de l'Art de Persuader', in *De l'Art de Parler* (Paris : André Pralard, 1676), p. 311.

increased dominance of women in society and a growing sentimentality, the statement that the passions were '*le ressort de l'âme*' (the spring-board of the soul) took on quite a different impact. The passions had been recognized and accepted, not regarded – or presented in literature – as the honour and glory of man. They had been exposed and attacked, and often ridiculed – all of them, including love. Now, though some satirical authors continued, like their predecessors, to subject all sorts of emotions to ridicule, others, focusing especially on love, presented an alluring, if not always a pleasant and happy, picture. The difference in attitude is perhaps the difference between a Phèdre created by Racine in 1677 and a Des Grieux created by Prévost in 1731. Though both are ravaged by love, no one, probably, would choose to change places with Phèdre, whereas many a man would put up with Des Grieux's sufferings in return for the rewards that were his.

Love was treated roughly only by some satirical or 'witty' writers in our period; for the most part the cutting analysis, which would need to be at the heart of their presentation, yielded to sentimentality. Nor was this due to any dearth of clever writers, but only to a shift of value and emphasis. Even so brilliant an author as Marivaux often allowed wit to yield to sentiment in his comedies. The same may be said of Voltaire, in the tragedy of *Zaïre*, and of many novels of the time. Love is treated as separate from the rest of the passions, placed in a sacred realm by a society which, in 1730, was far less Christian than the society of a half century earlier.

The conception of a fated love, all-powerful and ineluctable, points forward much more than it points back. Mme de Tencin points to Alfred de Musset, and more than one writer of both prose and poetry in this 'pre-romantic' period around 1730 expressed the ruling ideas of the 1830s, yielding nothing, in sentimentality and violence, to the Romantic writers of a century later. But let us listen now to a few of our authors for a notion of the place of sentiment and sentimentality in the literature of our period.

L'Abbé Prévost, best known as the author of *Manon Lescaut*, states in his periodical, *Pour et Contre*:

'Add the fact that in the realm of the emotions, there are

few nations which are as capable of them as they [the English]. Fathers and married couples are ardent, tender and loyal in England. In England tenderness of heart is the virtue of all classes, and that is what they express so well by the word *goodnatur'd*.'[4]

Prévost's note, after a story about an abandoned wife who dies, very melodramatically, of a broken heart:

'In English *broken heart*. This word literally translated means a heart broken. It is the ultimate effect of mortal sorrow. The English are more subject to this illness than other nationalities, because their strong imagination renders them more susceptible to a great passion.'[5]

'Note this well: true joy has the same symptoms as extreme sorrow. It excites tears, it prevents the use of the voice, it causes a delicious languor, it forces the soul to consider the cause of its emotions; as between two men, one overcome by joy, the other by sorrow, I do not know which would more willingly allow himself to be deprived of the feeling which he is enjoying.'[6]

The difference between recognizing the importance of emotion, as accepted in the Classical age, and wallowing in it, which was to become common in the eighteenth century, may be seen by comparing the first of the following statements

[4] 'Ajoutez que pour les sentimens, il y a peu de Nations qui en soient aussi capables qu'eux. Les Peres et les Epoux y sont tendres, ardens et fideles. En Angleterre la tendresse de cœur est la vertu de tous les états, et c'est ce qu'ils expriment si bien par le mot goodnatur'd.' Abbé Antoine-François Prévost, *Le Pour et Contre, Ouvrage périodique d'un goût nouveau* (20 vols; Paris: Didot, 1733-40), IV, No. 55 (1734), 227.

[5] 'En Anglois *broken heart*. Ce mot traduit litteralement, signifie *cœur brisé*. C'est le dernier effet d'une mortelle douleur. Les Anglois sont plus sujets à cette maladie que les autres Peuples, parce que leur imagination forte sert à les rendre plus sensibles à une grande passion.' *Ibid.*, I, No. 14 (1733), 234.

[6] 'Qu'on y fasse attention: une véritable joie a les mêmes symptômes qu'une excessive douleur. Elle excite des larmes, elle ôte l'usage de la voix, elle cause une délicieuse langueur, elle attache l'ame à considérer la cause de ses émotions, et de deux hommes transportés l'un de joie, et l'autre de douleur, je ne sais lequel souffriroit le plus volontiers qu'on lui arrachât le sentiment dont il jouit.' Prévost, *Le Philosophe anglais, ou Histoire de Monsieur Cleveland, fils naturel de Cromwell, écrite par lui-mesme,* liv. 4, in *Œuvres choisies de Prévost* (39 vols; Paris: Hôtel Serpente, 1783-85), V, 74.

with the rest, even the last of which, under the pretence of assuaging passion's pains, shows an obvious pleasure in indulging them.

'It is the emotions which do and which undo everything. If reason dominated the world, nothing would happen. It is said that pilots are most afraid of the still waters they cannot navigate, and that they wish wind, even at the risk of having storms. Feelings are in men the winds that are necessary to set everything in motion, even though they often cause tempests.'[7]

'I take pleasure in my suffering and find that it is sweet to suffer for the most lovable and most charming person in the world.'[8]

'How greatly a solitary life in places where one has seen the person one loves fortifies one's passion! Mine is of an order which nothing can express; each tree in this wood, each place where I spoke to you, increases it.'[9]

'The pains of the heart and of the spirit do not disappear of themselves; solitude nourishes them and their characteristics

[7] 'Ce sont les passions qui font et qui défont tout. Si la raison dominait sur la terre il ne s'y passerait rien. On dit que les pilotes craignent au dernier point ces mers pacifiques où l'on ne peut naviguer, et qu'ils veulent du vent au hasard d'avoir des tempêtes. Les passions sont chez les hommes des vents qui sont nécessaires pour mettre tout en mouvement, quoiqu'ils causent souvent des orages.' Bernard Le Bovier de Fontenelle, 'Hérostrate, Démétrios de Phalère', *Nouveaux Dialogues des Morts* (1683), ed. Donald Schier, University of North Carolina Studies in Romance Languages and Literatures, No. 55 (Chapel Hill: University of North Carolina Press, 1965), p. 111.

[8] 'Je me plais dans ma souffrance, et je trouve qu'il m'est doux d'endurer pour l'objet le plus aimable, et la personne la plus charmante du monde.' Anon., *Réponses du Chevalier de C. aux Lettres d'Amour d'une religieuse en Portugal*, in Anne Ferrand (?), *Lettres d'Amour d'une Religieuse portugaise . . . augmentees de plusieurs nouvelles lettres* . . . (The Hague: A. DeHondt, 1701), 1st letter, p. 100. Though the *Réponses* remain anonymous, we now know that the author of the *Lettres d'Amour d'une religieuse portugaise*, more properly called *Lettres portugaises*, was Gabriel-Joseph de Lavergne, Seigneur de Guilleragues. See Guilleragues, *Lettres portugaises, Valentins et autres œuvres* (1669), ed. F. Deloffre and J. Rougeot (Paris: Garnier Frères, 1962).

[9] 'Qu'une vie solitaire dans les lieux où l'on a vu ce qu'on aime est propre à fortifier une passion! La mienne est ici d'une ardeur que rien ne peut exprimer; chaque arbre dans ce bois, chaque lieu où je vous ai parlé l'augmente.' *Ibid.*, p. 217.

only impress themselves more deeply. When one is troubled by something, all one's thoughts, all one's inner movements concentrate upon it. It is a brazier which cannot be extinguished, because one continually feeds it. We need someone to confide in, and prudent friendship will always tell us who that should be. Sorrows seem to be assuaged, to be shared as one confides them to a loyal friend. . . . He wipes away our tears, reminding us that he has wept for similar reasons.'[10]

Almost a definition of *sensibilité* is provided us by Nivelle de La Chaussée, the famous writer of the tear-jerking *comédies larmoyantes*. In *Mélanide*, one of his most successful plays, we find the following eulogy of emotionalism, beginning with perhaps a conscious alteration of the Cartesian *cogito ergo sum*.

'The more deeply I feel, the more I feel that I am.
Evenness of temperament comes from indifference
And whatever you may say in its defence,
Insensitivity cannot be considered beneficial.
What! Never to be moved, to be affected by nothing,
To remain throughout one's life at the same emotional level,

.   .   .   .

To have but one sentiment, but one uniform pleasure,
To be always oneself? Can one resist?
Is that living? No. It is scarcely to exist.'[11]

Perhaps more striking than any single passage is the case of

[10] 'Les peines de cœur et d'esprit ne se dissipent point d'elles-mêmes ; la solitude les nourrit ; leurs traits ne font que s'y graver plus profondément. Est-on saisi d'un objet affligeant, toutes les pensées, tous les mouvements intérieurs se rapportent là. C'est un brasier qui ne peut s'éteindre, parce que sans cesse on l'entretient. Alors il nous faut des confidents ; l'amitié bien placée nous les indique, et ne nous trompe jamais. Les peines semblent s'adoucir, et se partager, à mesure qu'on les dépose dans le sein d'un ami, en qui l'on a confiance. . . . Il essuye nos larmes, en nous rappelant celles qu'en des cas pareils il a versées lui-même.' A. Pecquet, *Pensées diverses sur l'homme* (Paris : Nyon fils, 1738), p. 271.

[11] 'Plus je sens vivement, plus je sens que je suis./L'égalité d'humeur vient de l'indifférence ;/Et quoi que vous puissiez dire pour sa défense,/L'insensibilité ne sauroit être un bien./Quoi! jamais n'être ému, n'être affecté de rien ;/Rester au même point tout le temps de sa vie,/. . ./N'avoir qu'un sentiment, qu'un plaisir uniforme ;/Etre toujours soi-même? Y peut-on résister?/Est-ce là vivre? Non. C'est à peine exister.' Nivelle de la Chaussée, *Mélanide* I, iv, speech of Darviane, in *Répertoire général du théâtre français* (Paris : Veuve Dabo, 1822), Vol. IX.

Les Mémoires du Comte de Comminge (1735), by Mme de Tencin. Here was a novel in which religion, love, and death were mingled in a manner that would have been outlawed by the canons of propriety in the classic age. Above all, no high-born lady of the time of Louis XIV would have dared record – and in the first person – the violence of her emotional life and the struggles of her tortured soul, all in detail and all dripping with sentiment. As an exemplification of the idea of writing with the aim of provoking tears, it is as convincing in the field of the novel as La Chaussée's plays were in the drama. The excellent reception it had is indicative of public taste, and in turn Mme de Tencin's social status, her superior intellect, and her excellent style made her book very influential on other writers.

From Italy came, among other influences, that of Metastasio, whose drama presented a combination of watered-down Cornelian heroics and an extreme of self-conscious indulgence in sentiment. His *Artaserse* (1730), not unlike others of his works, is filled with 'mutual signs exchanged', 'tenderness', 'first fond looks', 'sighs of love', and 'inward pangs'. In the following conversation, the three principals vie for the distinction of suffering most, a trademark of the period. The Italian audiences which cheered Metastasio were not, it appears, far different from the French which acclaimed La Chaussée as a great dramatist. If Metastasio had more to draw on in Italian literature than La Chaussée had in French, if Sannazaro's adolescent shepherdesses gave him more inspiration than La Chaussée could find in Racine's grown-up heroines, France was to show that it could equal and even surpass her neighbour to the south in sentimentality once she took to that road.

'*Semira*:   Remember . . .
Mandane: . . . rigor is the throne's support.
Semira: . . . reflect that mercy is its base.
Mandane: O let the sorrows of a wretched daughter
                   Excite your indignation !
Semira: Let the tears
                   Of an afflicted sister calm your anger.

.   .   .   .

Artaxerxes: Rise – O Heaven! –
Rise both: how are your pains surpassed by mine!
Semira fears the rigor of my justice,
Mandane fears my mercy. Artaxerxes,
At once a friend and son, feels both your pangs,
And trembles with Mandane and Semira.'[12]

Did our French writers take this brand of sentimentality seriously? Some, as we might expect, did, entirely; but others were not beyond laughing at it (and at themselves). Robert Chasles, the author of the widely-read *Illustres Françoises*, was in the first camp. Here is his hero, Des Ronais, telling of his return to his beloved, after a particularly lachrymose letter from her:

'You cannot imagine the tenderness of the embraces which we gave each other, embraces so ardently awaited by both of us. We both wept for joy, I overcome with emotion at her feet and she scarcely less enraptured than I. At last we recovered our senses again and I resolved to make a final effort to marry her at all costs.'[13]

And here he is, after his unsuccessful conversation with the girl's father, a conversation filled with *'fureur'* and *'idolâtrie'*:

'Indeed I went out and joined her. I found her in tears; I needed consolation, but her sorrow touched me more than my own. We spoke to each other with spontaneity, resolving to

---

[12] Semira: Rammenta . . ./Mandane: . . . che sostegno del trono/Solo è il rigor./Semira:... che la clemenza è base./Mandane: D'una misera figlia/Deh! t'irriti il dolor./Semira: Ti plachi il pianto/D'un afflitta germana./.../Artaserse: Sorgete, oh Dio! sorgete. Il vostro affano/Quanto è minor del mio! Teme Semira/ Il mio rigor; Mandane/Teme la mia clemenza: e amico e figlio/Artaserse sospira/ Nel timor di Mandane e di Semira.' Pietro Metastasio, *Artaserse*, II.ix, in *Opere*, ed. Fausto Nicolini (3 vols; Bari: Gius. Laterza & Figli, 1912–14), II, 132.

[13] 'Vous ne scauriez concevoir la tendresse des embrassemens qu'elle et moi nous donnâmes à ce retour, si ardemment attendu des deux côtés. Nous pleurâmes de joye l'un et l'autre: je restai presque sans sentiment à ses pieds, et je m'aperçus qu'elle n'étoit guère mieux que moi. Nous reprîmes bientôt nos sens, et enfin je résolus de faire un dernier effort, pour l'épouser à quelque prix que ce fût.' Robert Chasles, *Les Illustres Françoises, histoires véritables* (1713), ed. F. Deloffre (2 vols; Paris: Société d'édition 'Les belles lettres', 1959), I, 32.

C

love each other eternally, in spite of the obstacles which her father put in our way.'[14]

It seems likely that Chasles, whose work went through many editions, was read by Marivaux and Prévost and had some influence on them. But as writers Marivaux and Prévost were far superior, and Marivaux at least had a sense of humour about this sentimental literature. In his 'Entre le Zist et le Zest', in *L'Indigent philosophe* (1728), the gay drunkard who tells his life story refers to the literature of the time in terms that must have delighted at least some readers:

'. . . she loved me in earnest, but with a story-book love, a love accompanied by endless sighs, sweet nothings, and endless sentimental languor. We talked of nothing but the sublime value of loving tenderly. I think, to tell the truth, that that sort of thing is lovely if it appeals to you, but I did not find that kind of loveliness very appealing; her tender spirituality made me yawn. It seemed to me that she spent all her time admiring the delicacy of the sentiments she felt. I believe that my lack of gratitude amused her, for that was how she described my lack of attention and tenderness . . . her heart delighted in her reproaches. All this would have touched my soul, if I had been able to understand any of it. Ah! fine feelings! That was all she offered me. All I had to feast upon was this heart-stuff, and that was it.'[15]

[14] 'Je sortis effectivement et vins la rejoindre. Je la trouvai toute en larmes, j'avois besoin d'être consolé, mais sa douleur me toucha plus que la mienne. Nous nous dîmes l'un à l'autre tout ce qui nous vint à la bouche, et nous ne conclûmes rien, que de nous aimer éternellement, malgré les traverses que son Père nous suscitoit.' *Ibid.*, p. 38.

[15] '. . . elle m'aima tout de bon, mais d'un amour de roman, de cet amour qui fait soupirer, qui a des délicatesses à n'en plus finir, des langueurs de sentiment à perte de vue . . . nous ne traitions que de cela ensemble, et du mérite sublime qu'il y a d'aimer bien tendrement. Je crois, en effet, que cela est beau, quand on veut s'en entêter; mais moi, je ne trouvais point de prise à ce genre de beau; sa tendre spiritualité me faisait bâiller. Il me semblait qu'elle passait tout son temps à admirer la finesse des choses qu'elle sentait. Je crois que mon ingratitude l'amusait; car c'est ainsi qu'elle appelait mon défaut d'attention et de délicatesse . . . son cœur se délectait dans les reproches qu'elle me faisait. Cela m'aurait pénétré l'âme, si j'avais pu y entendre quelque chose. Ah! les admirables sentiments! mais je n'en eus que cela; il ne tint qu'à mon cœur de faire bonne chère, et voilà tout.' Pierre Carlet de Chamblain de Marivaux, 'Entre le Zist et le Zest', *L'Indigent Philosophe*, in *Romans* (Paris: Gallimard-Pléiade, 1949), p. 989.

FAINTINGS AND TEARS

If now we examine the literature of our period for serious applications of the belief in *sensibilité*, we shall find – as we shall later also in our study of confessions – that the purest representative, as well as one of the most prolific of them all, was l'Abbé Prévost. Known to English readers almost exclusively as the author of *Manon Lescaut* (1731), Prévost also wrote the *Memoirs and Adventures of a Gentleman* (1728–31), of which *Manon Lescaut* is the seventh volume, *The English Philosopher*, or *The History of Mr Cleveland, Natural Son of Cromwell* (1731–34), *The Dean of Killerine* (1735–40), and *The Story of a Modern Greek Lady* (1740), as well as histories both ancient and modern, and a gazette, *Le Pour et Contre* (1733–40). In the course of his restless career, embracing army, church, and the world of gallantry, Prévost spent long stretches in England, with whose history and literature he became well acquainted. He published French translations of works of Dryden, Richardson, and others, and is one of the figures responsible for both the growing interest in English literature and the development of French romantic prose.

Prévost liked to claim that he was guided by reason as well as by emotion in his voluminous outpouring of sentimentality and that his writings would be (as indeed they were, at the time) very widely acceptable. 'Those with sensitive hearts,' he wrote, 'those with reasonable minds – in a word, all those who, without following a rigid philosophy, have a taste for virtue, wisdom, and truth – will find some pleasure in reading this work [the *Memoirs and Adventures of a Gentleman*]. It is for them alone that I write.'[16] Whether the claim is just may be readily judged from a few representative quotations, without, mercifully, a reading of volume after volume.

A key to the fever of Prévost's sentimental writings lies in what was, at bottom, his low regard for the place of passion in man's life. It is ironic that this leading exponent of *sensibilité*

---

[16] 'Les cœurs sensibles, les esprits raisonnables, tous ceux, en un mot, qui sans suivre une philosophie trop sévère, ont du goût pour la vertu, la sagesse et la vérité, pourront trouver quelque plaisir dans la lecture de cet ouvrage. C'est pour eux seulement que j'écris.' Prévost, *Mémoires et aventures d'un homme de qualité qui s'est reitiré du monde*, liv. 6, in *Œuvres*, I, 330.

did not really – like Racine, for example, or the purer of the
Romantics later – consider passion as an overriding, inevitable
force. Rather, there are indications, both in his discussions
and in his fiction, that he did not look upon the emotions as
self-generating and self-propelling, and that he considered
constant stimulation necessary to maintain them at the high
level required for effective fiction. In the weeping and swooning
of which we shall presently see a sampling, there is a strong
admixture of systematic self-pity and an almost conscious
determination to give way to sentiment. Prévost seemed to
know that, without these elements applied both to himself and
to his characters, there might be little basis for his passionate
prose.

By no means contradictory to this assertion, but rather
serving as a philosophical rationalization of his novels, is
Prévost's theory that the show of sentiment is a mark of
nobility. In deference to tradition, his characters often attempt
restraint, or even feel a little ashamed of their tears; but under
the steady guidance of their creator they are invariably
overcome, and the result is the more convincing for the
prior resistance and hesitation.

The following passages will, it is hoped, present a fair
picture of *sensibilité* as Prévost practised it and as he believed
in it. After a few passages of a general and introductory
nature, we shall move to faintings and tears, two of the pillars
of the sentimental structure.

' "Alas! my dear brother," Patrice said to me, "piety
makes you too calm, and your mind is too far above the
weaknesses of love for you to imagine how cruel and crushing
this news is to me. . . . You do not know that the sovereign
good of the lover is the presence of the one he loves. You do
not know that there is no rest for a heart removed from the
object that gives it life and breath; without that necessary
solace, life is languor; boredom, poison; and impatience is
martyrdom. . . ." ' [17]

[17] 'Helas! mon cher frère, la piété vous rend trop tranquille, et votre esprit
est trop supérieur aux foiblesses de l'amour, pour concevoir tout ce qu'il y avoit
de cruel et d'accablant pour moi dans cette nouvelle . . . vous ne savez pas que
le souverain bien d'un amant est la présence de ce qu'il aime. Vous ignorez qu'il

'We are all constituted this way; our hearts being incapable of an infinite feeling, it is certain that an emotion which daily diminishes in one respect or another moves toward termination, and that it will soon be extinguished completely.'[18]

'The separation of a few months could only increase the delight of meeting again. Such is our nature that we sometimes need this protection against the cooling of love. . . . The wellspring of love will never die in a heart by nature tender and constant; but the familiarity with the one we love and constantly seeing each other threaten sooner or later to lessen love's power.'[19]

'Upon rereading his letter, I was struck by the turn which his justification took; and I saw that strong emotion, in a violent man, can carry him to excesses which reason condemns but does not have the power to control. If his honour is great enough to struggle against them and to repress at least some of their effects, this mitigation of the evil speaks well of his character and perhaps shows that he deserves more pity than scorn and hatred.'[20]

---

n'y a point de repos pour un cœur loin de l'objet dans lequel il vit et respire; que . . . sans un soulagement si nécessaire, la vie est une langueur; l'ennui un poison; l'impatience un martyr. . . .' Prévost, *Le doyen de Killerine,* liv. 2, in *Œuvres,* VIII, 219–20.

[18] 'Nous sommes tous faits de cette manière; notre cœur n'étant point capable d'un sentiment infini, il est certain qu'une passion, qui diminue tous les jours dans quelqu'une de ses parties, tend à sa fin, et qu'elle s'éteint bientôt tout-à-fait.' Prévost, *Mém. d'un homme de qualité,* liv. 9, in *Œuvres,* II, 111.

[19] 'Quelques mois d'absence ne pouvoient servir qu'à nous faire éprouver de nouvelles douceurs à nous revoir. Faits comme nous sommes, nous avons besoin quelquefois de ce préservatif contre le refroidissement de l'amour. . . . Le fond des sentimens ne s'éteint jamais dans un cœur naturellement tendre et constant; mais la familiarité avec ce qu'on aime, et l'habitude continuelle de se voir, fait perdre tôt ou tard à l'amour quelque chose de sa vivacité.' Prévost, *Cleveland,* liv. 5, in *Œuvres,* V, 318–19.

[20] 'En relisant sa lettre, je fus touché du tour qu'il donnoit à sa justification; et je conçus qu'en effet, une passion ardente dans un homme violent, peut le porter à bien des excès que sa raison condamne sans avoir la force de les arrêter. Si son honneur en conserve assez pour le combattre et pour en réprimer du moins certains effets, c'est une modération dans le mal, qui doit faire juger favorablement de son caractère, et qui lui fait peut-être mériter plus de pitié que de mépris et d'aversion.' Prévost, *Killerine,* liv. 6, in *Œuvres,* IX, 111.

The following faintings give a taste only. They could be multiplied many times over in the works of Prévost.

'But this unfortunate girl, frightened by the murder of her father and by her own danger, fell into a swoon so deep that, despairing of awakening her, they hastened to flee.'[21]

'We were no sooner around him, than he fell unconscious at our feet. Help being near, it did not take long to revive him.'[22]

'Rose fell swooning with joy and astonishment. I confess that, because of the surprise which overcame me, I was utterly confused for a few moments.'[23]

'Merely the telling of the peril which she had just escaped caused her to fall into such a deep swoon that we feared for her life.'[24]

'I remained alone with my sad traveling-companion, who soon justified my fears by falling into a deep swoon.'[25]

'I saw . . . Mademoiselle de L—— lying on the ground without any sign of consciousness.'[26]

'My sister-in-law had resisted the tumults which I have

[21] 'Mais cette malheureuse fille épouvantée du meurtre de son père et de son propre péril, tomba dans un évanouissement si profond que désespérant de lui faire rappeler ses esprits, ils se hâtèrent de fuir.' *Ibid.*, liv. 3, in *Œuvres*, VIII, 246.

[22] '. . . nous ne fûmes pas plutôt autour de lui, qu'il tomba à nos pieds sans connoissance et sans sentiment.
'Les secours n'étant point éloignés, on ne fut pas longtems à lui faire rappeler ses esprits.' *Ibid.*, p. 304.

[23] 'Rose tomba évanouie de joie et d'étonnement. J'avoue que dans la surprise que je ressentis moi-même, tous mes esprits furent quelques momens dans la dernière confusion.' *Ibid.*, liv. 5, in *Œuvres*, IX, 21.

[24] 'La seule relation du péril qu'elle venoit d'éviter la fit tomber dans un évanouissement si profond, qu'il nous fit craindre quelque chose pour sa vie.' *Ibid.*, pp. 39–40.

[25] 'Je demeurai seul avec la triste compagne de mon voyage, qui justifia aussitôt mes craintes en tombant dans un profond évanouissement.' *Ibid.*, liv. 6, in *Œuvres*, IX, 188.

[26] 'Je vis . . . mademoiselle de L—— étendue sans aucun signe de connoissance.' *Ibid.*, pp. 202–3.

described; but this new treachery overcame her steadiness. She fell in a swoon upon her chair.'[27]

'As nothing had ever happened to me which had caused me the slightest disturbance, and as I had always seen my mother as controlled as myself, her tears, the confused manner in which she had begun to speak, and the word father which I had never heard spoken, made such a great impression on me that I fell unconscious. . . . When she had finished, I found myself in a sort of delirium which prevented me for some time from being aware of what was happening around me.'[28]

The last passage, besides its fainting interest, indicates what seems to have been a preoccupation of Prévost with a 'mother figure', the idea of a benevolent and protecting mother watching over the young man surrounded by danger. The similarity to the case of Rousseau, who probably read *Cleveland* at the time that he was being 'cared for' by Mme de Warens, will impress itself on readers of the *Confessions*.

'It was then that, feeling more than ever that I was lost, betrayed, scorned by Milord Axminster, and abandoned by Fanny, I fell without strength and feeling at the feet of Madame Lallin.'[29]

'In a moment, the cruel stirrings which were breaking my heart reached my brain: I felt that my reason was being obscured suddenly. . . . Indeed, I fell . . . all feeling and consciousness gone.'[30]

[27] 'Ma belle-sœur avoit résisté aux agitations que j'ai dépeintes; mais cette nouvelle trahison surmonta sa constance. Elle tomba, évanouie sur sa chaise.' *Ibid.*, liv. 7, in *Œuvres*, IX, 299.

[28] 'Comme il ne m'étoit jamais rien arrivé qui m'eût causé le moindre trouble, et que j'avois toujours vu ma mère aussi tranquille que moi, ses larmes, le désordre avec lequel elle avoit commencé à parler, et le nom de père, que je n'avois jamais entendu prononcer, firent sur moi une si forte impression, que je tombai sans connoissance. . . . Je me trouvai, lorsqu'elle [ma mère] eut fini, dans une espèce de transport qui m'empêcha durant quelque temps d'être attentif à ce qui se passoit auprès de moi.' Prévost, *Cleveland*, liv. 1, in *Œuvres*, IV, 12–13.

[29] 'Ce fut alors que sentant mieux que jamais que j'étois perdu, trahi, méprisé de milord Axminster, abandonné de Fanny, je tombai sans force et sans sentiment aux pieds de madame Lallin.' *Ibid.*, liv. 3, in *Œuvres*, IV, 249–50.

[30] 'Les mouvemens cruels qui me déchiroient le cœur, se communiquèrent en un moment au cerveau ; je sentis que ma raison s'obscurcissoit tout d'un coup. . . .

We may now examine Prévost's theory and practice of tears. The elements of self-pity and autostimulation will be visible in these excerpts, as generally in Prévost's novels. Moreover, tears are seen to come from pleasure as well as from grief, as Metastasio pointed out for the writers of our period (*Artaserse*, II, xii), and in both cases the tears are in turn a source of pleasure.

'These signs of tenderness . . . do honour to your character. A cruel, unyielding heart does not feel sweetness in weeping. Tears, shed in taste and moderation, are proof of a sensitive and generous character; they never dishonour.'[31]

'Everyone struck by ill fortune knows all too well that the gentle consolation of a great sorrow is to have the freedom to complain and to appear afflicted. The heart of an unhappy person dotes upon its sorrow as that of a happy man is preoccupied with its good fortune. If silence and solitude are agreeable in adversity, it is because one welcomes them and feels the sweetness of constant grief.'[32]

'The tragic event which I am about to relate needs no introduction or embellishment to move the refined reader who feels no shame in being a man; that is, one sensitive to the impulses of a just compassion.'[33]

'On the very first day [after being rejected by her husband],

---

En effet, je tombai . . . sans le moindre reste de sentiment et de connoissance.' *Ibid.*, liv. 5, in *Œuvres*, V, 363.

[31] '. . . ces marques de tendresse . . . font honneur à votre bon naturel. Les cœurs durs et cruels ne sentent point de douceur à pleurer. Des larmes, répandues avec bienséance et avec modération, sont la preuve d'un caractère sensible et genereux; elles ne déshonorent jamais.' Prévost, *Mém. d'un homme de qualité*, liv. 12, in *Œuvres*, II, 414.

[32] '. . . tous les infortunés savent trop bien que la plus douce consolation d'une grande douleur, est d'avoir la liberté de se plaindre et de paroître affligé. Le cœur d'un malheureux est idolâtre de sa tristesse, autant qu'un cœur heureux et satisfait, l'est de ses plaisirs. Si le silence et la solitude sont agréables dans l'affliction, c'est qu'on s'y recueille en quelque sorte au milieu de ses peines, et qu'on y a la douceur de gémir sans être interrompu.' Prévost, *Cleveland*, liv. 1, in *Œuvres*, IV, 3.

[33] 'L'événement tragique que je suis au moment de raconter, n'a besoin ni de préparations, ni d'ornemens pour émouvoir un lecteur qui n'est pas né barbare, et qui n'a point honte d'être homme, c'est-à-dire, sensible aux mouvemens d'une juste compassion.' *Ibid.*, liv. 5, in *Œuvres*, V, 210.

she shut herself in her apartment, no longer admitting anyone.
Her servants scarcely dared approach her to serve her. She
spent entire days without food. She wept incessantly.'³⁴

'On both sides of the table were two small round tables
which supported the lamps which were to light this mournful
place constantly. . . . Such was the arrangement in this sort
of tomb in which I had resolved to bury myself alive.

'If tears and sighs cannot be called pleasures, it is nonetheless
true that they have infinite sweetness for the mortally afflicted
person. All of the moments which I devoted to my sorrow
were so dear to me that in order to prolong them I scarcely
slept at all. Two months passed without my thinking of
throwing myself on my bed.'³⁵

'. . . the memory of that dear mother touched me so much
that my eyes filled with tears. I interrupted my story in order
to wipe the tears from my eyes and, looking at the captain, I
was astonished to see that while looking closely at me, he too
was weeping.'³⁶

'I saw nothing clearly, and in the confusion of so many
painful sensations my eyes had already poured forth a stream
of tears before I began to feel them.'³⁷

---

³⁴ 'Dès le premier jour elle se renferma dans son appartement, où elle n'admit
plus personne. A peine ses femmes osoient-elles s'en approcher pour la servir.
Elle passoit des jours entiers sans nourriture. Elle pleuroit sans cesse.' Prévost,
Killerine, liv. 6, in *Œuvres*, IX, 133.

³⁵ 'Aux deux côtés de la table étoient deux guéridons qui soutenoient les flam-
beaux, dont ce triste lieu devoit être sans cesse éclairé. . . . Telle étoit la disposition
de cette espèce de tombeau, dans lequel j'avois résolu de m'ensevelir tout vivant.
'Si les pleurs et les soupirs ne peuvent porter le nom de plaisirs, il est vrai néanmoins qu'ils ont une douceur infinie pour une personne mortellement affligée.
Tous les moments que je donnois à ma douleur, m'étoient si chers, que pour les
prolonger je ne prenois presque aucun sommeil. Deux mois se passèrent, sans
que je pensasse même à me jeter sur mon lit.' Prévost, *Mém. d'un homme de qualité*,
liv. 5, in *Œuvres*, I, 264.

³⁶ '. . . le souvenir de cette chère mère acheva tellement de m'attendrir, que
mes yeux se couvrirent de pleurs. J'interrompis mon récit pour les essuyer, et,
les levant ensuite sur le capitaine, je fus étonné d'appercevoir qu'en me regardant
attentivement, il en versoit aussi.' Prévost, *Cleveland*, liv. 3, in *Œuvres*, IV, 269–70.

³⁷ 'Je ne me représentois rien distinctement; et dans la confusion de tant de
sensations douloureuses, mes yeux avoient déjà versé un ruisseau de larmes, que
je n'avois pas encore commencé à les sentir couler.' Prévost, *Killerine*, liv. 3, in
Œuvres, VIII, 287.

'My heart was simultaneously beset by tenderness and rage, torn by the one and stirred by the other, so that I wept a stream of tears each time I embraced my dear friends. I could not find words sufficient to express these two emotions; anger prevented my affection from manifesting itself, while my affection seemed to stop the expression of my rage.'[38]

'The feeling of sorrow which accompanied these words was so profound and so bitter that I felt tears flow from my eyes. I was ashamed of them and promptly wiped them away. Madame was touched, for the natural expression of violent grief is seldom witnessed without emotion; I even saw a few tears moisten her eyes.'[39]

'Tears fell from my eyes in spite of myself upon seeing so many objects either sad or sweet, but all infinitely touching; and I could not distinguish in particular by which sentiment I was moved the more.'[40]

It would be tedious to quote widely from the literature to show how highly esteemed faintings and tears were in our period, or how avidly the writers sought this kind of expression. The obscure Du Castre d'Auvigny spoke for many when he said: 'We are so strongly attracted to sadness that we complain of our fate at the slightest provocation.'[41] But tears, as we shall see, were not necessarily associated with sadness; the point was

[38] 'Mon cœur étoit en proie tout à la fois à la tendresse et à la fureur, déchiré par l'une et touché par l'autre jusqu'à verser un ruisseau de larmes, en recommençant mille fois d'embrasser mes chers amis. Je ne trouvois point de paroles qui pussent suffire à ces deux transports, la fureur empêchoit ma tendresse de s'exprimer, et ma tendresse sembloit arrêter toutes les expressions de ma fureur.' Prévost, *Cleveland*, liv. 3, in *Œuvres*, IV, 457–58.

[39] 'Le sentiment de douleur qui accompagna ces paroles fut si vif et si amer, que je sentis couler des pleurs de mes yeux. J'en eus honte, et je les essuyai promptement. Madame en fut touchée; car les expressions naturelles d'une violente affliction, ne s'entendent guères sans émotion: je vis même quelques larmes s'avancer au bord de ses paupières.' *Ibid.*, liv. 6, in *Œuvres*, V, 498.

[40] 'Les larmes me tomboient des yeux malgré moi, à la vue de tant d'objets ou tristes, ou tendres, mais tous infiniment touchants; et je ne pouvois distinguer en particulier par quel sentiment j'étois le plus attendri.' Prévost, *Mém. d'un homme de qualité*, liv. 8, in *Œuvres*, II, 63.

[41] 'Nous avons tant d'inclination de nous chagriner, que les moindres choses amènent des reproches contre le sort.' Jean du Castre d'Auvigny, *Mémoires du Comte de Comminville* (Paris: Josse, 1735), p. 40.

to weep. Several quotations from Marivaux and Defoe, two of the most perceptive writers of the time, will give an idea of the importance of *sensibilité*; the sharpness of analysis which we find in them was not often equalled.

Defoe and his principal characters were always aware of their reactions and saw to it that responses were in line with the prevailing mode. The Romantic poets of the nineteenth century can scarcely be said to have observed their emotional crises in more detail than Robinson Crusoe or to have appreciated the relationship of tears to joy and sorrow more than Colonel Jack:

'He spoke this with so much Affection, that his Face was ever smiling when he talked of it, and yet his Eyes had Tears standing in them, at the same Time, and all the Time; for he had a delightful Sorrow, if that be a proper Expression in speaking of it.'[42]

'This is the delightful Sorrow, says he, I spoke of just now; and this makes Smiles sit on my Face, while Tears run from my Eyes, a Joy that I cannot otherwise express, than by telling you, Sir, that I never liv'd a happy Day since I came to an Age of acting in the World, till I landed in this Country, and work'd in your Plantation, naked and hungry.'[43]

Marivaux, as we have seen already, is rather distinctive by virtue of his light touch. Although his characters behave in the standard pre-Enlightenment manner, Marivaux's intelligence, good taste, and sense of humour created a wide gulf between them and the Romantics of the next century. The following paragraph from *La Vie de Marianne* (1731) emphasizes the contagion of tears and is, at the same time, typical of Marivaux's engaging novelistic style.

'. . . I said so much more, that I wore myself out; only tears were left me, and never has anyone shed them so abundantly. The good woman, seeing this, also began to weep from the bottom of her heart.

[42] Daniel Defoe, *The History of Colonel Jack* (1721), Vols V–VI of *The Shakespeare Head Edition of the Novels and Selected Writings of Daniel Defoe* (Oxford: Basil Blackwell, 1927), V, 198.
[43] *Ibid.*, p. 200.

'Thereupon Toinon entered to tell us that dinner was ready: and Toinon, who was a great conformist, wept, because we were weeping. For my part, after all these tears, and being soothed by the kindnesses that they both showed me, I calmed myself, felt consoled, and forgot the whole thing.'[44]

THE USES OF CONFESSION

The emotional revolution of the period which we are studying is nowhere seen more clearly than in the growing propensity to 'confess'. While everyone is acquainted with the acme of eighteenth-century confessions, those of Rousseau, few readers are aware of the long period during which lesser writers first cultivated the genre and prepared the public taste for the master-work of Jean-Jacques. Nor were these always second-rate authors; but in the matter of the confessional, their mastery had yet to be asserted.

The growth of confessions occurred above all in novels written in the first person. Not that an author presented a frank and full report of the events of his own life; but as soon as he was launched he often found it difficult not to indulge his personal experiences, and if he did not actually relate his own past, he entered into his hero's with such gusto that we must at the very least recognize the adventures as ones which the author might have, or would have, enjoyed experiencing. The degree of involvement, or detachment, varies widely among the authors of our period. Lesage remains distinct from Gil Blas; Crébillon *fils* has his hero, Meilcour, in *Les Egarements du cœur et de l'esprit* (1736–38), write his memoirs some years after the events depicted, thus allowing time for maturing and for the development of perspective and psychological analysis; Prévost eschews all detachment and enters

[44] '. . . j'en dis encore tant, que j'épuisai mes forces; il ne me resta plus que des pleurs, jamais on n'en a tant versé; et la bonne femme, voyant cela, se mit à pleurer aussi du meilleur de son cœur.
'Là-dessus Toinon entra pour nous dire que le dîner était prêt: et Toinon, qui était de l'avis de tout le monde, pleura, parce que nous pleurions, et moi, après tant de larmes, attendrie par les douceurs qu'elles me dirent toutes deux, je m'apaisai, je me consolai, j'oubliai tout.' Marivaux, *La Vie de Marianne*, Part I, in *Romans*, pp. 114–15.

fully and unrestrainedly into the sufferings of his characters – and it is for that reason that *Manon Lescaut*, without being Rousseau's 'source', is, of the novels of our period, surely the closest in spirit to the *Confessions*. What Des Grieux gives us in *Manon Lescaut* is not a mere reminiscence; nor is he motivated by a desire to entertain. He is consumed by a need to set the world right by communicating to others the trials and tribulations of his love; it is his own, not our welfare which is at stake. 'Nothing,' Prévost says in one place, 'does violence as much as being afflicted without daring to communicate one's pains,'[45] and this view applies generally, both in his writings and in others. 'I put my adventures on paper,' says the Marquis d'Argens, 'for my own satisfaction. I am sure that they will never see the light of day; nothing has persuaded me to adorn or disguise the truth.'[46]

In the century of Louis XIV, the dissection of the emotions of seventeen-year-old Des Grieux might well have evoked laughter more often than tears, but by 1730 the *sensibilité* of the reading public was quite another thing, the misfortunes of an infatuated youth having become a subject of wide and serious interest. Yet, lest we lose perspective and regard all readers and writers of the time as intoxicated with lachrymose confessions, we must quote from two authors who expressed their doubts. One of these, Mme de Lambert, attributing the frankness of the literature to the dominance of women in matters of taste, rebelled at the trends of the time:

'In this exchange, has society gained by the taste of women? They have put debauchery in the place of knowledge; the precious, for which they have been so much reproached, has given way to indecency. In the process they have degraded themselves, fallen from their erstwhile dignity.'[47]

---

[45] '. . . rien n'est si violent que d'être affligé, sans oser communiquer ses peines.' Prévost, *Mém. d'un homme de qualité*, liv. 11, in *Œuvres*, II, 361.

[46] 'Je ne couche mes aventures sur le papier que pour ma satisfaction. Je suis assuré qu'elles ne verront jamais le jour; rien n'a pu m'obliger à farder, ni a déguiser la vérité.' J.-B. du Boyer, Marquis d'Argens, *Mémoires* (1735) (new edn; Paris: F. Buisson, 1807), liv. 1, beginning.

[47] 'La société a-t-elle gagné dans cet échange du goût des femmes? Elles ont mis la débauche à la place du savoir; le précieux qu'on leur a tant reproché, elles l'ont changé en indécence. Par là elles se sont dégradées, et sont déchues

The other, the anonymous author of the *Mémoires du Chevalier de T——*, sometimes expressed doubts, but not without also subscribing in good measure to the *sensibilité* of the time. He does, to be sure, criticize the confessionals which were popular in the period: 'The young men of our day make a point of confessing all their weaknesses; nothing is so dangerous, for it is shame alone which can correct us, and easy confession does not cause shame.'[48] However, since this is an attack only on 'easy confession', the author is able to proceed to the usual justification of the sentimental literature, the effect of which probably was to leave the way open for confessions that were deep and sincere and to carry most readers along on the sentimental journey: 'Advice on love is useless, for it speaks only to the mind; the heart recognizes no laws but its own.'[49]

The confessions of our period were justified mainly as honest, truthful expressions of the heart, as a means of finding tranquility, and as a school for morality. The ratio of sincerity to sensationalism varies a great deal from author to author, but in general it is safe to say that, with the most serious intentions, our writers tended, as they worked, to let the former be overshadowed by the latter. Here are a number of excerpts which will give the reader a notion of how the authors themselves looked upon their books of confessions. The first will touch upon truthfulness, the second upon tranquility, and the next on the confessions as moral instruction.

'What I had composed only for my own amusement was destined either to bore or to amuse the public. I admit that, if the pleasure of the public requires a web of romanesque invention, these memoirs (which I surely did not intend for the public) will not be to its liking. . . . I have been content to

de leur dignité. . . .' Mme de Lambert, *Réflexions sur les femmes* (1730), in *Œuvres Morales de la Marquise de Lambert* (Paris: Bibliothèque des Bibliophiles, 1883), p. 147.

[48] 'Les jeunes gens d'aprésent se font une mérite d'avouer tous leurs défauts: rien n'est si dangereux, il n'y a que la honte qui puisse corriger. Quand on fait cet aveu si facilement, on n'en rougit pas.' Anon., *Les Mémoires du Chevalier de T——* (The Hague: Pierre Gosse, 1738), p. 40.

[49] 'Les conseils sur l'amour sont inutiles, ils ne vont qu'à l'esprit, et le cœur ne reçoit des loix que de lui-même.' *Ibid.*, p. 42.

let my heart speak. Though the language may sometimes seem too full of tenderness, in fact my expression is unable to render completely the tenderness of my feelings.[50]

'This story will be read only if it is found worthy of being read. I write of my misfortunes only for my own satisfaction; thus I will be content if the reward for my work consists of a measure of tranquility during the moments that I plan to devote to it. . . . With a heart fashioned in a certain way, one can lead a very unhappy life indeed.'[51]

'I set about to depict the strangest life-story that ever was . . . and I find myself forced, as it were, to detail a chain of adventures so extraordinary that they will deserve the care which I am going to take in writing them, in order to make them useful for the instruction of the public.'[52]

The contradiction between the last two statements by Prévost – 'for my own satisfaction', as against 'the instruction of the public' – is accounted for by an interval of some years between them. Prévost's earlier, more personal view seems to have yielded to one containing a larger ingredient of moral utility.

Some authors, on the other hand, deliberately disavowed any moral intentions, and though that approach is not as

---

[50] 'Ce que je n'avois composé que pour mon seul amusement fut destiné, ou à ennuyer, ou à amuser le public. J'avoue que si, pour lui plaire, il faut un tissu de fictions Romanesques, ces Mémoires, qu'assurément je ne lui réservois pas, ne seront point de son goût. . . . Je me suis contentée de laisser parler mon cœur ; peut-être ce langage paroîtra-t-il quelquefois bien tendre : mais quoiqu'il [*sic*] en soit, mes expressions ne sçauroient rendre toute la tendresse de mes sentimens.' Abbé Claude-François Lambert, *La Nouvelle Marianne, ou les Mémoires de la Baronne de* ——— (The Hague : P. de Hondt, 1740), Preface, p. 6.

[51] 'On lira cette histoire, si l'on trouve qu'elle mérite d'être lue. Je n'écris mes malheurs que pour ma propre satisfaction ; ainsi je serai content, si je retire, pour fruit de mon ouvrage, un peu de tranquillité dans les moments que j'ai dessein d'y employer. . . . On peut mener . . . une vie très-malheureuse, quand on a le cœur formé d'une certaine façon.' Prévost, *Mém. d'un homme de qualité*, in *Œuvres*, I, 1–2.

[52] 'J'allois commencer le genre de vie le plus étrange dont il y ait jamais eu d'exemple . . . et me trouver comme forcé à le suivre, par un enchaînement d'aventures si extraordinaires, qu'elles mérite bien le soin que je vais prendre de les écrire, pour les rendre utiles à l'instruction du public.' Prévost, *Killerine*, liv. i, in *Œuvres*, VIII, 38–39.

common as Prévost's second position, it occurs enough to merit illustration:

'Moreover, my purpose in writing these memoirs has been only to entertain the reader, and not to edify him by examples of virtue. . . . Though Madame de Borville sins in the course of this story, I will show her neither as repentant nor as punished for her sin, since in fact she was neither the one nor the other.'[53]

A further motive that appears in the confessions is self-justification, either as a real need of the author or as an excuse for accounts of salacious adventures. Since the genre by its logic demanded vice more than virtue, the process of self-justification often involved detailed and vivid presentations of the acts which were (falsely, of course) attributed to the author. Thus, a writer like Bonneval, despite his protestations that his sole concern was to cleanse his reputation, in the end dwelt more on secret trysts and seductions than on the falsity of the accusations against him. Yet his stated intention was distinct from that of the rest: whereas Bonneval set about to clear his name, the others were resigned to besmirching theirs. Their view was that they would speak out in spite of the damage, for the dictates of the heart and the need to communicate their sufferings overshadowed the petty considerations of personal vanity. This latter attitude, represented by Prévost below, was more common than that of Bonneval.

Some account needs to be taken of the fact that a successful confession of one's sins, by showing the author as a thorough-going rake or adventurer, might give him a certain appeal. Laments about the emotional strain of confessing and the damage to the author's good name are probably not to be taken without consideration of a possible reward with sections of the reading public.

'The boredom of solitude, to which my evil star and the malice of my enemies reduced me, and the desire to make

[53] 'D'ailleurs je ne me suis proposé pour but en écrivant mes Mémoires, que d'amuser le Lecteur et non de l'édifier par des exemples vertueux . . . quoique Madame de Borville péche dans la suite de cette Histoire, je ne la montrerai, ni repentante, ni punie de sa faute, parce qu'elle ne fut ni l'une ni l'autre.' Auvigny, *Mémoires de Comminville*, pp. 32–33.

known to all the world my innocence and the falsity of the
accusations by which I was blackened . . . these and other
considerations which I shall not here elaborate, have impelled
me to take pen in hand.'[54]

'However, they [the thoughts of immediate danger] did not
remove the force or freedom of mind that I needed at so
menacing a juncture. In this I can say that I have always
been different from other men; it is this which I would name
as my most basic character trait. I do not know whether stating
this publicly will be taken as ostentation, but even if it were
to bring me consideration, it would have cost me too dearly
to inspire in me a sentiment as frivolous as that which is
called vanity.'[55]

The genre of confessions, like any other genre, quickly
developed a set of conventions. There is a high degree of
predictability which, for a modern reader who is acquainted
with the literature, makes the books tedious, but their success
in the eighteenth century, when they were newer, is indisput-
able. Some of the emotional qualities that characterize this
literature and that gave it its appeal should now be examined.
We will follow these with sundry other themes which seem to
us to represent the genre, even if some of these themes are
only loosely associated with the 'emotional revolution' of the
period. In most cases, needless to say, the quotations could be
multiplied many times over.

The reader of Rousseau's *Confessions* may recall how the
youth, hitherto timid and inexperienced, is astonished at his

[54] 'L'ennui de la solitude à laquelle ma mauvaise étoile et la malice de mes
ennemis m'ont réduit, l'envie de faire connaître à toute la terre mon innocence et
la fausseté des accusations dont on m'a noirci . . . tout cela et d'autres considérations, que je ne m'amuserai point à développer, m'ont fait prendre la plume.'
Claude-Alexandre, Comte de Bonneval, *Mémoires du comte de Bonneval, Officier-
Général au service de Louis XIV* (1737), ed. Guyot Desherbiers (2 vols ; Paris : Capelle
et Renand, 1806), I, 1,

[55] 'Cependent elles ne m'ôtèrent point la force et la liberté d'esprit dont j'avois
besoin dans une si dangereuse conjoncture. C'est en quoi je puis dire que j'ai
toujours été différent des autres hommes, et ce que je puis nommer véritablement
le fond de mon caractère. Je ne sais si l'on trouvera qu'il y ait de l'ostentation à le
publier ; mais quand j'aurois quelque gloire à espérer de ces sortes d'aveux, elle
m'auroit coûté trop cher pour me faire naître un sentiment aussi frivole que celui
qu'on appelle vanité.' Prévost, *Cleveland*, liv. 4, in *Œuvres*, V, 35.

D

boldness toward Mme De Warens. Love accomplished the transformation, and regularly our young men find themselves, in the presence of their beloved, suddenly raised to new levels of emotional maturity and awareness in matters of love. The following sentences from *Manon Lescaut* are typical:

'She [Manon] looked so charming to me that I, who had never thought of the difference between the sexes nor looked at a girl closely – I, I say – . . . found myself burning with passion. I had the fault of being overtimid and easily disconcerted; but on this occasion, far from being stopped by that weakness, I went straight toward the mistress of my heart.'[56]

'I soon realized that I was less of a child than I had thought; my heart was opened to a thousand pleasurable emotions of which I had never had any idea. A gentle warmth filled my veins; I was in a kind of transport. . . .'[57]

Difficulty of expression is a motif that we encounter continually. Most of our heroes allege that it is exceedingly hard or painful to detail for us the episodes of their love affairs and their effects upon them. In actual fact, they are seldom hampered by lack of words, by failure of memory, or by reticence, and statements like the following are largely in the realm of convention. There is no doubt that the difficulty is designed, at least in part, to emphasize the depth of feeling.

'I would like to be able to overlook this sad point in my story. I feel that it will be difficult for me to present so painful a scene as it occurred. It will seem surprising – and justly so – that I should experience this difficulty, I who, after so many sad events that I have either lived or witnessed, should have

---

[56] 'Elle me parut si charmante, que moi, qui n'avois jamais pensé à la différence des sexes, ni regardé une fille avec un peu d'attention : moi, dis-je . . . je me trouvai enflammé tout d'un coup jusqu'au transport. J'avois le défaut d'être excessivement timide et facile à déconcerter ; mais loin d'être arrêté alors par cette foiblesse, je m'avançai vers la maîtresse de mon cœur.' Prévost, *Manon Lescaut*, in *Œuvres*, III, 245–46.

[57] 'Je reconnus bientôt que j'étois moins enfant que je ne le croyois. Mon cœur s'ouvrit à mille sentimens de plaisir, dont je n'avois jamais eu l'idée. Une douce chaleur se répandit dans toutes mes veines. J'étois dans une espèce de transport. . . .' *Ibid.*, pp. 248–49.

become accustomed to speak the language of sadness and sorrow. May the explanation not lie in the fact that my heart, having suffered sadness unceasingly, is filled with such an excess of grief that I can no longer find words capable of expressing it?'[58]

The heroes and heroines of the literature of confession consistently express a feeling of isolation from the world. They are either literally alone, without friends and relations who care about them, or spiritually isolated in spite of people physically close to them, and frequently both at the same time. A significant result of true solitude, as we shall see in the third extract below, is that it is excellent for inducing the writing of confessions. Though aloneness became a convention, it was not a mere convention; there is no doubt that Marivaux wrote the passages given below with great sincerity and compassion. The famous banter, or *'marivaudage'*, which is associated with his name does not appear in passages like these. The state of mind depicted foreshadows Rousseau's in the *Lettres à M. de Malesherbes*, the Rousseau of the *Promeneur solitaire*; it is the state of mind which in French literature produced Chateaubriand's *René* and Vigny's *Chatterton* at the beginning of the nineteenth century. These characters of Marivaux, with their sad solitude, were thus to have a brighter future in French letters than the hardier heroes like Gil Blas, the French counterpart of the adventurers of the English picaresque novels of the time.

'The more people and movement I saw in that prodigious city of Paris, the more silence and solitude I found for myself; a forest would have seemed to me less deserted; I would have felt less alone, less lost. I would have been able to get out of the forest, but how find my way out of the wilderness in which

[58] 'Je voudrois pouvoir éviter ce triste endroit de mon histoire. Je sens qu'il me sera difficile de représenter au naturel une scène si douloureuse. On sera surpris avec raison que j'y trouve cette difficulté, moi que tant d'événemens tristes, dont j'ai été le sujet ou le témoin, devroient avoir accoutûmé à parler le langage de la tristesse et de la douleur. N'est-ce pas peut-être aussi que mon cœur, en ayant fait une expérience presque continuelle, en porte le sentiment à des excès auxquels je ne trouve plus d'expressions qui puissent atteindre?' Prévost, *Mém. d'un homme de qualité*, liv. 8, in *Œuvres*, II, 75.

I found myself? The whole world was a wasteland to me, since I had no bond with a single person.'[59]

'I was but an unknown wretch on this earth; I had now only enemies in the world, for to have no ties with anyone is to be at war with all men, to be unwanted everywhere.'[60]

'I live in the country, whither I have withdrawn and where my leisure inspires a spirit of reflection which I propose to apply to the events of my life. I shall write these down as best I can; every man has his own way of expressing himself, which comes from his way of feeling.'[61]

This feeling of solitude is not unrelated to the convention of multiplication of confessions. Not only does the principal character make his confession to us, but each new character must tell his life story to one or more of his colleagues, to the point where we often dread the introduction of a new person or the return of an old acquaintance: 'We thus spent most of the night telling him the reasons that we too had for complaining of our fortune. . . . It was almost day when we left him.'[62] This tradition, assuredly, is as old as Homer, but there have been few periods, if any, in which writers indulged the autobiographical bent of their characters to the same extent as the authors of the early eighteenth century. There are two explanations for this. First, the point already made, that

---

[59] 'Plus je voyais de monde et de mouvement dans cette prodigieuse ville de Paris, plus j'y trouvais de silence et de solitude pour moi : une forêt m'aurait paru moins déserte ; je m'y serais sentie moins seule, moins égarée. De cette forêt, j'aurais pu m'en tirer ; mais comment sortir du désert où je me trouvais? Tout l'univers en était un pour moi, puisque je n'y tenais par aucun lien à personne.' Marivaux, *Marianne*, Part III, in *Romans*, p. 183.

[60] 'Je n'étais plus sur la terre qu'un malheureux inconnu ; je n'avais plus que des ennemis dans le monde, car n'y tenir à qui que ce soit, c'est avoir à y combattre tous les hommes, c'est être de trop partout.' Marivaux, *Le Spectateur français* (1725), ed. Paul Bonnefon (Paris : Editions Bossard, 1921), feuille 25, p. 311.

[61] 'Je vis dans une campagne où je me suis retiré, et où mon loisir m'inspire un esprit de réflexion que je vais exercer sur les événments de ma vie. Je les écrirai du mieux que je pourrai ; chacun a sa façon de s'exprimer, qui vient de sa façon de sentir.' Marivaux, *Le Paysan parvenu*, Part I, in *Romans*, p. 568.

[62] 'Nous passâmes donc la plus grande partie de la nuit à lui raconter les sujets que nous avions eus de nous plaindre aussi de la fortune. . . . Il était presque jour lorsque nous le quittâmes.' Prévost, *Mém. d'un homme de qualité*, liv. 9, in *Œuvres*, II, 179.

characters are isolated and therefore grasp the opportunity to communicate whenever it presents itself; second, that in an age when readers tolerated – even enjoyed – ten-volume novels, these multiple confessions made convenient copy. The quotation above spares the reader the account itself; usually he does not get off with so summary a statement!

Poverty, to which we have seen reference before, is common, though by no means universal, in these confessions. As a literary device, it served to evoke the reader's sympathy and to underline the confessor's total misery; but it also served to publicize the fact that the majority of citizens lived in dire poverty. It was part of pre-Revolutionary social propaganda; and this was as true in England as in France. As an illustration, we can read a few sentences from *The Compleat Mendicant*, by 'Peregrine', a first-person 'confession' novel which is both an early example of the type and a book of superior readability. The narrator, an innocent and pleasing man stricken by poverty, successfully engages both our sympathy and our sustained interest.

'I can see no reason why the fabulous Life of a Vertuous Mendicant should not be as acceptable to the World as an English Rogue, a Gusman Lazarillo, or any other Romantick History of Villanous Tricks, etc.'[63]

'It must necessarily be allowed, that the greater part and generality of Mankind are but one bare remove at best from flat and substantial Misery . . . but my own woful Experience shall not urge me into complaints, or a long Introduction.'[64]

'Indeed I have been amazed to see with what indifference and satisfaction some of our wealthy Cormorants have beheld their own humane Nature pining and starving in the Person of their poor Brother, tho' at the same time perhaps they have been burthen'd with an excess of another kind, and might be relieved against both by a more equal distribution.'[65]

[63] Peregrine (pseud.), *The Compleat Mendicant* (London: E. Harris, 1699), 'To the Reader'.
[64] *Ibid.*, pp. 2–3.
[65] *Ibid.*, pp. 4–5.

The quest for sympathy, whether based on material poverty or on emotional suffering, is fairly universal in the confession literature of our period. It is, as the following passages from two separate books by the Abbé Prévost will show, one of the real aims of these writings.

'I want to inform you, not only of my misfortunes and sorrows, but also of my licentiousness and my most shameful weaknesses. I am sure that while condemning me, you will be obliged to feel pity for me.'[66]

'I enter upon the immense sea of my misfortunes. I begin a narration which will be accompanied by tears and which will make the reader's flow as well. This thought gives me some satisfaction; I shall win the pity of tender hearts. I make them the judge of my sorrows; it is at their tribunal that I present them.'[67]

Appeals like these – and there are many dozens, if not hundreds, in the early eighteenth century – presuppose a tender heart and a susceptibility to a fellow-man's pain, which was part of the growing *sensibilité* of the time. Personal emotions and an unashamedly subjective outlook on the world became increasingly acceptable. If these are often expressed awkwardly, in comparison to the writings of the Diderots, Bernardin de Saint-Pierres and Chéniers of a later age, they nonetheless indicate an important shift in values in the direction of the lyric, the personal. The coldness of some of the material which we shall quote is less important than what the writers were trying to get at, and what at first looks like artificiality was often the result of inexperience and ineptness, not of insincerity. Even writers on political subjects, especially the

---

[66] 'Je veux vous apprendre, non seulement mes malheurs et mes peines, mais encore mes désordres et mes plus honteuses foiblesses. Je suis sûr qu'en me condamnant vous ne pourrez pas vous empêcher de me plaindre.' Prévost, *Manon*, in *Œuvres*, III, 243.

[67] 'J'entre dans la mer immense de mes infortunes. Je commence une narration que je vais accompagner de mes larmes, et qui en fera couler des yeux de mes lecteurs. Cette pensée me cause quelque satisfaction en écrivant; j'obtiendrai la pitié des cœurs tendres; je les fais Juges de mes peines; c'est à leur tribunal que je les présente.' Prévost, *Cleveland*, liv. 3, in *Œuvres*, IV, 229.

Abbé de Saint-Pierre, infused their arguments with a personal passion which is at bottom inseparable from the *sensibilité* of the age. Intimately linked with *sensibilité* and lyricism is the great interest in nature and the elements, which, as Professor Atkinson has shown in *Le sentiment de la nature*, loomed ever larger in this period.

'Walking is my third occupation. As I walk I consider the works of nature and admire their variety. My efforts contribute to the birth and growth of some flowers and fruits which I have taken into my charge. I let my eyes wander over the peaceful landscape which surrounds me. I note the distance from earth to sky; and I sometimes lament the weight which prevents me from rising to those happy climes.'[68]

'The sun, the rain, the wind seem to me fire, flood, and tempest; at last [knowing you to be alive and well] I breathe.'[69]

> 'Our heart is but care, our mind but fantasy;
> Our body is but misery;
> What is birth? It is suffering.
> What is life? It is dying.'[70]

'Inhuman Célimène, I see, has no weakness or tenderness for me. How little the fire of my love reaches the cruel one! Can she too not burn, and love me? Oh god of love, cause the unbending one to respond, show her your invincible power. Let her this day be chained. Avenge yourself, avenge me.'[71]

[68] 'La promenade fait ma troisième occupation. Je marche, en considérant les ouvrages de la nature, et j'admire leur variété. J'aide, par mes soins, à la naissance et à l'accroissement de quelques fleurs et de quelques fruits, dont j'ai pris la direction. Je promène mes regards sur le paysage tranquille qui m'environne. Je mesure des yeux la distance du ciel à la terre ; et je gémis quelquefois de la pesanteur qui m'empêche de m'élever à cette région de félicité.' Prévost, *Mém. d'un homme de qualité*, liv. 15, in *Œuvres*, III, 184.

[69] 'Le soleil, la pluie, les vents, me paroissent des embrasemens, des inondations, des ouragans ; enfin, j'ai respiré [en vous sachant saine et sauve chez vous].' Mlle Catherine-Elisabeth Aïssé, *Lettres* (Paris : La Grange, 1787), Letter I, 1726.

[70] 'Nôtre cœur n'est que soin, nôtre esprit que chimère ;/Et nôtre corps n'est que misère ;/Qu'est-ce que naître? c'est souffrir,/Qu'est-ce que vivre? c'est mourir.' Antoine-Louis Le Brun, 'L'Homme', in *Les Pensées ingénieuses, ou les Epigrammes d'Owen, traduits en vers françois* (Paris and Brussels : Jean Léonard, 1710).

[71] 'L'Inhumaine/Célimène,/Je le voi,/N'a pour moi/Ni foiblesse,/Ni tendresse :/

The case of the Abbé Chaulieu, one of our very worldly eighteenth-century priests, with a sinful enough past, is especially interesting in the matter of lyricism. His felicitous combination of the light touch and the sincere, personal note in the following poems, written at an advanced age, is unmistakable.

'Alas ! Why does a cruel law decree
    That the youth of the seasons,
    Which gives our trees
    And bushes their green cover,
Is unable to revive our worn body,
To infuse my blood with its erstwhile fire,
And my limbs and senses with the vigour of their youth?[72]

'I who feel old age advancing . . .
I take pleasure in the spring, in the sun, in a fair day;
I live for myself, more happy with my lazy life
Than with wealth, fortune, and high place.
    Should my taste run to some fair lass,
I take my pleasure there, and fear no harm;
    I will but drink with her,
    And laugh at my rivals.'[73]

The role of the out-of-doors in relation to confessions has already been mentioned; and we have seen Paris considered as a poor place for our heroes and heroines to live and express

---

Que mon feu/Touche peu/La cruelle !/Ne peut-elle/S'enflammer,/Et m'aimer?/ Rens sensible/L'inflexible,/Fais-lui voir/Ton pouvoir/Invincible,/Dieu d'Amour,/ Qu'elle prenne/En ce jour/Une chaîne :/Venge-toi,/Venge-moi.' Le Brun, *Odes Galantes et Bacchiques* (Paris : G. Cavelier fils, 1719), p. 84.

[72] 'Hélas ! pourquoi faut-il, par une loi trop dure,/Que la jeunesse des saisons,/ Qui rend la verte chevelure/A nos arbres, à nos buissons,/Ne puisse ranimer notre machine usée ;/Rendre à mon sang glacé son ancienne chaleur ;/A mon corps, à mes sens, leur première vigeur. . . .' L'Abbé Guillaume Amphrye de Chaulieu, 'A madame la marquise de Lassai' (1705), in *Œuvres* (new edn ; 2 vols ; Paris : David ; Prault fils ; Durand ; 1757), II, 290.

[73] 'Moi, qui sens qu'à grand pas la vieillesse s'avance . . ./Je jouis du printemps, du soleil, d'un beau jour ;/Je vis pour moi, content que ma seule indolence/ Me tienne lieu de biens, de fortune et de cour./Si je vois encore quelque belle,/ J'y trouve des plaisirs, et n'en crains point de maux./Je ne veux que boire avec elle,/Et me moquer de mes rivaux.' Chaulieu, 'A Monsieur l'abbé Courtin (1703), in *ibid.*, pp. 311-12.

themselves in (see note 59, above). We cannot always tell, in our novels, what the grounds are for hating Paris, but that there is a common revulsion for the capital (in contrast to the attitude of writers in the sixteenth and seventeenth centuries) is certain. Sometimes the crowds highlight one's solitude; sometimes it is a simple matter of loving the country because one is more used to it or because it is healthier; sometimes – and here the confessions are at one with the contemporary picaresque novels – it is wanderlust that draws our characters away. Whatever the explanation, the love of country over city shows itself plainly in the literature of the early eighteenth century, and we easily feel that we are on the way to Rousseau and Romanticism.

'. . . the air healthy, the ground good, the view limited but beautiful, a little brook nearby making the only sound that can be heard; the house small, comfortable, and neatly furnished; the garden proportioned to the house and cultivated by the owner's own hand. . . . I saw the effect of all this; I saw Mr Temple, healthy and cheerful, who, in spite of the gout and his advanced age, left me behind as we walked, and were it not for the rain which began to fall, I would have been forced to ask for quarter. You may well believe that I did not see all this without sighing more than once, or without asking myself what I was doing there, why I had come to disturb other people's quiet.'[74]

. . . Mr Temple's secluded home and its little garden were ever in my mind and made me think of the pleasure of a quiet, secluded life.'[75]

[74] '. . . l'air sain, le terroir bon, la vuë bornée, mais belle, un petit Ruisseau qui coule près de là, et qui fait le seul bruit qu'on y entend; la Maison petite, commode et proprement meublée; le Jardin proportionné à la Maison et cultivé de la main du maître. . . . Je vis aussi l'effet de tout cela; je vis Monsieur *Temple* sain et gai, qui, quoi-que gouteux et dans un âge assez avancé, me lassa à la Promenade, et qui, sans la pluie qui survint, m'auroit, je crois, réduit à lui demander quartier. Vous croiez bien que je ne vis pas tout cela sans soupirer plus d'une fois, ni sans me demander à moi-même, ce que je faisois là, pourquoi je venois troubler la Retraite des autres.' Béat-Louis de Muralt, *Lettres sur les Anglois et les François et sur les voiages* (1725), ed. Charles Gould and Charles Oldham (Paris: Champion, 1933), p. 162.
[75] '. . . la Maison retirée et le petit Jardin de Monsr. Temple se présentoient

'I was hardly seven when, following certain impulses that I could not control, I began to escape from the family residence. My excursions were not really very extensive, because of my age and strength . . . my parents often had to come to get me in the outlying districts. . . . Gradually, as I grew up, I even adopted the habit of getting out of sight of Paris.'[76]

'. . . I was no sooner on the pavement of Paris, than I was tired of being there. All I thought of were voyages, and the longer and more perilous they were, the better I liked them. Not to leave one's country, not to know what the rest of the world is like, I considered that good for women.'[77]

A great deal of attention is paid in the confession literature to bodily detail, and it is not uncommon for the narrator to suffer from some infirmity (although the multiplication of deformities described in the quotation below from *The Dean of Killerine* is rare). Vividness of physical detail was justified in the confessions by the fact that emotional suffering affected, and sometimes almost destroyed, the body. The devastating effects of the pangs of passion, often best put in terms of physical decline, could be most conveniently seen and gauged by the reader if he had a clear picture of the person's size, colouring, and so forth. Prévost excels in presenting these details, as he excelled in so many other departments of the literature of confession and *sensibilité*.

'The marquis was well proportioned, had prominent black eyes which were alert and bright, but full of gentleness; his

---

à moi sans cesse, et me faisoient rêver au plaisir d'une Vie cachée et tranquille.' *Ibid.*, p. 163.

[76] 'A peine avois-je sept ans que je commençay, par certains mouvemens dont je n'étois pas le maître, à m'échapper de la maison paternelle. Mes courses à la vérité n'étoient pas bien longues, parce que mon âge et mes forces ne me le permettoient pas . . . je donnois souvent à mes parents la peine de me venir chercher aux Fauxbourgs . . . peu à peu et à mesure que je croissois je m'accoûtumay même à perdre Paris de vûë.' Raveneau de Lussan, *Journal du voyage fait à la mer du Sud, avec les Flibustiers de l'Amérique en 1684 et années suivantes* (Paris: J.-B. Coignard, 1690), pp. 1-2.

[77] '. . . je ne fus pas plus tôt sur le pavé de Paris, que je me lassay d'y être. Je n'avois que voyages en tête, les plus longs et les plus perilleux me sembloient les plus beaux. Ne point sortir de son païs, et ne sçavoir comment le reste de la Terre est fait, je trouvois cela bien pour une femme.' *Ibid.*, pp. 3-4.

complexion was remarkably light and intense at the same time. A forest of light-brown hair hung down to his waist. With all this he had, as if by nature, the bearing and manners of a man of distinction, and an indefinable playfulness that endeared him immediately. Thus, I was not a bit surprised to find that our beautiful hostess had become attracted to him.'[78]

'. . . heaven had early [taught me] to hate the world and to love solitude. I had entered the world with three infirmities, from which no care or remedy was able to deliver me. My legs were crooked – though strong enough, and nearly enough equal in length to allow me to walk straight. Further, I had a hump not only in back but also in front, and to top all this off, my face was disfigured by warts which were regularly spaced above my eyes and on my forehead in the shape of two horns. Add the fact that my head was big and my torso full, short, and stocky.'[79]

'The sorrows that I had endured for more than a year had changed me completely. I had lost interest in food and sleep. Thus, attempts at cure, regaining a great departure from habits which I had acquired when ill, were of slight value. However, Christian hope fortified my soul even as my health declined. I was already more than forty years old.'[80]

[78] 'Le marquis avoit la taille très-bien prise, de grands yeux noirs à fleur de tête, vifs et brillants, quoiqu'ils fussent pleins de douceur ; le teint d'une blancheur admirable, et en même tems fort animé. Une forêt de cheveux, châtain-clair lui descendoit jusqu'à la ceinture. Il avoit avec cela naturellement le port et les manières d'un homme de distinction, et je ne sais quel air enjoué et mutin qui le faisoit trouver aimable au premier coup d'œil ; de sorte que je ne fus point surpris que notre belle hôtesse fut devenue sensible pour lui.' Prévost, *Mém. d'un homme de qualité*, liv. 6, in *Œuvres*, I, 335–36.

[79] 'Le ciel . . . de bonne heure la haine du monde et le goût de la solitude. J'avois apporté en naissant trois infirmités, dont tous les soins et les remèdes de l'art n'avoient pu me délivrer. Mes jambes étoient crochues, quoique fermes d'ailleurs, et de longueur assez égale pour ne pas m'empêcher de marcher droit. J'étois bossu avec cela par devant et par derrière ; et pour comble de disgrâce, j'avois le visage défiguré par des verrues qui étoient plantées régulièrement au-dessus de mes yeux, et qui s'avançoient sur mon front avec l'apparence de deux cornes. Ajoutez que j'avois la tête fort grosse, la taille pleine, mais ramassée et extrêmement courte.' Prévost, *Killerine*, liv. 1, in *Œuvres*, VIII, 5–6.

[80] ' . . . les chagrins que j'avois essuyés depuis plus d'un an, altéroient jusqu'à mon sang et mes forces. J'en avois perdu le sommeil et l'appétit. Ainsi le dédom-magement étoit d'un autre ordre que les peines, et n'avoit pas la même force pour se faire sentir. Cependant l'espérance chrétienne fortifioit mon ame à mesure que

Our characters are sad most of the time, think of suicide often, and have the idea sometimes that their misery is contagious. Somewhat in the style of René and Hernani a century later, Mlle de Bernay, in a story by Robert Chasles, speaks as follows of the contagion she spreads, as well as of the possibility of ending it all by suicide:

'Do you not marvel at our unhappiness, dear lover? You would always have been happy, had you not become attached to me. My misfortunes spread to any that come near me. . . . I am spending the best years of my life in sorrow. No matter; my love is proof against all. My only fear is that time and sorrow will dishearten you and will dim the lustre of that beauty and youth which you have often praised. I fear being no longer lovable to you. That is my sole concern. . . . If you cease loving me, I will myself end my miseries. I will punish myself for the crime of my father and of time, which will have removed from me all that you loved.'[81]

Though in exotic writings the French, along with other Europeans, were developing notions of the 'noble savage', and had been doing so since the sixteenth century, and though these notions were to have an effect on the renowned optimism of eighteenth-century thought, in the more personal realm represented by the literature that we are examining, a stark pessimism reigned. Occasionally the natural tendency of one man to love another asserts itself, as in the third excerpt below, but the pessimism of the first two excerpts is much more representative. This pessimism usually applies to both human nature and the world in general, as we might well expect in

---

ma santé s'affoiblissoit. Mon âge passoit déjà quarante ans.' *Ibid.*, liv. 2, in *Œuvres*, VIII, 134.

[81] 'N'admirez-vous point notre malheur, mon cher Amant? Vous auriez toujours été heureux, si vous ne vous étiez point attaché à moi. Mes malheurs se répandent sur tout ce qui m'approche. . . . Ce sont les plus belles années de ma vie que je passe dans les douleurs. Il n'importe, mon amour est à l'épreuve de tout. Tout ce que je crains, c'est que les chagrins et le tems ne vous rebutent, et ne ternissent l'éclat de beauté et de jeunesse que je vous ai vû vanter. Je crains de n'être pas toujours aimable à vos yeux. C'est le seul soin qui m'occupe. . . . Si vous cessez de m'aimer, je finirai moi-même mes malheurs. Je me punirai du crime de mon Père et du tems, qui m'auront enlevé tout ce que vous aimez.' Chasles, *Illustres Françoises*, I, 153–54.

books filled with forced marriages, betrayals, and every form of heartbreak.

'In all my life, nothing has contributed so much to my errors and sorrows as my naïve tendency to make favourable assumptions about the virtue of others, especially when, thanks to a little close observation so as to get at a person's basic character, I thought I discovered natural principles of honesty and goodness. I have not known the great passions by experience, and without that key one never enters perfectly into the human heart. . . . Thus, I have always relied on the character of other people almost as much as on my own – . . . a false notion which credits men with either too much goodness or too much evil, and with a consistency in the one or the other that nature seldom provides.'[82]

'I buried myself in the woods near my daughter's house. 'There I surveyed the long unhappy years which had elapsed since . . . my childhood. Wherever I looked in that long passage of time, I found marks of misfortune and sorrow. I could scarcely find a few moments of pleasure in it; and even among those short fleeting moments I saw none that was not followed by untold bitterness. One after another, I had seen death or fortune take from me everything that represented esteem, tenderness, and attachment.'[83]

[82] 'Dans toute ma vie, rien n'a tant contribué à mes erreurs et à mes peines, que ce penchant trop crédule à présumer favorablement de la vertu d'autrui ; sur-tout lorsqu'avec un peu d'étude pour démêler le fond d'un caractère, je croyois y découvrir des principes naturels de droiture et d'inclination pour le bien. Je n'ai pas connu les grandes passions par expérience ; et sans cette clef, l'on n'entre jamais parfaitement dans la science du cœur humain. . . . Ainsi je me suis toujours reposé sur le charactère d'autrui presqu'autant que sur le mien . . . fausse idée, qui suppose dans les hommes trop de bonté ou de malice, avec une constance dans l'une ou dans l'autre dont la nature est rarement capable.' Prévost, *Killerine*, liv. 2, in *Œuvres*, VIII, 96.

[83] 'Je m'enfonçai dans le bois, qui est voisin de la maison de ma fille. 'Là, je jetai les yeux sur cette longue et malheureuse suite d'années qui s'étoient écoulées pour moi, depuis . . . mon enfance. Dans quelque partie de cette vaste carrière que je portasse mes regards, j'y apercevois des vestiges d'infortune et de douleur. A peine y pouvois-je compter quelques moments de plaisir ; et parmi ces courts et légers instants, je n'en voyois aucun qui n'eût été suivi par d'innombrables amertumes. Je m'étois vu enlever successivement, par la mort, ou par la fortune, tout ce qu'on appelle objets d'estime, de tendresse et d'attachement.' Prévost, *Mém. d'un homme de qualité*, liv. 12, in *Œuvres*, II, 430–33.

'We embraced warmly and became friends, for no reason but the goodness of our hearts and a natural impulse which leads a sensitive and generous man to love another who is like him.'[84]

If, in the matter of optimism and pessimism, our writers can lay little claim to paving the way for the Enlightenment, the same cannot be said of their social or religious doctrine. Here a great many of the writers of the early part of the eighteenth century, major as well as minor, writers of confessions as well as writers of disquisitions, foreshadowed the liberal propaganda efforts of Voltaire, Rousseau, and the *Encyclopedia*. We have already seen examples of sympathy for the poor. Here is one more strong statement, from La Hontan. This will be followed by a rather typical remark of Marivaux's Marianne on religion. Marianne's view that religion is not for the young, that God means little to people who find themselves in circumstances of emotional turmoil, is very much the assumption underlying a large part of the literature of the early eighteenth century. Marianne and the other sufferers and confessers of our books do indeed, for the most part, believe in 'the things of this world'.

'. . . but tell me, I beg you, what difference there is between sleeping in a good hut and in a palace, between sleeping on beaver-skins and on mattresses between two sheets; between eating roast-meat and soup, or between dirty crusts and stews prepared by dirty scullions. . . . Oh, how many there are among you who sleep on straw, under roofs or in attics where rain has free entry, and who have a hard time finding bread and water? I have been in France and speak from first-hand observation.'[85]

---

[84] 'Nous nous embrassâmes avec tendresse, nous devînmes amis, sans autre raison que la bonté de nos cœurs, et une simple disposition qui porte un homme tendre et généreux à aimer un autre homme qui lui ressemble.' Prévost, *Manon*, in *Œuvres*, III, 351.

[85] '. . . mais di-moy, je t'en conjure, quelle différence il y a de coucher sous une bonne Cabane, ou sous un Palais ; de dormir sur des peaux de Castor, ou sur des matelats entre deux draps ; de manger du rosti et du boüilli, ou de sales pâtez et ragoûts, aprêtez par des Marmitons crasseux? . . . Hé ! combien y en a-t-il parmi vous, qui couchent sur la paille, sous des toits ou des greniers que la pluye traverse de toutes parts, et qui ont de la peine à trouver du pain et de l'eau?

'. . . the point is that I was not religious enough and that a person of eighteen thinks all is lost and feels quite hopeless when told that in such a case only God can help; this is a grave, serious idea which upsets her little bit of confidence, for at that age one trusts only what one sees, one knows only the things of this world.'[86]

TREATMENT OF LOVE

Of the many attitudes mirrored in literature, the treatment of love underwent perhaps the greatest transformation between the period of French classicism and the early eighteenth century. Elements that were not previously allowed in sophisticated literature appear in the eighteenth century, and others appear in new contexts. Not that there was anything new – in love there is certainly nothing new under the sun – but we do observe, first, the elevation of a whole category of material which, a generation earlier, would have been regarded as too vulgar to find its way into the works of serious writers, and second, a sympathetic approach to both characters and events which would have been thought fit for mockery and laughter only.

We shall make great use of Robert Chasles, who, though much less known than the Abbé Prévost and Marivaux, was both a successful and a rather good author. Writing earlier than the others (his *Illustres Françoises*, from which our quotations will be taken, date from 1720, Prévost's *Manon* from 1735, and the early parts of Marivaux's *Vie de Marianne* from 1731–35), Chasles lacked the finesse which his successors were to develop in dealing with love, but his interests and values were fairly representative of the whole period. Without multiplying quotations excessively, we shall reinforce his

---

J'ay esté en France, j'en parle pour l'avoir veu.' Louis-Armand Lahontan, *Dialogues curieux entre l'auteur et un sauvage* (1703), ed. G. Chinard (Baltimore Md.: Johns Hopkins Press and Oxford University Press, 1931), p. 202.

[86] '. . . c'est que je n'étais pas assez dévote, et qu'une âme de dix-huite ans croit tout perdu, tout désespéré, quand on lui dit en pareil cas qu'il n'y a plus que Dieu que lui reste: c'est une idée grave et sérieuse qui effarouche sa petite confiance; à cet âge on ne se fie guère qu'à ce qu'on voit, on ne connaît guère que les choses de la terre.' Marivaux, *Marianne*, Part III, in *Romans*, p. 193.

statements with quotations from other writers, in order to give what we hope will be an adequate picture of the treatment of love. We shall not prejudge the extent of the 'emotional revolution' by presenting only things that differ from the preceding age; we shall rather attempt a faithful representation of the handling of love in the literary works of our period.

The 'History of Des Frans and Silvie', one of the stories in Robert Chasles's series of *Illustrious Frenchwomen*, presents us material that is surprising from several points of view. Silvie, the heroine, is of unknown birth, like Marivaux's Marianne. Like Marianne also, Silvie, courted by a young man of noble family, finds herself falsely accused of misconduct and is later vindicated – all in striking similarity to Marivaux's novel. After a happy marriage, the details of which are more frankly sensual than in Marivaux or Prévost, we encounter a scene which reminds us of *Manon Lescaut* but in one or two respects goes beyond anything in that book.

The hero, Des Frans, returns home after an absence of several months and, entering his bedroom, finds his wife in bed with a friend of the family. His first thought is of violence against the adulterous couple, but

'. . . a movement that she made disarmed me. I gazed at that bosom which I idolized. All my fury left me; the only effect of my rage was for me to lament my misfortune. Can one be capable of such weakness? I feared that I would cover her with shame if I burst out then and there. I respected her honour at the very moment that she was so cruelly outraging mine. I could not bring myself to get revenge by a cruelty which, though justified at the moment, so ill befit the tenderness of my love and the generosity of my feelings. . . .

'This thought, which I took as a pure impulse of magnanimity and which was in reality only a cover for my weakness, settled things for me. I satisfied myself with taking my unfaithful one's necklace, which lay unclasped. I took it away, to show her that I had caught her in the greatest crime that a woman can commit; and I went out.'[87]

[87] 'Un mouvement qu'elle fit me désarma. Je jettai les yeux sur ce sein que j'idolâtrois. Toute ma fureur m'abandonna, je n'écoutai plus ma rage que pour

This, surely, is the state of mind and way of thinking of Des Grieux in *Manon Lescaut*. Prévost's art precluded the description of an unfaithful Manon in the arms of a rival – and it might be maintained that Des Grieux's passion is the better conveyed by leaving the details of the perfidy to the reader's imagination. But the portrayal of a passion that leaves no room for honour or for a lover's wrath, but does carry with it an awareness of degradation, is common to these two stories. 'I reproached myself,' says Des Frans, 'for the condition to which my madness had brought me, but it was not the only time that love led me to acts of madness. My love dominated all, I sacrificed everything on its altar – honour, virtue, family, fortune, personal tastes; I looked at nothing except as it related to that love.'[88] Chasles need not be read as a source of Marivaux or Prévost: all three might have been inspired by another, unknown, fourth writer altogether; or, more likely, they independently arrived at the same view of the lover's reaction, through personal experience or otherwise. The possibility of influence among these writers has been suggested by Henri Roddier and others;[89] but what is most important for us is that in this period from 1720 to 1735, the loss of classical and Christian principles permitted the open and serious expression of emotions and values which in the Grand Century would have been found entertaining. Des Frans, fifty years earlier, could only have been a comic figure.

---

plaindre mon malheur. Peut-on être capable d'une si grande foiblesse? J'appréhendai de la couvrir de honte, si j'éclatois dans le moment. Je respectai son honneur dans le tems même qu'elle outrageois si cruellement le mien. Je ne pûs me résoudre à me vanger par une cruauté qui, quoique légitime dans ce moment, s'accordoit si mal avec la tendresse de mon amour, et la générosité de mon cœur. . . .

'Cette pensée, que je pris pour un pur mouvement de générosité, et qui n'étoit en effet qu'une illusion de ma foiblesse, me détermina. Je me contentai de prendre le colier de mon infidèle qui étoit dénoüé. Je l'emportai pour la convaincre que je l'avois surprise dans le plus grand des crimes qu'une Femme puisse commettre; et je sortis.' Chasles, *Illustres Françoises*, II, 382–83.

[88] 'Je me voulois mal à moi-même,' says Des Frans, 'de l'état où me réduisoit ma folie, mais ce n'est pas la seule que l'amour m'a fait faire. Il étoit le plus fort, je lui sacrifiai tout, honneur, vertu, parens, fortune, inclination; je ne regardois rien que par rapport à lui.' Chasles, 'Histoire de Monsieur Des Frans et de Silvie', *ibid.*, p. 299.

[89] See, for example, Henri Roddier, *L'Abbé Prévost – l'homme et l'œuvre* (Paris: Hatier-Boivin, 1955), p. 117.

E

Chasles was much given to descriptions of his characters,
far more than either Marivaux or Prévost, and perhaps more
than any of his contemporaries with the possible exception
of Defoe describing his man Friday. Here is a description of
Silvie, whom we have met above in a compromising position,
which is not without its touch of humour. It will be followed
by a description of Mlle Fenoüil, the heroine of another story
in the *Illustres Françoises*, whom we shall also see caught in
bed with her lover. (Mlle Fenoüil and her lover have, however,
pledged their troth and regard themselves as married.)

'She was at most nineteen. . . . Her hair was a good foot
longer than she was tall, curly, and of the most beautiful
brown imaginable. . . . Her bosom, rising and falling regularly
as she breathed, showed both the agitation of her heart and
her perfect health. Her breasts were small but firm; she sometimes said jestingly to me that a woman's breasts are big
enough if they will fill a gentleman's hands.'[90]

'Mlle Fenoüil was tall and well proportioned, with a pleasant
figure and a delicate white complexion; she had black eyes,
eyebrows, and hair, large, deep-set, animated eyes which the
least sorrow left languid, asking for the heart of all she looked
upon. A wide and smooth forehead, a well-formed nose, the
face oval-shaped, a dimple on the chin, a small and rosy
mouth, white, well-set teeth, a narrow and slightly aquiline
nose, a finely formed neck, a high and ample bosom, well-
formed arms, and the most beautiful hand that ever a woman
might possess. You see from her portrait that I may be excused for loving her to the point of risking everything for
her.'[91]

---

[90] 'Elle n'avoit au plus que dix-neuf ans. . . . Ses cheveux étoient plus longs
qu'elle d'un grand pié, annelez, et du plus beau châtain qu'on puisse voir. . . . Le
sein montroit par ses mouvemens réglez l'agitation du cœur dans sa respiration,
et indiquoit une santé parfaite. Elle en avoit peu, mais ferme ; et elle me disoit
quelquefois en plaisantant, qu'une femme en a toûjours assez quand elle en a de
quoi remplir la main d'un honnête homme.' Chasles, 'Des Frans et Silvie', *Illustres
Françoises*, II, 291–92.

[91] 'Mademoiselle Fenoüil étoit grande et bien faite, la taille aisée, la peau
délicate et fort blanche, aussi bien que le teint ; elle avoit les yeux, les sourcils et
les cheveux noirs, les yeux grands et bien fendus naturellement vifs, mais le moindre
chagrin les rendoit languissans, pour lors ils sembloient demander le cœur de tous

'We made a promise of marriage; a piece of paper sufficing us, we swore to be ever faithful, and from that day on we lived as man and wife.'[92]

'. . . seeing that she was not in Paris, though I cannot tell you how they discovered the route we had taken, they did discover it, they followed us, and they came upon us when we were still in bed. I defended myself as best I could, but I was overwhelmed by the number of our enemies. I was treated roughly but was less concerned about what they were doing to me than what I saw them doing to her. The man in whose hands we were could, by the right of birth, exercise authority over her; but he abused that right. I was in despair but unable to avenge her except by my grief. . . . I was bound like the most dangerous of criminals. In vain did she cry out that I was her husband. . . .'[93]

Chasles's details are frequently vivid, as when the woman who initiates one of the young heroes of the *Illustres Françoises* into the ways of love 'uncovered to my sight, among other things, a throat and a pair of breasts as beautiful as any I have ever in my life seen'.[94] Sometimes they are more restrained, as in the following suggestive lines on a honeymoon:

---

ceux qu'elle regardoit. Le front large et uni, le nez bien fait, la forme du visage ovale, une fossette au menton, la bouche fort petite et vermeille, les dents blanches et bien rangées, le nez serré et un peu aquilin, la gorge faite au tour, le sein haut et rempli, les bras comme la gorge, et la plus belle main que femme puisse avoir. Vous voyez par son portrait que je suis excusable de l'avoir aimée, jusques au point de tout hazarder pour elle.' Chasles, 'Histoire de Monsieur de Jussy et de Mademoiselle Fenoüil', *ibid.*, I, 174.

[92] 'Nous nous fîmes chacun une promesse de mariage ; et un morceau de papier nous tenant lieu de tout nous nous jurâmes une fidélité éternelle, et vécûmes dès ce jour-là comme mari et femme.' *Ibid.*, p. 184.

[93] '. . . comme on vit qu'elle n'étoit point à Paris, sans vous dire comment notre route fut découverte, on la sçut, on nous suivit, et on nous surprit que nous étions encore au lit. Je me défendis le plus qu'il me fut possible ; mais je fus accablé par le nombre de mes ennemis. Je fus maltraité et fus moins sensible à tout ce qu'on me faisoit qu'à ce que je voyois qu'on lui faisoit à elle. L'homme entre les mains de qui nous étions pouvoit par sa naissance prendre quelque autorité sur elle, il en abusa. J'en fus au désespoir, mais je n'étois point en état de la vanger que par ma douleur. . . . Je fus lié comme le plus scélerat de tous les criminels. Ce fut en vain qu'elle cria que j'étois son mari. . . .' *Ibid.*, p. 188.

[94] '. . . elle me découvrit entr'autres choses, une gorge et une paire de tetons aussi beaux que j'en aye vû de ma vie.' Chasles, 'Histoire de Monsieur Dupuis et de Madame de Londé', *ibid.*, II, 414.

'We had a good lunch again. Everyone left us, and she and I went to bed. Imagine the rest, between people who are in love. I spent a week with her without leaving the room except to go to mass, and I did that so early that upon my return I could go back to bed again. What a life! A man would be happy if it could last!'[95]

Chasles shows, or his characters show, signs of believing in a fated love. Young men and women are born for each other, and though this is no guarantee of happiness (more often the opposite), it gives assurance that they will be drawn together. Chasles and Prévost, in the first two passages below, express in very similar terms this view which was to become steadily stronger through the eighteenth and early nineteenth centuries. It was reinforced, in many of our writers, by a more general view that the course of our lives is divinely determined, by our 'star' – of this view we shall give several samples.

'. . . we were surely born for each other . . . [witness] our immediate attraction for each other the moment we fell in love, the transformation which I had undertaken rather than leave her, the failure of the attempt to separate us . . . besides, she had in her favour the virtue of generosity, of having given and sacrificed everything for me . . . all this presaged a marriage decreed by Heaven and Fate. God had certainly brought us into the world for each other; the ceremony that had consummated our union had but fulfilled his will, which must be respected.'[96]

---

[95] 'Nous déjeunâmes encore bien, chacun prit congé de nous et nous nous mîmes au lit elle et moi, imaginez-vous le reste, entre deux personnes qui s'aiment.

'Je passai huit jours avec elle sans sortir du tout que pour aller à la messe, et de si bon matin qu'à mon retour je me remettois au lit. Quelle vie! Un homme seroit heureux, si elle pouvoit durer long-temps!' Chasles, 'Des Frans et Silvie', *ibid.*, II, 360.

[96] '. . . nous étions assurément nez l'un pour l'autre . . . cette prompte inclination que nous avions euë tout d'un coup l'un pour l'autre dès le moment que nous nous étions aimez; la métamorphose à quoi je m'étois réduit, plutôt que de la quitter; la vaine entreprise qu'on avoit tentée pour nous désunir . . . outre cela, elle avoit de son côté le mérite de la générosité de m'avoir tout donné et tout sacrifié . . . tout cela ensemble faisoit voir un mariage du Ciel et de destinée. Que Dieu nous avoit certainement fait naître l'un pour l'autre; et que le sacrement qui avoit achevé de nous unir, n'avoit fait qu'accomplir sa volonté qui devoit être respectée.' *Ibid.*, pp. 373–74.

'I cannot doubt, after my experience, that there are hearts which are made for one another, which would never fall in love if they did not have the good fortune of meeting each other. It takes two such hearts but a moment's meeting to realize that they need each other, that their happiness depends on remaining always united. A secret force leads them to fall in love; they recognize each other, one might say, at first sight, and without the help of protestations, proofs, or oaths, a trust is quickly born between them, which leads them to give themselves completely. This is a picture of what happened between Sélima and me.'[97]

'These two lovers heaped thanks upon her [Angélique] for her kindness. . . . [She] answered pleasantly that marriages were contracted in heaven before the principals know each other on earth, and that besides, the impulses of our hearts are not in our control.'[98]

'I had to stay in Paris through the autumn and winter, unfortunately. I say unfortunately, for if I had been elsewhere I would not have ruined myself, as I did, through my own fault, but as if forced by some power which I do not understand. This makes me believe that, though our actions are quite voluntary, at least one may say that our life is not always governed by our will alone, but that our star guides its principal motions and directions.'[99]

[97] 'Je ne saurois douter, après l'expérience que j'en ai faite, qu'il n'y ait des cœurs formés les uns pour les autres, et qui n'aimeroient jamais rien s'ils n'étoient assez heureux pour se rencontrer. Mais il suffit aussi que deux cœurs de cette nature se rencontrent un moment, pour sentir qu'ils sont nécessaires l'un à l'autre, et que leur bonheur dépend de ne se séparer jamais. Une force secrète les entraîne à s'aimer; ils se reconnoissent, pour ainsi dire, aux premières approches; et sans le secours des protestations, des épreuves, des serments, la confiance naît entre eux tout-d'un-coup, et les porte à se livrer sans reserve. C'est l'image de ce qui se passa entre Sélima et moi.' Prévost, *Mém. d'un homme de qualité*, liv. 4, in *Œuvres*, I, 183.
[98] 'Ces deux amans la remercièrent de ses bontez, et lui firent mille amitiez. . . . [Elle] lui dit agréablement que les mariages étoient arrêtez au Ciel avant qu'on se connût sur terre; et qu'outre cela ,les mouvemens de notre cœur ne dépendoient pas de nous.' Chasles, 'Histoire de Monsieur de Contamine et d'Angélique', *Illustres Françoises*, I, 111.
[99] '. . . je fus obligé de rester à Paris l'automne et l'hiver pour mon malheur. Je dis pour mon malheur; car si j'avois été partout ailleurs, je ne me serois pas perdu par ma propre faute comme j'ai fait, mais comme forcé par une certaine

' "The controlling star under which I was born was so firmly opposed to my recovery that, being assured of misfortune, I went about seeking a violent remedy, when you intervened." "Alas !" said Julie, "alas, my brother ! That star which you complain of did me no less harm than it did you. . . . Hypolite, I love you; indeed, I love you too much, since you are my brother. . . ." '[100]

Chasles shows concern lest his characters, overpowered by love, lose control of themselves. Here, for example, is a young man speaking to the father of his beloved: 'Come what may, sir, I shall follow the example of your daughter and tell you nothing, for fear that the deep feeling that stirs me may cause me to forget the respect that I owe the father of a young lady whom I love to the point of madness and idolatry.'[101] We have already spoken of the sacrifice of pride and honour because of love, and have seen some of the uncontrolled faintings and tears to which love brings its victims. Without being quite as excessive as Prévost and some others, Chasles was well on the way, as the following sentences will demonstrate:

'They were in each other's arms for more than a quarter-hour without speaking a word, and it was a good thing that she was on a chair, for when Jussy let go of her she was unconscious. She was brought to, and they embraced again, but

---

puissance que je ne comprens point ; et qui me fait croire, que si nos actions sont tout-à-fait volontaires, du moins peut-on dire que nôtre vie n'est pas toûjours gouvernée par nôtre seule volonté, et que l'Etoile en règle les principaux mouvemens et la disposition.' Chasles, 'Des Frans et Silvie', *ibid.*, II, 289.

[100] 'L'Astre fatal sous lequel je suis né, s'est opposé si fortement à ma guérison, que ne pouvant plus douter de mon malheur, j'y allois chercher un remède violent quand vous vous êtes opposée. Hélas ! reprit Julie ; hélas, mon Frère ! cet Astre duquel vous vous plaignez, ne m'a pas fait moins de mal qu'à vous. . . . Hypolite, je vous aime, et je vous aime trop, puisque vous êtes mon Frère. . . .' Marie Catherine Comtesse d'Aulnoy, *Histoire d'Hypolite, Comte de Duglas*, (new edn ; Brussels : G. de Backer, 1713), p. 40. For another example of incest see note 106, below.

[101] Quoi qu'il en soit, Monsieur, je suivrai l'exemple de Mademsoiselle votre Fille, et ne vous dirai rien, de crainte que la passion dont je suis animé ne me fît sortir du respect que je dois au père d'une fille que j'aime jusqu'à la fureur et à l'idolatrie.' Chasles, 'Histoire de Monsieur Des Ronais et de Mademoiselle Dupuis', *Illustres Françoises*, I, 38.

as I feared she might pass out again, I did not allow them the time for a repeat performance; I separated them. They both had tears in their eyes, and joy had such power over them that they did not have the strength to open their mouths. Truly, what a pleasure to find themselves faithful to each other after so many hardships and so long a separation !'[102]

Strong reactions like these remain superficial in Chasles. They are not indicative of any true soul union, and the idealism of love that would be developed later in the eighteenth century and in the nineteenth is generally lacking in his writings. In his *Journal of a Voyage to the East Indies* (written for the most part on shipboard, 1690–91), Chasles states what appears to be his real, materialistic and hedonistic, view of love – the faintings and tears in his stories notwithstanding. His attitude is reminiscent of Molière's *Misanthrope*, which indeed Chasles quotes in one place.

'A man has to be utterly mad to go so far as to risk his health. . . . These Celadon-like love bouts are devilishly shocking to me, because in my opinion a man of sense should look upon women as no more than simple amusement; it is pure folly to become attached to them to the extent of losing one's peace of mind.'[103]

There are many cases, other than those cited from Chasles, of a frivolous, or at least of a less than solemn, approach to

[102] 'Ils furent plus d'un quart d'heure entre les bras l'un de l'autre sans dire un mot, et bien leur prit qu'elle étoit sur une chaise, car lorsque Jussy la quitta, elle étoit évanoüie. On la fit revenir, ils s'embrassèrent encore; mais comme je craignois pour eux une nouvelle foiblesse, je ne leur donnai pas le tems de se défaire de nouveau. Je les séparai. Ils avoient tous deux les larmes aux yeux, et la joie les saisissoit tellement, qu'ils n'avoient pas la force d'ouvrir la bouche; en effet quel plaisir de se trouver fidèles après tant de traverses, et une absence si longue !' Chasles, 'M. de Jussy et Mlle Fenoüil', *ibid.*, I, 197.

[103] 'Il faut qu'un homme soit diablement fou, pour se livrer jusques à intéresser sa santé. . . . Ces sortes d'amour à la Céladon me choquent comme le Diable; parce que je crois qu'un homme d'esprit ne doit regarder les Dames que comme un simple amusement, et que c'est pure folie de s'y attacher jusques à en perdre le repos.' Chasles, *Journal d'un voyage aux Indes Orientales* (3 vols; Rouen: J.-B. Machuel le Jeune, 1721), II, 37. The modern edition of this work, *Voyage aux Indes d'une escadre française, 1690–1691*, edited by A. Augustin-Thierry (Paris: Plon, 1933), contains but a fraction of the whole and includes very few of the passages used in this study; I have therefore retained the references to the original edition of 1721, even though it is less accessible.

love. The Rabelaisian vein, the *'esprit gaulois'*, which has never been absent from French literature, persisted in our period as well. That love was treated as an amusement can be gleaned not only from many books but from titles and names of characters. One amusing instance, although the book itself is not worth reading, is an *Account of a Trip of Ursuline Nuns of Rouen to New Orleans*,[104] in which there is a Jesuit father named Boulanger, or Baker, and a nun named Tranchepain, or Breadknife. The author of another book of this type tells us that 'it would take a book as big as the world to describe all the happy encounters of love . . . for there is no occupation or individual that has not experienced some good fortune in love; there are even apothecaries and barber-surgeons who have'.[105] The search for the sensational, including a great deal of incest and adultery, is visible in authors both poor and superior. Prévost, for example, gave a great amount of space in his periodical, *Pour et Contre*, to a story of incest in Jamaica. Though Prévost claimed to be summarizing 'a rather long account which has just been published by Cox', it is possible that Prévost is the real author. Here is his story of a Spaniard in Jamaica who, in order to protect his twelve-year-old daughter from marriage to either a local savage or one of the Spanish servants, has her marry her own brother. The story bears some resemblance to several later tales, especially to the part of *Cleveland*, by Prévost himself, which takes place on the isle of Saint Helena, as well as to *Pierre et Virginie*, by Bernardin de Saint-Pierre, and Chateaubriand's *Atala*.

'. . . my children conceived so violent an attraction for each other that I could not prevail upon them to cease acting like a married couple. I sometimes marvelled at their ardent affection, which it was no longer in my power to stop. I considered whether Nature could be offended by a union which must

---

[104] Marie Madeleine Hachard, *Relation de Voyage des Dames religieuses Uruslines de Rouen à la Nouvelle Orléans* (Rouen: Antoine le Prévost, 1738).

[105] 'Il faudroit un livre aussi gros que le monde pour pouvoir décrire toutes les heureuses rencontres d'Amour. . . . Car il n'y a point de métier ni de personne particulière à qui il ne soit arrivé quelque bonne fortune en Amour; il n'est pas même jusqu'aux Apoticaires et aux Chirurgiens qui n'en ayent quelques favorables.' A.-G.-J.-B. de Roquelaure, *Roger Bontemps, en belle humeur* (new edn, 2 vols; Cologne: Pierre Marteau, gendre d'Antoine l'Enclume, 1730), II, 164.

have been necessary in the infancy of the human race, and without which men would not have been able to multiply. But I soon concluded that however one might explain the past, what is today forbidden by laws both human and divine could not be innocent. . . . I only hope that honour and religion will be reasons strong enough to persuade my son and daughter to give each other up; it is in order to stir them by shame that I am revealing to you, in their presence, the whole truth of our adventure.'[106]

Adultery probably occurs no more and no less in the literature of our period than of others. A vivid example can be selected from the *Love Letters of a Portuguese Nun . . . Enriched and Enlarged by a number of new Tender and Moving Letters of Mme F. to Baron B.*: 'I am writing to you right after your departure. . . . But no! No one has ever experienced what I have just felt . . . but my husband is coming in. Lord! What cruelty to be forced to see the man one hates just after leaving the man one loves!'[107]

The following instances of love scenes that border on the erotic or sensual are not unusual in our period. They do not necessarily point to a lower regard for love than is customary, but they may help us keep perspective when reading some of the loftier-sounding writers whom we will sample soon.

[106] '. . . mes enfants conçurent une si violente inclination l'un pour l'autre, qu'il me fut impossible de les faire renoncer à la qualité d'Epoux. J'admirois quelque fois cette tendresse ardente, qu'il ne dépendoit plus de moi d'arrêter. J'examinois si la Nature pouvoit être blessée d'une union qui doit avoir été nécessaire dans l'origine du Genre Humain, et sans laquelle on ne conçoit pas que les Hommes ayent pû se multiplier. Mais je n'étois pas longtems à reconnoître, que dans quelque sens qu'on explique le passé, ce qui est défendu aujourd'hui par les Loix divines et humaines, ne sçauroit être innocent. . . . J'espere seulement que l'honneur et la Religion vont être des motifs assez forts pour faire consentir mon fils et ma fille à renoncer l'un à l'autre : et c'est pour commencer à les exciter par la honte, que je vous découvre en leur présence toute la vérité de notre aventure.' Prévost, *Pour et Contre*, IV, No. 53 (1734), 173-74. For another example of incest, see note 100, above.

[107] 'Je commence à vous écrire aussi-tôt que vous venez de me quitter. . . . Mais non, personne n'a jamais connu comme moi ce que je viens de sentir . . . mais mon mari entre. Dieux! quelle cruauté d'être obligée de voir ce que l'on hait, en quittant ce que l'on aime!' Anne Ferrand (?), *Nouvelles Lettres fort tendres et passionnées de la Présidente F. à Mr. le Baron de B.*, in *Lettres d'Amour d'une religieuse portugaise, augmentées de plusieurs nouvelles lettres* (The Hague: A. DeHondt, 1701), p. 232.

'Expect me tonight between the sheets.
There, I assure you, I will believe you faithful,
As long, Phyllis, as you are in my arms.'[108]

'He [the Count of Canaple, accidentally finding himself in bed with his friend's wife] knew, from the softness of a foot which rested upon him, that he was in bed with a woman. He was young and emotional. . . . Moments like these are not for thought; nor was the Count of Canaple guilty of any. He took advantage of the good fortune which had come his way. . . . [Next morning:] He saw, with astonishment and fright, that he had just betrayed his friend. . . . His soul was rent asunder.'[109]

Passages like these have the virtue of being readable, which is more than can be said of many passages of poetry, drama, and prose that have conventional love language but no ring of sincerity. It is language like the following that has given the eighteenth century the reputation of being particularly lacking in lyricism:

'Thus Iris spoke to me one day;
It bodes well for my love
And is a sure pledge of her affection,
The greatest she can give.
But after all, one is more in love
With those to whom one wants to give oneself.'[110]

'He has just sworn that he loves me, adores me;
That he has found in my eyes a flame which devours him;

---

[108] 'Attendez-moi ce soir entre deux draps./Là, sur ma foi, je vous croirai fidèle,/Tant que serez, Phyllis, entre mes bras.' Chaulieu, 'A Mme D.', in *Poésies*.

[109] '. . . il comprit, par la delicatesse d'un pied qui vint s'appuyer sur lui, qu'il était couché avec une femme ; il étoit jeune et sensible. . . . De pareils moments ne sont pas ceux de la réflexion. Le comte de Canaple n'en fit aucune, et profita du bonheur qui venoit s'offrir à lui. . . . Il vit, avec étonnement et effroi, qu'il venoit de trahir son ami. . . . Son âme étoit déchirée. . . .' Claudine-Alexandrine Guérin de Tencin, *Le Siège de Calais* (1739) (bound together with *Mémoires du Comte de Comminge*; Paris : A. Quantin, 1885), pp. 160–61.

[110] 'Iris un jour me tenait ce langage ;/De mon amour c'est un heureux présage,/De sa tendresse un infaillible gage,/Et le plus grand qu'elle puisse donner ;/Mais après tout on aime davantage/Ceux avec qui on veut se damner.' Quoted from Abbé Régnier Desmarais, *Poésies françoises* (The Hague, 1716), in *Nouvelles de la République des Lettres*, January–February, 1716, Article III.

So moving a homage cannot be expressed
In words more flattering, sweet, and charming.
The incense one offers the gods does not say as much as his
    words.
    Alas ! It is the language of lovers.
In Azor's mouth, what charm it would have had !
And what sighs and tears it would have spared me !

'I find myself again in a state that I love.
How sweet it is ! Oh, Nadine, in truth I am enjoying
A happiness which I think the greatest in life.
At these moments, always too fleeting,
The future, the past, all is obscured and forgotten;
My sorrows are so completely destroyed or suspended,
That I do not recall ever having had any.'[111]

The true bridge, perhaps, between the frivolous, hedonistic
view of love and the solemn, romantic view which was to gain
ground through the eighteenth century, was the Abbé Prévost,
who had a thorough appreciation of both. The following
passage, spoken by Des Grieux in *Manon Lescaut*, is a remarkably acute expression of the libertine approach to love on the
part of a young man who was to become famous as one of
Venus' most complete salves.

'Considering what we are like, it is certain that our happiness
lies in pleasure; I am wary of people's forming any other
idea of it. Now, the heart has no need of long pondering to
feel that, of all the pleasures, that of love is the sweetest. It
soon realizes that it is being deceived when greater pleasures
are promised it elsewhere, and that deception causes it to
distrust the most solidly grounded promises. Preachers, you

---

[111] 'Il vient de me jurer qu'il m'aime, qu'il m'adore ;/Qu'il a pris dans mes
yeux un feu qui le dévore :/En termes plus flatteurs, plus doux, et plus charmans,/
On ne peut jamais rendre un si sensible hommage./L'encens qu'on offre aux
Dieux ne vaut pas ce langage./Hélas ! c'est celui des Amans./Dans la bouche
d'Azor qu'il auroit eu de charmes !/Et qu'il m'épargneroit de soupirs et de larmes !/
. . ./Je me retrouve alors dans un état que j'aime./Qu'il est doux ! Ah ! Nadine,
en effet, je jouis/Du bonheur que je crois le plus grand de la vie./Dans ces momens,
toujours trop tôt évanouis,/L'avenir, le passé, tout se perd et s'oublie ;/Mes
chagrins sont si bien détruits ou suspendus,/Qu'il ne me souvient pas d'en avoir
jamais eus.' La Chaussée, *Amour pour Amour* (1742), II.ii.

who desire to lead men back to virtue, tell me that virtue is absolutely necessary; but do not hide from me the fact that it is severe and painful.'[112]

Love, and even marriage, were separated by Prévost from religion. Union of heart and soul in love, yes; sanction of the Church, when convenient, yes; but for the Church to arrogate to itself any rights, privileges, or veto power, emphatically no. The tone with which Prévost repeatedly makes this point can be gathered from the following examples:

' "When we arrived on this island," I said to him in a tone as proud as his, "we laid claim to all the rights of its inhabitants, especially the two principal rights of freedom and equality. If we recognize any authority as superior to ourselves, it is not that of an individual whose only function is to recite prayers in church; it is solely that of the general assembly of the colony. So, sir," I added, "leave that imperious and haughty manner, which becomes you less than anyone. We shall explain our actions [choosing wives and swearing to be faithful to them, without church ceremony] to those who have a right to ask for explanations." The minister's pride was much shaken by this answer.'[113]

'We were born free. Nothing has seemed to us as unjust and as ill-conceived as that odious ceremony of chance, to

[112] 'De la manière dont nous sommes faits, il est certain que notre félicité consiste dans le plaisir ; je me défie qu'on s'en forme une autre idée : or, le cœur n'a pas besoin de se consulter long-tems, pour sentir que de tous les plaisirs les plus doux, ce sont ceux de l'amour. Il s'aperçoit bientôt qu'on le trompe, lorsqu'on lui en promet ailleurs de plus charmans ; et cette tromperie le dispose à se défier des promesses les plus solides. Prédicateurs, qui voulez me ramener à la vertu, dites-moi qu'elle est indispensablement nécessaire ; mais ne me déguisez pas qu'elle est sévère et pénible.' Prévost, *Manon*, in *Œuvres*, III, 339.

[113] 'Lorsque nous sommes venus dans cette île, lui dis-je d'un ton aussi fier que le sien, nous avons prétendu y entrer dans tous les droits des habitants, et sur-tout dans les deux principaux, qui sont la liberté et l'égalité. Si nous y reconnoissons une autorité supérieure à nous, ce n'est pas celle d'un particulier, qui n'a point ici d'autre emploi que de réciter les prières à l'église, c'est uniquement celle de l'assemblée générale de la colonie. Ainsi, monsieur, ajoutai-je, retranchez cet air impérieux et hautain qui vous convient moins qu'à personne : nous rendrons compte de nos actions à ceux qui ont droit de le demander. L'orgueil du ministre fut extrêmement déconcerté par cette réponse.' Prévost, *Cleveland*, liv. 3, in *Œuvres*, IV, 367.

which, if you had your way, we would owe our wives. English-
men and Frenchmen do not allow anyone to tyrannize their
hearts. We exercised our rights in making our own choice of
the dear and loving mates who would henceforth share our pains
and pleasures. . . .'114

' "I have thought about the fact that we have no minister,"
he [Lord Axminster] added, "but that difficulty will not stop
me from giving you my daughter. Religious authority adds
nothing essential to a father's. My consent and my blessing
will take the place of church ceremonies, and in the future
we can have a more religious celebration." '115

'He had us add to the vows a promise that we would present
ourselves at an altar as soon as we would be in a position to,
so as to receive the blessing of a minister; he then gave us his
own, with the clearest marks of affection and pleasure.'116

The writers of our period strove to show love as an all-
powerful, irresistible force which dominates life throughout
and is the principal source of pleasure and pain. Its first
discovery, usually in a context of youth and innocence, is
often a profound experience, as the following passages from
Prévost will effectively demonstrate:

'I soon realized that I was less of a child than I had thought.
My heart was opened to a thousand pleasurable impulses

114 'Nous sommes nés libres : rien ne nous a paru si injuste et si mal conçu, que
cette odieuse cérémonie du sort, à laquelle vous avez voulu que nous fussions
redevables de nos épouses. Des anglois et des françois ne souffrent point qu'on
tyrannise leur cœur. Nous sommes rentrés dans nos droits en nous choisissant
nous-mêmes de chères et aimables moitiés qui partageront désormais nos peines
et nos plaisirs. . . .' *Ibid.*, p. 368.
115 'J'ai fait réflexion, ajouta-t-il, que nous sommes sans ministre : mais cette
difficulté n'empêchera point que je ne vous donne ici ma fille. L'autorité sacer-
dotale n'ajoute rien d'essentiel à celle d'un père. Mon consentement et ma béné-
diction suppléeront au défaut des cérémonies de l'église, et nous le réparerons
dans la suite par une célébration plus canonique.' *Ibid.*, liv. 4, in *Œuvres*, V, 85.
116 'Il nous fit ajouter à ce serment la promesse de nous présenter aux pieds
des autels aussi-tôt que nous en aurions la commodité, pour y recevoir la béné-
diction d'un ministre, et il nous donna ensuite la sienne, avec les plus vives marques
de tendresse et de satisfaction.' *Ibid.*, p. 90.

which I had never dreamed of. A gentle warmth pervaded my veins. I was in a veritable rapture. . . .'[117]

'[Love] took command of my heart by a surprise attack; but I was not alarmed to see it happen. I was convinced, in accord with the philosophical principles that I had learned from my mother, that the simple impulses of nature, when it has not been corrupted by practices of vice, never contain anything contrary to virtue. They do not need to be repressed, but only regulated by reason.'[118]

'But it appeared to me, after sincere examination, that, the rights of nature being the most basic of all rights, nothing was strong enough to prescribe against them; that love was one of the most sacred, since it is, as it were, the heart and soul of everything alive; thus, all that reason or the order established among men could do against it was to prohibit certain effects, without ever being able to condemn it at its source.'[119]

' "I was so surprised and so delighted . . . that never has a truth appeared to me so much like a dream. The impulses that my heart felt appeared to me different from those one feels in a state of wakefulness. It was something above nature, it was . . . I cannot express it, and the most delicious moment of my life was the one in which I experienced it." '[120]

[117] 'Je reconnus bientôt que j'étois moins enfant que je ne le croyois. Mon cœur s'ouvrit à mille sentimens de plaisir, dont je n'avois jamais eu l'idée. Une douce chaleur se répandit dans toutes mes veines. J'étois dans une espèce de transport. . . .' Prévost, *Manon*, in *Œuvres*, III, 248–49.

[118] '. . . il s'empara de mon cœur par une espèce de surprise, mais je ne m'effrayai point de l'y appercevoir. J'étois persuadé, suivant les principes de la philosophie de ma mère, que les mouvemens simples de la nature, quand elle n'a point été corrompue par l'habitude du vice, n'ont jamais rien de contraire à l'innocence. Ils ne demandent point d'être réprimés, mais seulement d'être réglés par raison.' Prévost, *Cleveland*, liv. 1, in *Œuvres*, IV, 137.

[119] 'Mais il me parut, après un sincère examen, que les droits de la nature étant les premiers de tous les droits, rien n'étoit assez fort pour prescrire contre eux; que l'amour en étoit un des plus sacrés, puisqu'il est comme l'ame de tout ce qui subsiste, et qu'ainsi tout ce que la raison ou l'ordre établi parmi les hommes pouvoient faire contre lui, étoit d'interdire certains effets, sans pouvoir jamais le condamner dans sa source.' *Ibid.*, p. 145.

[120] 'J'étois si surpris, et si charmé . . . que jamais une vérité ne me parut approcher si fort d'un songe. Les mouvemens mêmes que mon cœur ressentoit, me paroissoient d'une autre espèce que ceux qu'on éprouve en veillant. C'étoit quelque chose de supérieur à la nature, c'étoit . . . il est impossible que je l'exprime,

Life without love is not thinkable, and its dominion, whether for good or ill, cannot be gainsaid:

'All my emotions, in truth, came down to that one. . . . It was the sweetness of my life, the charm of my sufferings, and the reward for the perpetual constraint that I set on all my other desires. Reason, duty, natural bent of an infinitely sensitive heart – everything conspired to make love necessary for my happiness. Therefore, I had made so sweet a habit of it that, just as one must breathe to live, so I had to love Fanny and be loved by her in order to be happy.'[121]

'The joy that he showed . . . made clear to me for the first time what I have never felt by experience, but what I have since seen confirmed by other cases, namely, that . . . love is a violent emotion, that it dominates the imagination as completely as it does the heart, and that, extending its tyranny over the body and the soul, it affects the blood and the reason at one and the same time.'[122]

Nor do men's ruses – much less their willpower – suffice to turn love from its appointed, and often fated, course. Thus, a young French marquis, after falling in love with a young man from Turkey and being properly upbraided by his governor for his 'simple passion', happily learns, eventually, that the young man is a girl, who for complicated reasons has had to take a male disguise. Love could not mislead him after all: 'Her face was so charming in that outfit that one would have

---

et le plus délicieux moment de ma vie fut celui auquel je l'éprouvai.' *Ibid.*, liv. 2, in *Œuvres*, IV, 220–21.

[121] 'Toutes mes passions en effet se réduisoient à celle-là. . . . C'étoit toute la douceur de ma vie, le charme de mes peines, et le dédommagement de la contrainte perpetuelle où je tenois tous mes autres désirs. Raison, devoir, penchant naturel d'un cœur infiniment sensible, tout s'accordoit à rendre l'amour nécessaire à mon bonheur. Aussi m'en étois-je fait une si douce habitude, que de même qu'il faut respirer pour vivre, il me falloit aimer Fanny et être aimé d'elle, pour être heureux.' *Ibid.*, liv. 5, in *Œuvres*, V, 359.

[122] 'La joie qu'il fit paroître . . . me fit connoître alors pour la première fois ce que je n'ai jamais senti par expérience, mais ce qu'une infinité d'autres exemples ne m'ont que trop confirmé dans la suite ; je veux dire que . . . l'amour est une passion violente, mais qu'elle s'empare de l'imagination aussi souverainement que du cœur ; et qu'étendant sa tyrannie sur le corps et sur l'ame, elle trouble tout à la fois le sang et la raison.' Prévost, *Killerine*, liv. 1, in *Œuvres*, VIII, 49.

had to be either more or less than human not to be moved by it.'[123]

Though sadness and depression appear no less in the love literature of this period than of others, our characters frequently affirm that nothing in life is more important or more satisfying than love, somewhat in the tone of the following outburst: 'Without sorrow do I abandon the frivolous glory that battles bring or high office awards; what triumph can equal the sweetness of mine !'[124]

The predominance of sensuality in this literature was, at least in part, dictated by public taste. The authors themselves, and their main characters, often protest that soul union, and not physical pleasure, is the true aim of love; but, as the history of Platonic love in the Renaissance has taught us, the line is hard to draw between sense fulfilment *per se* and sense fulfilment in the service of a nobler ideal. Here are two typical expressions of the aim of love, followed by a quotation from Marivaux, whose depth and clarity produce a statement far more piercing than most.

'There is a pleasure more moving and more lasting than the union of the senses: that is the union of hearts, that secret yearning which impels you toward the one you love.'[125]

'But what have I ever sought in love? Is it sensual pleasure? That lowers man to the level of the beasts. No, it is the sweet union of two hearts that are harmonious in their feelings; it is the love of perfection, the inexpressible enchantment of tender affection.'[126]

'A man who desires you more than he loves you is a mean

---

[123] 'Sa figure étoit si charmante en cet équipage, qu'il falloit être plus ou moins qu'homme pour n'en être pas ému.' Prévost, *Mém. d'un homme de qualité*, liv. 10, in *Œuvres*, II, 266.

[124] 'J'abandonne sans peine la gloire frivole que l'on acquiert dans les combats, et par des emplois brillans; quel triomphe peut égaler la douceur du mien!' Auvigny, *Mémoires de Comminville*, p. 29.

[125] 'Il y a un plaisir plus touchant et plus durable que la liaison des sens, c'est l'union des cœurs; ce penchant secret qui vous porte vers ce que vous aimez. . . .' Mme de Lambert, *Réflexions sur les femmes*, in *Œuvres Morales*, pp. 167–68.

[126] 'Mais qu'ai-je jamais cherché dans l'amour? Est-ce le plaisir des sens? Il abaisse l'homme au rang des bêtes. Non, c'est la douce union de deux cœurs qui s'accordent dans tous leurs sentimens; c'est le goût du mérite, c'est le charme inexprimable de la tendresse. . . .' Prévost, *Cleveland*, liv. 6, in *Œuvres*, V, 524.

lover. Not that the most delicate lover will not desire you, in his way; but the difference is that in his case the dictates of the heart and those of the senses are commingled, all melted into one – which creates a tender, not a sinful, love, though it is in truth capable of sin; for in matters of love people are constantly using refinement to perform lowly acts; but that is not the point.'[127]

[127] '. . . c'est un vilain amant qu'un homme qui vous désire plus qu'il ne vous aime : non pas que l'amant le plus délicat ne désire à sa manière, mais du moins c'est que chez lui les sentiments du cœur se mêlent avec les sens ; tout cela se fond ensemble : ce qui fait un amour tendre, et non pas vicieux, quoi-que à la vérité capable du vice ; car tous les jours, en fait d'amour, on fait très-délicatement des choses fort grossières : mais il ne s'agit point de cela.' Marivaux, *Marianne*, Part I, in *Romans*, p. 109.

CHAPTER 2

Literary Attitudes and Stance

UNREASON plays a big part in our period. The works of many authors, and many parts of the works of others, including the most balanced and perceptive, present a striking divorce from the real world. Though some of these writings, by men like Prévost and Marivaux, must be deemed first-rate from the viewpoint of credibility, naturalness, realism, and other such prosaic virtues, these masters sinned only somewhat less than their contemporaries.

EXAGGERATED 'LITERARY' SENTIMENTS

It is understandable that the frank revelation of certain thoughts and emotions, which at least on such a scale was a departure from the past, should lead to excess and exaggeration on the part of innovators – which, let us not forget, the writers of this period really were. The fast growth in the public consumption of literature, moreover, was a temptation to lower aesthetic and intellectual levels, a phenomenon with which readers of the present age will be familiar, so that even the best writers sometimes look like hacks. As students of later French literature will recognize, some of the developments during this period were to bear fruit and earn a respected place in the fine writings of the Romantic era and later, but the early eighteenth century was not able to handle these literary processes with the effectiveness of the early nineteenth. What seems exaggeration may thus often be due to groping and stumbling; surely our authors did not want to appear unbelievable or unconvincing. And yet . . .

The level on which our authors operated much of the time can be gathered from a few sample glances at *Les Mémoires du Comte de Comminge*, a book written by Mme de Tencin, a lady of distinction and taste and some notoriety. Young Comminge, because of his refusal to marry as his father dictated, is forced to live in an isolated tower of his family's castle, where he torments himself with the reading and rereading of a letter from his beloved, which tells him of her forthcoming marriage; for, matching the heartlessness of the young man's father, the girl's father has forced her to choose one of a specified list of suitors. Unable to have her count because of family feuding, she has chosen the most frightful of the group. When the count escapes from his prison in a frenzied attempt to stop the marriage, or to 'die at her feet', he learns that she has already married the ogre. Disguising himself as a workman, he succeeds in penetrating the household of his beloved and her husband. There ensue discoveries, duels, and deaths (both pseudo and real), with very little that a reasonable reader could regard as credible. The book had a great vogue, with many editions in the eighteenth century and in the early nineteenth.

The extent to which all this was accepted – or considered unavoidable – at the time can be seen in the following comments from a review of a *Secret History of the Galant Ladies of Antiquity*, a three-volume opus published in 1732. The reviewer obviously wants more than melodrama, but he is not so bold, or perhaps so foolish, as to fight it.

'. . . this book is not merely a new combination of miraculous understandings, invincible drives, moving declarations, and dangerous meetings; of alarms, jealousies, kidnappings, and absences; of shipwrecks, recognitions, and all those common-places of which novels are made up and which speak only to the readers' imagination. The anonymous author has chosen a more reasonable and useful goal . . . the fulfillment of which demanded a distrust of the testimony of poets and a reliance on that of historians.'[1]

---

[1] '. . . ce livre n'est point uniquement une nouvelle combinaison de sympathies merveilleuses, de penchants invincibles, de déclarations touchantes, d'entrevûës hazardeuses, d'allarmes, de jalousies, d'enlevemens, d'absences, de naufrages, de reconnoissances et de tous ces lieux communs qui composent les Romans, et qui ne parlent qu'à l'imagination des Lecteurs. L'inconnu qui l'a composé, s'y propose un but plus raisonnable et plus utile. . . . Pour remplir ce dessein, il falloit se défier du témoignage des Poëtes et recourir à celui des Historiens.' Review of *Histoire secrette des Femmes galantes de l'Antiquité* (1732), in *Journal des Sçavans*, November, 1732, p. 369.

Here is part of an author's résumé of his own novel, published in 1732, the same year as the preceding: 'It is about a woman who, born and raised in a strange manner, and after a great many adventures in the world, finally married, in Flanders, the second son of Jean Olden de Barneveldt. . . . Though clothed in male attire during the early years of her life, Mme de Barneveldt in no way offends modesty.'[2] This book, which could almost have served as a model for *Candide* twenty-five years later, contains murders and enslavements, arrests and escapes, the dead coming alive, and all the rest of the melodramatic menu, the whole seasoned with plenty of disguises and mistaken identities. The most amusing moment (for us) comes when the heroine, who in consideration of her male disguise has had to reject a number of attractive young ladies, finally falls in love with one. Happily, it develops that this young lady is really a man dressed as a girl, so that a quick exchange of costumes permits a proper Florentine marriage – after which occur some of the heart-rending adventures referred to above. (This change of sex in Castre d'Auvigny's book is very similar to an episode in Prévost's *Mémoires d'un homme de qualité*, Book X.)

A rather less happy outcome of this kind of sex mix-up occurs in the Comtesse d'Aulnoy's *Histoire d'Hypolite, Comte de Duglas*. Here a fair lady, Julie, disguised as a pilgrim (male), captures the love of a marquise, who takes her for a handsome young man (*un jeune homme si beau*). One night, having followed Julie (alias Silvio), the marquise finds her asleep (fully dressed so as to keep the mistake going, no doubt) and bends over to steal a kiss. The unexpected arrival of the marquise's husband on the scene puts an end to the infatuation: he stabs his wife to death and, after wounding Julie, has her-him imprisoned.[3]

When, in the midst of all this excitement, there is a period of quiet, it is sure to be short and unstable. Prévost spoke for

---

[2] 'Il s'agit ici de la vie d'une femme, qui née et élevée d'une façon très-singulière, après avoir eu un grand nombre d'aventures dans le monde, épousa enfin en Flandre le second fils de Jean Olden de Barneveldt. . . . Sous l'habit d'homme que Madame de Barneveldt porte les premières années de sa vie, il ne lui échappe rien de contraire à la pudeur.' Jean du Castre d'Auvigny, *Mémoires de Madame de Barneveldt* (2 vols; Paris: Gandouin et Giffart, 1732), Avertissement.

[3] Aulnoy, *Histoire d'Hypolite*, pp. 35–51.

a multitude of his contemporaries when he wrote: 'However, all that structure of peace and happiness was a vain illusion, which had built up by degrees only to vanish in a moment. My name was inscribed on the darkest, saddest page of the book of destiny, where it was followed by a list of terrible sentences which I was condemned to suffer one after another.'[4]

Robert Chasles participated fully, and expertly, in the melodrama and excitement that filled this literature. His 'History of Monsieur de Terny and Mademoiselle de Bernay', one of the stories in his *Illustrious Frenchwomen*, contains the following typical account, by the hero, of a ceremony at which his beloved, a nun in a convent, was to take the religious vows:

'The ceremony continued; I was too unaware of what was going on to be able to describe it to you. My thoughts and my eyes were only on Clémence, who, when asked what she desired, answered firmly, as we had agreed: "I want the Count de Terny for my husband if he is willing to have me for his wife," and saying this, she threw herself madly into my arms. My friends and Monsieur de Lutry's men, by pre-arrangement, surrounded us and kept the crowd away. . . . The nuns were frightfully scandalized and the whole clergy shocked. A loud and disrespectful murmur arose in front of the Blessed Sacrament, which was left exposed. I had received Clémence in my arms, and had kissed and embraced her before everyone, openly, in church.'[5]

[4] 'Cependant, tout cet édifice de tranqullité et de bonheur étoit un vain fantôme, qui s'étoit formé par degrés pour s'évanouir en un moment. Mon nom étoit écrit dans la page la plus noire et la plus funeste du livre des destinées; il y étoit accompagné d'une multitude d'arrêts terribles, que j'étois condamné à subir successivement.' Prévost, *Cleveland*, liv. 2, in *Œuvres*, IV, 228.

[5] 'La cérémonie fut poursuivie; j'y pris trop peu de part pour vous en faire le récit. Je ne songeais et ne regardois que Clémence, qui lorsqu'on lui demanda ce qu'elle vouloit, répondit fort résolument, comme nous en étions convenus.

—Je demande Monsieur le Comte de Terny pour mon Epoux s'il veut bien de moi pour sa Femme, et en même tems elle se jetta à corps perdu dans mes bras. Mes Amis et les gens de Monsieur de Lutry qui avoient apparemment l'ordre, nous entourèrent et écartèrent la presse. . . . Les Religieuses en furent terriblement scandalisées, et tout le Clergé surpris. Il se fit un murmure très-grand et très-peu respectueux, devant le Saint Sacrement qui étoit exposé. J'avois reçu Clémence entre mes bras; je l'avois baisée et embrassée devant tout le monde en pleine Eglise.' Chasles, *Illustres Françoises*, I, 165–66.

In another story, 'Histoire de Monsieur de Jussy et de Mademoiselle Fenoüil', Chasles makes effective use of a suicide threat uttered by the heroine to test her lover. The melodramatic tone of the story will appear from the following lines:

'Finishing these words, she took from a little box a folded paper in which there was a yellow powder that I was un-acquainted with. . . . This she mixed with some preserves, which she fed to a little dog of hers. Hardly had the little animal swallowed this than it fell stone dead . . . but when I saw her take that goblet and bring it to her mouth, all my senses revived. I leaped at it, spilled part of it on the floor, and the rest I hurled out into the courtyard. A big dog which belonged to Ivonne's coachman came and licked the con-coction, and died a moment later.'[6]

An amusing variation within this body of melodrama is occasional restraint on the part of a character. Given the assumptions to which the reader becomes accustomed, the failure of a character to react with customary violence, swoon-ings, or outcries must have been a welcome, as well as effective, departure. Thus, in Chasles's 'Histoire de Monsieur Des Frans et de Silvie', in a passage quoted in Chapter I, what would normally have been a single or double murder, with perhaps a suicide added, turns out to be a scene of quiet suffering – a bit incredible but refreshing. Entering the bedroom and seeing his wife asleep with a friend of the family, the hero first has an impulse of revenge – but, overcome by an impulse of tenderness, spares her life and only takes her necklace which lay unclasped.[7]

One saving grace of the melodramatic writing of this period

---

[6] 'En achevant ces paroles elle tira d'un petit coffret un papier plié, dans lequel il y avoit d'une poudre jaune que je ne connoissois pas . . . qu'elle mêla avec des confitures, et les fit manger à une petite Chienne qu'elle avoit. A peine ce petit animal en eut-il dans le corps qu'il tomba mort sans branler . . . mais lorsque je lui vis prendre ce gobelet et le porter à sa bouche, tous mes sens me revinrent. Je me jettai dessus, j'en répandis une partie à terre, et je jettai le reste dans la Cour. Un gros Chien qui appartenoit au Cocher d'Ivonne, vint lécher cette composition, et mourut un moment après.' Chasles, 'Histoire de M. de Jussy et de Mlle Fenoüil', *ibid.*, I, 186–87.

[7] For the full quote and translation, see p. 64 and note.

is its internationalism. The authenticity of the multitudinous exotic scenes is usually dubious, but as an element which added interest and flavour to the succession of sad stories, their value at the time was immeasurable. Sometimes, as in *The Life of Madame de Beaumont*, by Pénélope Aubin, a Protestant refugee in England, we are taken to the caves of Great Britain, as well as to London and the English forests, which contained plenty of rustic huts in which a villain could incarcerate an innocent woman, and which afforded plenty of room for bandits to batter the defenses of female virtue. Sometimes, as in the same Mme Aubin's *The Noble Slaves*, we meet Persians on the coast of Mexico and have escapes in Japanese ships and pursuits by North African pirates. Prévost's flight of Des Grieux and Manon through the wilds of North America and of a servant turned pirate through the forests of Corsica with a noble lady in his charge (*Mémoires d'un homme de qualité*, Book VIII) are better-known examples of adventures tinged with the exoticism of the time.

Occasionally our authors recognized that they were doing little more than following the conventions of the period, but, as we can see in a frank passage from Du Castre d'Auvigny's *Mémoires du Comte de Comminville* (1735), this did not deter them from staying in the main stream.

'. . . the coasts were infected with pirates from Tunis and Morocco. . . . You can already see me as a slave in Morocco or Tunis; in that I am like almost all the heroes of our modern novels; but is it my fault if the pirates are so diligent? I would very much have liked not to meet them; but they came and, like hungry wolves, swooped down on our little boat . . . and put us in chains. . . .'[8]

The fated quality of love appears many times in the novels. The following example, which points to many Romantic

[8] '. . . les Côtes étoient infestées de Corsaires de Tunis et de Maroc . . . on me voit déjà esclave à Maroc ou à Tunis; je ressemble en cela à presque tous les Héros de nos Romans modernes; mais est-ce ma faute si les Corsaires sont si diligens? J'aurois voulu pour beaucoup ne les avoir point rencontrés; ils vinrent fondre, comme des loups affamés, sur ma petite barque . . . on nous chargea de chaînes. . . .' Auvigny, *Mémoires de Comminville*, p. 105.

expressions of the same idea later, comes from one of the leading writers:

' "How admirable that is! And then you ask me whether I love you! But could it be otherwise? Do you not see that my love, born by divine prophecy, was determined before we were born? Nothing could be clearer." "Truly, you speak marvellously," she answered, "and it seems to me that God has furnished you the means of convincing me. Yes, my friend, I do not doubt that you are the one to whom God wants me to be attached; you are the man I was seeking, with whom I must live, and I shall give myself to you." '[9]

Sudden and surprising deaths are a frequent part of the melodramatic pattern of the time, such as this one in the *Mémoires du Chevalier de T——*:

'One night when she had seemed to me more ill than usual. . . . "Ah, dear Count," she said to me in a dying voice, "I look upon you for the last time!" I rushed to her, and saw her expire in my arms.'[10]

Often the surviving lover talks to the deceased, and if he is lucky, as in the third quotation below, she will come back to life; if not, he will die with her, as in the last:

'I took the body in my arms, and when I could open my mouth I called Julie by name, unable to believe that I had lost her for good. I spoke to her as though she could hear me. But alas! My dear, lovely Julie was alive no longer; her beautiful soul was already in the bosom of the Lord; for

---

[9] '. . . que cela est admirable! Et puis vous me demandez si je vous aime? Eh! mais cela se peut-il autrement? Ne voyez-vous pas bien que mon affection se trouve là par une prophétie divine, et que cela était décidé avant nous? Il n'y a rien de si visible.

—En vérité, tu dis à merveille, me répondit-elle, et il semble que Dieu te fournisse de quoi achever de me convaincre. Allons, mon fils, je n'en doute pas, tu es celui à qui Dieu veut que je m'attache, tu es l'homme que je cherchais, avec qui je dois vivre, et je me donnerai à toi.' Marivaux, *Paysan parvenu*, Part II, in *Romans*, p. 646.

[10] 'Une nuit qu'elle m'avoit paru plus mal qu'à l'ordinaire. . . . Ah, mon cher Comte, me dit-elle d'une voix mourante, je vous vois pour la dernière fois! Je courus à elle, et je la vis expirer dans mes bras.' Anon., *Mémoires du Chevalier de T——*, pp. 205–6.

where else could it have gone, with so much innocence and virtue?'[11]

'I remained more than twenty-four hours with my mouth pressed to the face and hands of my dear Manon. My plan was to die there; but at the start of the second day, I reflected that after my death her body would be left exposed and become the prey of wild beasts. I resolved to bury her and await death at her grave.'[12]

'Picking her up by her clothes, he carried her until he was able to put her down on the island which was nearby. But it is not possible to describe the extent of his sorrow when he saw that her eyes were closed and that a deathly pallor covered her face; she was without movement . . . "Julie, dear Julie, what will become of me?" Having said these words, he embraced her closely, put his lips on hers, and was about to die of the extreme sorrow that filled his breast. But his burning sighs and the flood of tears with which he bathed her face soon drew her out of the unconsciousness into which fear, and nothing more, had thrown her.'[13]

'He addressed a thousand tender words to the spirit which appeared to him in imagination, and his soul, making a

---

[11] 'Je pris le corps dans mes bras, et lorsque je pus ouvrir la bouche, j'appelois Julie par son nom, ne pouvant me persuader que je l'eusse perdue tout à fait. Je lui parlois, comme si elle eût été en état de m'entendre. Mais hélas ! ma chère et trop aimable Julie ne vivoit plus ; sa belle âme étoit déjà dans le sein de Dieu : car où seroit-elle allée avec tant d'innocence et de vertu ?' Prévost, *Mém. d'un homme de qualité*, liv. 1, in *Œuvres*, I, 39.

[12] 'Je demeurai, plus de vingt-quatre heures, la bouche attachée sur le visage et sur les mains de ma chère Manon. Mon dessein étoit d'y mourir ; mais je fis réflexion, au commencement du second jour, que son corps seroit exposé après mon trépas, à devenir la pâture des bêtes sauvages. Je formai la résolution de l'enterrer, et d'attendre la mort sur sa fosse.' Prévost, *Manon*, in *Œuvres*, III, 478.

[13] 'L'ayant prise par ses habits, il ne la quitta point qu'il ne l'eût mise dans l'Isle dont ils n'étoient pas éloignez ; mais il n'est pas possible de bien représenter quel fut l'excès de sa douleur, lorsqu'il vit que ses yeux étoient ferméz, et qu'une pâleur mortelle lui couvroit le visage : elle étoit sans mouvement . . . —Julie, ma chère Julie, que vais-je devenir? En achevant ces mots il la serra étroitement en ses bras, il attacha sa bouche sur la sienne, et fut prêt d'expirer par la douleur extrême qu'il ressentoit, mais ses brûlants soupirs, et le deluge de larmes dont il lui mouilloit le visage, la tirèrent bien-tôt d'un état, où la seule frayeur l'avoit jettée.' Aulnoy, *Histoire d'Hypolite*, pp. 30-31.

great effort to join it, became loosed from his body, and he fell dead on the grave.'[14]

The prolonged contemplation of the portrait of a beloved from whom a hero or heroine has been forcibly separated, the caressing of some keepsake, and other traces of fetishism are present everywhere. The portrait and the clothing are most typical: 'I went in . . . to look at the picture . . . very life-like; I sat facing it and there spent a part of the day with a satisfaction known only to those who are in love.'[15] In Prévost's *Mémoires d'un homme de qualité* a young marquis has shirts made for himself of the last garments which his late beloved had worn. He treasures her hat, gloves, stockings, and so on, but these cannot readily be made into men's clothes. In another place we have a precious blood-stained handkerchief: 'I shall keep, till my last living moment, this sad monument of my love and misfortune; I have it from Philippa, who used it – alas without avail – to stop the blood of my poor, dying Clara.'[16]

We have already referred to an occasional display of objectivity on the part of our authors, an awareness of the conventional character of their fiction. There is even – though rarely – some evidence of a sense of humour, which must have provided the writers a moment of relief from the strained and plaintive style. The following touch, though not entirely without parallel, is not easily duplicated: 'I am tall and good-looking, with shiny black eyes. . . . My mouth is big when I laugh, small when I do not – but unfortunately I am always laughing. I have beautiful teeth, a pretty nose, and my throat . . .'[17]

[14] 'Il adressa aussi mille expressions tendres au Fantôme que son imagination lui representoit, et son ame fit tant d'efforts pour se hâter de le joindre, qu'elle se dégagea effectivement des liens du corps. Il tomba mort sur le tombeau.' Prévost, *Pour et Contre*, IV, No. 51 (1734), 143–44.

[15] 'J'allois dans l'appartement . . . pour contempler le portrait . . . très ressemblant: je m'y asseyois vis-à-vis, j'y passois une partie de la journée dans une satisfaction qui n'est connuë que de ceux qui aiment.' Anon., *Mémoires du Chevalier de T——*, p. 69.

[16] 'Je conserverai jusqu'au tombeau ce funeste monument de mon infortune et de mon amour: je le tiens de Philippa qui s'en est servie trop inutilement pour arrêter le sang et la vie de la malheureuse Clara.' Prévost, *Mém. d'un homme de qualité*, liv. 9, in *Œuvres*, II, 178.

[17] 'Je suis grande et de bonne mine; j'ay les yeux noirs et brillans . . . ma bouche est grande quand je ris, fort petite quand je ne ris point; mais par malheur pour elle, je ris toujours. J'ay les dents belles, le nez bien fait, la gorge. . . .' D'Alègre,

The grotesque has, in the authors of this period, a part which will assume larger proportions later. Its function is usually to provide a contrast between inner beauty and outer ugliness. The following description, quoted earlier in another connection, inevitably brings to mind Hugo's Quasimodo of a century after:

'Heaven had early taught me to hate the world and to love solitude. I had entered the world with three infirmities, from which no care or remedy was able to deliver me. My legs were crooked – though strong enough, and nearly enough equal in length to allow me to walk straight. Further, I had a hump not only in back but also in front, and to top all this off, my face was disfigured by warts which were regularly spaced above my eyes and on my forehead in the shape of two horns. Add the fact that my head was big and my torso full, short, and stocky.'[18]

Again in a manner which readers of French literature will recognize as early pre-Romantic, there is great concern for chastity and modesty, in the midst of a heavily suggestive and often erotic literature. On the one hand we have cases such as the young lady in Boursault's *Lettres à Babet et de Babet* (1697) who writes to her lover: 'Whether we sleep together, or at least in the same room, tomorrow depends on you,'[19] and who receives the following direct answer: 'You would be the first nice girl ever to have asked me to go to bed with her and received no for an answer.'[20] On the other hand there is great delicacy. In Prévost's *Cleveland*, for example, there is an episode in which the Indians of Virginia strip the clothes off all the Europeans, who make shift with such meagre belts and scanty 'tunics' as they can design with the reeds and grasses at hand. Our young man, eager to see his beloved

---

Les Aventures, ou mémoires de la Vie de Henriette Sylvie de Molière (Paris and Brussels: J. van Vlaenderen, 1707), beginning.

[18] For the French original, see Ch. I, Note 79.

[19] 'Il ne tiendra qu'à Toy que demain nous ne couchions ensemble ou du moins dans la mesme chambre.' Edme Boursault, *Lettres à Babet et de Babet* (Paris, 1697), p. 192.

[20] 'Tu serois la première honneste Fille qui m'ait jamais prié de coucher avec elle, que j'eusse refusée.' *Ibid.*, p. 195.

after a long absence, receives the following sensitive advice from his fellow European: 'I understand that you wish to see her, and I can assure you in advance that she will be delighted to find that you still have some affection for her. But in the state she is in, with Madame Riding and her women, I advise you, out of consideration for their modesty, to wait till night brings us darkness.'[21]

Considering the quantity of violence that fills the books from which we are quoting, it is to be expected that there will be considerable bloodthirstiness, including, as in the first passage below, a literal wallowing in blood.

'Sara lay stretched out, without any sign of feeling or consciousness; and her blood, which gushed forth, had covered the floor to such an extent that Patrice, from where he was standing with Mademoiselle de L——, could not take a step without treading on it . . . but seeing that in the haste with which he had got up he had stepped into the blood which he had just spilled and which he still saw flowing, he leaped over to the first place where he could sit down, as if he had been walking on burning irons whose heat his feet could not bear. He wiped them with his handkerchief, which was covered with blood, and he looked at it with a release of pain and consternation. His valet, who watched his movements . . . saw a stream of tears flowing down his cheeks.'[22]

'I went up to milady's apartment and found her seated and

[21] 'Je comprends que vous souhaitez de la voir, . . . et je puis vous répondre d'avance qu'elle sera charmée de vous retrouver de l'affection pour elle. Mais dans l'état où elle est avec madame Riding et ses femmes, je vous conseille, pour ménager leur modestie, d'attendre que la nuit nous amène l'obscurité.' Prévost, *Cleveland*, liv. 4, in *Œuvres*, V, 65.

[22] 'Sara étoit étendue sans aucun signe de connoissance ni de sentiment; et son sang, qui couloit à grands flots, s'étoit déja tellement répandu sur le plancher, que dans la situation où il [Patrice] étoit avec mademoiselle de L——, il ne pouvoit faire un pas sans le fouler aux pieds . . . mais s'appercevant que dans la précipitation avec laquelle il s'étoit levé, il avoit trempé ses pieds dans le sang qu'il venoit de répandre, et qu'il voyoit encore couler, il se jeta dans le premier endroit où il pût s'asseoir comme s'il eût marché sur un fer brûlant dont ses pieds n'eussent pu supporter l'ardeur; il les essuya de son mouchoir, qu'il retira, en effet, tout sanglant, et qu'il se mit à considérer avec un redoublement de douleur et de consternation. Son valet-de-chambre, qui observoit toutes ses démarches . . . avoit vu couler le long de ses joues un ruisseau de larmes.' Prévost, *Killerine*, liv. 8, in *Œuvres*, IX, 369–70.

all covered with blood, but there was still some life left in her.
Monsieur de B—— ... was stretched out and showed no sign
of life; his brain could be seen in several places on the floor.
My niece had fallen into a deep faint. ... I had the body of
Monsieur de B—— taken away. ...'[23]

ANTI-INTELLECTUALISM

Much of the foregoing suggests a sensationalism, an emotionalism, scarcely in keeping with the developing rationalism of the
time. The truth is that, in whatever direction one turns,
opposition to the growing forces of Enlightenment are visible
side by side with the harbingers of reason. It is as though – to
judge by some of our authors – they are fighting the three Rs
of reason, reform, and relativity before these can get well
started; the fact that the forces of light and reason were to
prevail should not blind us to the considerable body of literature which expressed reservations and which, in the long run,
was to keep doors ajar for the prophets of Romanticism.
Perhaps a study of this period merely confirms what we should
know about any period – that all opinions exist: historical
conditions help some to thrive and force others to flow under-
ground, for a time.

Doubts regarding the efficacy of reason were voiced by
many writers, often in balanced and sober terms. Often, in
keeping with established French practice dating at least from
Montaigne's time, there is no special opposition to reason, but
rather doubt as to its chance of gaining sway over mankind.
Reason is here equated with strength, and man's inability to
follow reason is a sign of weakness. Some writers, on the other
hand, are distrustful of reason altogether, or opposed to it,
quite aside from whether men can or cannot follow it. Better,
say these writers, to trust instinct and feeling. A number of
writers, as we might expect, demand only that the flight to

[23] 'Je montai à l'appartement de miladi, que je trouvai assise et toute sanglante,
mais à qui il restoit encore quelque sentiment de vie. M. de B—— étoit étendu
sans mouvement; sa cervelle paroissoit en plusieurs endroits sur le plancher.
Ma nièce étoit tombée dans un profond évanouissement. ... Je fis éloigner le
cadavre de M. de B——.' Prévost, *Mém d'un homme de qualité*, liv. 13, in *Œuvres*,
III, 35–36.

reason be tempered by recognition of man's emotional side. The following quotations are a fair representation of the comments on this subject. For some writers reason is good, but man is too weak to follow it:

'The mind is an ornament of man that is not acquired by our power; it is Nature that gives it to us, and by that token, as well as by the small number of persons to whom she makes this gift, she shows us clearly that it is not necessary for us to have it.'[24]

> 'Feeble Reason, much praised by man,
> Here is your true meaning and power:
> Ever vain, ever false, ever full of injustice,
> In all our speech we rail
> Against the emotions, weaknesses, and vices
> To which we always yield.'[25]

'A blade of grass that we trample underfoot is the stumbling block of the whole proud structure of philosophy. A peasant sees as much of it with his naked eye as a physicist after thirty years of study and contemplation, except perhaps that the physicist, with the help of a good microscope, will examine the surface of the blade of grass more intimately. . . . The basic causative factor, which creates the essence and nature of any body, is not within reach of optical apparatus or within the jurisdiction of the senses.'[26]

[24] 'L'Esprit est un Ornement de l'Homme, qu'il ne dépend pas de nous d'aquerir ; c'est la Nature qui nous le donne, et par là, aussi bien que par le petit nombre de personnes à qui elle fait ce present, elle nous prouve assés que ce n'est pas pour nous une necessité de l'avoir. . . .' Muralt, *Lettres sur les Anglois et les François*, p. 235.

[25] 'Foible Raison que l'homme vante,/Voilà quel est le fond qu'on peut faire sur vous :/Toujours vains, toujours faux, toujours pleins d'injustices,/Nous crions dans tous nos discours/Contre les passions, les foiblesses, les vices,/Où nous succombons tous les jours.' Review of *Histoire de la Philosophie païenne*, *Journal des Sçavans*, May, 1724, p. 552. The lines were written by 'une Dame célébre'.

[26] 'Un brin d'herbe, que nous foulons sous nos pieds, est l'écueil de tout le superbe apareil [*sic*] de la Philosophie. Un paysan en voit autant par ses yeux, qu'un Physicien en fait après trente années d'étude, et de contemplation : si ce n'est peut-être, que ce Physicien par le secours d'un bon microscope spéculera plus intimement la surface de ce brin d'herbe. . . . La cause formelle, qui fait l'essence, et la nature de quelque corps que ce soit, n'est point à la portée des machines de l'Optique, ni de la jurisdiction des sens.' C. Biron, *Curiositez de la Nature et de l'Art* (Paris : J. Moreau, 1703), pp. v–vi.

For other writers, reason and intellect are utterly ineffectual, or even positively dangerous to man:

'God did not create the universe as an object for our research. He made it so that we might seek him in it, so that we might recognize, in the silence of religious contemplation, his divinity and eternal power.'[27]

'A scholar who is considered of the first rank, even if he is indigent, looks upon himself as the lord of the intellectual world. A sensible man who does not pride himself on his learning, who knows only the things needed for living, such as how to earn enough to feed and clothe himself decently and comfortably and to give his children a start, and so forth, is a beggar in the eyes of the scholar. . . .'[28]

'. . . dogs do not reason about the education of their pups, as you women do about that of your children, and it does not occur to them to fight their instincts. . . . Is not that a thousand times more reasonable than our maxims? . . . To copy them in these matters would make us resemble them less than we do now.'[29]

> 'Mind, you seduce us; we admire you,
> But rarely will we love you:
> What will be truly moving
> Is what our hearts dictate;
> It is the words of our heart

[27] 'Dieu n'a point fait l'Univers pour être l'objet de nos recherches. Il l'a fait, afin que nous l'y cherchassions lui-même; et que nous y reconnussions dans le silence d'une contemplation Religieuse sa Divinité, sa Puissance éternelle.' *Ibid.*, p. xiii.

[28] 'Un Sçavant qu'on appelle du premier ordre, fût-il dans l'indigence, se regarde comme le Monarque de la Republique des Lettres. Un homme sensé, qui ne se pique pas de science, qui ne sçait que les choses nécessaires à la vie, comme gagner de quoi se nourrir et se vêtir honnêtement et commodément, de quoi établir ses enfans, et le reste, est un gueux pour le Sçavant.' Review of *Recueil de toutes les feuilles de la SPECTATRICE* (1730), in *Journal des Sçavans*, June, 1731, pp. 177–78.

[29] '. . . les Chiennes ne raisonnent point sur l'éducation de leurs petits, comme vous autres femmes sur celle de vos enfans, et elles ne s'avisent point de forcer leur instinct. . . . Cela n'est-il pas mille fois plus raisonnable que nos maximes? . . . Les copier dans ces choses-là, ce seroit leur ressembler moins que nous ne faisons.' *Ibid.*, pp. 183–84.

That seize the soul and stir it;
And you will never have the credit
Of causing tears to flow from our eyes.'[30]

'With the most cursory examination of Reason, it would be easy to refute those grandiose titles given out indiscriminately [to mathematicians]. Who will ever be convinced that from a confused mass of little lines, crosses, figures, etc., with which their books are studded . . . anybody could ever arrive at inventions useful to man and beneficial to society? . . . But perchance they will want to call upon experience. "Have we not invented the art of hurling bombs?" they will say to us. Ah, gentlemen, a little patience, I beg you. Most of those discoveries which you pride yourselves upon are due less to you than to the workmen . . . and you have simply taken the trouble to express what chance brought your way, and in that barbarous language that you call Algebra, Analysis, etc. . . .

'I conclude that the only advantage that comes from that study is the production of some rather peculiar machines.'[31]

'Whence comes it that in everyday life, to which we must needs return as the thing that will be decisive, whence comes it, I say, that Reasoning is something foreign there, that it scarcely enters into the familiar and simple exchange between two sensible people who know and love each other? It is undoubtedly because the natural way of men is not reasoning,

[30] 'Esprit ; tu séduis ; on t'admire,/Mais rarement on t'aimera :/Ce qui sûrement touchera/C'est ce que le cœur nous fait dire ;/C'est ce langage de nos cœurs/Qui saisit l'âme et qui l'agite ;/Et de faire couler nos pleurs/Tu n'auras jamais le mérite.' Chaulieu, 'Ode contre l'esprit' (1708), in *Poésies*.

[31] 'Pour peu qu'on voulût consulter la Raison, il seroit aisé de refuter ces Titres glorieux dispensez sans ménagements. Qui pourra jamais se persuader, que d'un amas confus de petites lignes, de Croix et de Chiffres etc. dont leurs livres sont hérissez . . . on puisse déduire des inventions utiles à l'Homme, et avantageuses pour la Société? . . . Mais ils voudront peut-être en appeler à l'expérience. N'avons-nous pas inventé l'art de jeter des Bombes, nous diront-ils? Eh! Messieurs, un peu de patience je vous prie. La plupart de ces découvertes dont vous vous glorifiez, sont dûës, moins à vous qu'aux Ouvriers . . . et vous avez eu soin seulement d'exprimer ce que le Sort vous a appris, dans ce langage barbare, que vous appelez Algèbre, Analyse, etc. . . .
'Je conclus que le seul avantage qu'on retire de cette étude, c'est la production de quelques Machines assez drôles.' 'Quelle étude est la plus utile, des Mathématiques, ou des belles Lettres?' in *Journal littéraire*, II (September–October, 1713), 189–90, 197.

because the heart does not reason, and because man's worth is in his heart, and not in his head.'[32]

'It is vain, miserable Knowledge that has led Christianity away from simplicity and converted it to Science and Opinions.'[33]

'We are reduced to reading and reasoning so much only because of our failure to cultivate the emotions that are in us. These would not be lacking if we were to let ourselves go, if we cultivated the humanity which produces them. The emotions are born in the heart, from a seed which is hidden there and which is animated only by the inclination toward good, when it is as strong as it should be. . . . Reasonings, when we give ourselves over to them, and when we make them our dominant way, stifle the emotions. . . . The simple man does not know the art of reasoning, and he who follows his true vocation ignores it.'[34]

A third, more balanced, view was that, though the intellectual processes are useful and their results often valid, they must be tempered or supplemented by the emotions:

'One observes, as between two men whose minds are equally ample, deep, and penetrating in purely intellectual matters, how superior that one is who has a sensitive soul, on matters

---

[32] 'Et d'où vient que dans l'ordinaire de la vie, à quoi enfin il en faut revenir, comme à ce qui peut décider la chose, d'où vient, dis-je, que le Raisonnement y est quelque chose d'étranger, qu'il n'en entre guère dans le Commerce familier et simple de deux Personnes sensées qui se connoissent et s'aiment? C'est sans contredit parce que le Langage naturel de l'Homme n'est pas le Raisonnement, que le Cœur ne raisonne pas, et que l'Homme vaut par le Cœur, et non par la Tête.' Béat-Louis Muralt, *Lettres fanatiques* (2 vols; London: Aux dépens de la compagnie, 1739), I, 54–55.

[33] 'C'est le vain, le malheureux Savoir, qui a tiré le Christianisme hors de la simplicité et l'a converti en Science et en Opinions.' *Ibid.*, II, 110.

[34] 'Nous ne sommes réduits à tant lire et à tant raisonner, que faute de cultiver les Sentimens qui sont en nous, et qui ne manqueroient pas si nous nous y laissions aller, si nous cultivions l'Humanité qui les produit. Les Sentimens naissent dans le Cœur, d'une Semence qui y est cachée, et que la seule Inclination pour le Bien, lorsqu'elle est forte autant qu'elle doit l'être, est capable d'animer. . . . Les Raisonnemens, lorsque nous nous y abandonnons, et que nous en faisons nôtre principal Langage, etouffent les Sentimens. . . . L'Homme simple ignore l'art de raisonner, et celui qui a sa veritable Occupation le néglige.' Muralt, 'Lettre sur les Voyages', in *Lettres sur les Anglois et les François*, p. 294.

G

in that category. How many ideas there are which are inaccessible to those whose emotions are cold! Sensitive souls may, because of warmth or impetuosity, make mistakes that orderly, systematic men would not commit; but they are far ahead because of all the good they do. Sensitive souls have a fuller existence than others: good and evil are multiplied for them. They have still another advantage for society, namely, that they are persuaded of truths of which the mind can only be convinced; conviction is often but passive, whereas persuasion is active, and the only true motive force is in what makes us act. The mind alone can and should form the upright man, sensitivity the virtuous man.'[35]

'It is not enough, my daughter, in order to be worthy, to submit outwardly to the rules of conduct: it is the emotions which form one's character and which guide the mind, which control our will and are responsible for the reality and permanence of all our virtues. What will be the principle of these emotions? Religion.'[36]

PRIMITIVISM

Eighteenth-century primitivism, which is commonly associated with Jean-Jacques Rousseau, who made it famous in modern

[35] 'On remarque entre deux hommes dont l'esprit est également étendu, profond et pénétrant sur des matières purement intellectuelles, quelle supériorité gagne celui dont l'âme est sensible, sur les sujets qui sont de cette classe-là. Qu'il y a d'idées inaccessibles à ceux qui ont le sentiment froid! Les âmes sensibles peuvent par vivacité et chaleur tomber dans les fautes que les hommes *à procédés* ne commettroient pas; mais elles l'emportent de beaucoup par la quantité de biens qu'elles produisent. Les âmes sensibles ont plus d'existence que les autres: les biens et les maux se multiplient â leur égard. Elles ont encore un avantage pour la société, c'est d'être persuadées des vérités dont l'esprit n'est que convaincu; la conviction n'est souvent que passive, la persuasion est active, et il n'y a de ressort que ce qui fait agir. L'esprit seul peut et doit faire l'homme de probité; la sensibilité prépare l'homme vertueux.' Charles Pinot Duclos, *Considérations sur les mœurs* (1750), ed. F. C. Green (Cambridge: Cambridge University Press, 1939), pp. 50–51.

[36] 'Il ne suffit pas, ma fille, pour être estimable, de s'assujetir extérieurement aux bienséances: ce sont les sentimens qui forment le caractère, qui conduisent l'esprit, qui gouvernent la volonté, qui répondent de la réalité et de la durée de toutes nos vertus. Quel sera le principe de ces sentimens? la religion. . . .' Mme Lambert, *Avis d'une mère à sa fille*, in *Œuvres morales* (Paris: Librairie des Bibliophiles, 1883), p. 48.

times, is much older than the *Discourse on Arts and Sciences* of
1749. Indeed, there has probably never been a time when men
did not regard their own society as inferior to societies of the
past. In the Renaissance, the discovery and exploration of
lands hitherto unknown to Europeans led easily to comparisons
which put modern European society in a bad light. Some of
these comparisons were in the beginning, and even later,
based on a combination of misinformation or misinterpretation
of life in the newly discovered regions and a desire to disparage
modern developments. The latter tendency seems a permanent
one among men; the former was a function of a new enthusiasm,
a desire to do justice to peoples whom on the surface a European
would be entitled to scorn. There was a steady search, covering
more than two centuries prior to Rousseau, for ways in which
the 'backward' peoples might be considered superior to the
'advanced', sometimes on abstract moral and idealistic
grounds, sometimes on the basis of European values themselves, as we shall see. To anyone who is acquainted with the
Renaissance literature on the subject[37] the surprise is that by
our period the discussion had changed so little and that the
vastly increased contact and knowledge had exerted so little
influence on the nature of the argument. It is a question
whether our writers had much to add to what Montaigne had
written; but the huge volume of writings on the subject is
another matter and reflects an enormous growth of interest in
primitivism, if not a superior understanding of primitive
peoples.

We shall see later that the literature of our period is not
entirely without some sound, first-hand, unromantic accounts
of life among the Indians of the New World, written by an
occasional traveller or missionary. But overwhelmingly the
picture of the Indians was one drawn by novelists and therefore
much less inspired by truth or observation, even second-hand,
than by the genre of moralistic imaginary voyages inherited
from the late seventeenth century.

A time-honoured technique, which had been successfully
used many times, involved putting a speech against civilization

[37] See Geoffroy Atkinson, *Les Nouveaux horizons de la Renaissance française* (Paris :
Droz, 1935).

into the mouth of a 'savage' visiting Europe. The device proved as effective in the eighteenth century as it had earlier. In the first of the two passages given below, Prévost has an Indian sage speak at the English court; in the second Lahontan uses a 'savage' who is well travelled in Europe for an attack on the French legal system.

'What you call happiness and abundance does not appear to us worthy of that name. We have for a long time known about the luxury and vanity that infect Europe; far from wishing that they extend to us, we fear them as the greatest of all evils. But in the servitude in which you find yourselves, under the dominion of two such cruel masters, we had until now thought you more worthy of pity than of scorn. Now that you assure us that your misfortune is voluntary, and that – though able to be as free and happy as we are, after the example of your ancestors – it is by your own choice and by the cultivation of your passions rather than of your talents that you have renounced the advantages that we enjoy, do not be surprised to see our esteem and compassion dwindle.'[38]

'We live simply, under the laws of instinct and of the innocent guidance which wise Nature has impressed upon us from the cradle. . . . Thus, we spend our lives in so perfect a harmony that lawsuits, disputes, and quarrels are unknown among us. Ah, you poor people, how you are to be pitied, exposed to laws that are contravened by your ignorant, unjust, and vicious judges, contravened as much in their own conduct as in the execution of their official duties. They are the fair-minded judges, who are without rectitude, who use their public office for their private advantage, who aim at

[38] 'Ce que vous nommez bonheur et abondance ne nous paroît pas digne de ce nom. Il y a longtems que nous connoissons le luxe et la vanité, qui infectent l'Europe; loin de souhaiter qu'ils s'étendent jusqu'à nous, nous les redoutons comme les plus grands de tous les maux. Mais dans la servitude où vous êtes, sous l'empire de deux tyrans si cruels, nous avions crû jusqu'à présent que vous étiez moins à mépriser qu'à plaindre. Aujourd'hui que vous nous assûrez vous-mêmes que votre malheur est volontaire, et que pouvant être aussi libres et aussi heureux que nous à l'exemple de vos Ancêtres, c'est par votre choix et par la culture de vos Passions plutôt que de vos Talens, que vous avez renoncé aux avantages dont nous joüissons, ne soyez pas surpris que notre estime et notre compassion diminuent.' Prévost, *Pour et Contre*, IV, No. 56, 256–57.

nothing but to enrich themselves, who are unapproachable except by the demon of money, who administer justice by the light of avarice or passion, who authorize crime and exterminate justice and good faith, giving free rein instead to deceit, trickery, prolonged lawsuits, abuse and violation of oaths, and endless other disorders.'[39]

In large measure, the high regard for the primitive originated with Frenchmen abroad, though not necessarily in America. Some of the reasons for this admiration – reasons not always sound – can be seen in the following quotations from Prévost, whose rather undisciplined interest in far-away lands and peoples received considerable stimulation during sojourns (1728–30 and several years in the 1730's) in England; a more scientific approach to exoticism was to express itself only twenty years later, with the publication of his *Histoire générale des voyages*. Prévost never visited America. In the quotations given below we note, first, the view that the Indians are in need of very little law in the European sense, thanks to the simplicity of life among them and the beneficence of nature:

'As for laws, I did not think I should establish a great number. Nature's laws were sufficient, and their most important features were already included in the order that I established in families. Live in union; be as gentle and patient to one another as each wishes the rest to be to him; such was the sole political law that I tried to have the Abaquis appreciate.'[40]

[39] 'Nous vivons simplement sous les Loix de l'instinct, et de la conduite innocente que la Nature sage nous a imprimées dès le berceau. . . . Ainsi, nous passons la vie dans une si parfaite intelligence, qu'on ne voit parmi nous ni procez, ni disputes, ni chicanes. Ha! malheureux, que vous estes à plaindre d'estre exposez à des Loix auxquelles vos Juges ignorans, injustes et vicieux contreviennent autant par leur conduite particulière qu'en l'administration de leurs Charges. Ce sont là ces équitables Juges qui manquent de droiture, qui ne raportent leur Emploi qu'à leurs interêts, qui n'ont en veüe que de s'enrichir, qui ne sont accessibles qu'au démon de l'argent, qui n'administrent la justice que par un principe d'avarice, ou par passion, qui autorisent le crime, exterminent la justice et la bonne foy, pour donner cours à la tromperie, à la chicane, à la longueur des procez, à l'abus et à la violation des sermens, et à une infinité d'autres désordres.' Lahontan, *Dialogues curieux*, p. 188.

[40] 'Pour ce qui regardoit les loix, je ne crus pas devoir en établir un grand nombre. Celles de la nature suffisoient, et leur plus importante partie se trouvoit déjà comprise dans l'ordre que je mettois dans les familles. Vivez dans l'union; ayez les uns pour les autres les mêmes égards de douceur et de patience que chacun

Nor is their religion to be scorned, being simple and to the point:

'I expected to see them set up some altar and add to their oath some idolatrous and superstitious rites; but I was happy to observe that nothing could be simpler than the worship that they offered to the sun. They had neither priests nor other religious paraphernalia. The whole thing consisted in recognizing the sun as their god, and each person was free to honour it in his own way, without following any prescribed form. . . . I had a better opinion than ever of this religious people, and I had no doubt whatever that I would succeed in civilizing and governing them happily.'[41]

Much emphasis is given to the absence of theft and adultery among the Indians. Moreover, because of their innocence, the issue of nudity (a topic much discussed in eighteenth-century literature) could safely cease to be a subject of moral discussion.

'It is a shocking thing for a European to see them naked, both men and women, with scarcely any thought of modesty . . . they had available an incredible supply of skins of tigers, leopards, and other animals which they killed on the hunt, but, because they had the habit of wearing these during the winter . . . it was only necessary to have them adopt that practice in the summertime. . . . Modesty, which was the only reason I had for wishing them clothed, did not seem to me as strong an argument as the disadvantages that would inevitably follow from the adoption of clothes. Looking at the matter closely, the shame of being nude is not a natural reaction. It is a prejudice which comes from upbringing and is a clear result of habit. I had sure proof of this before my eyes in these

---

souhaite qu'on ait pour lui-même : telle fut la seule loi politique que je tâchai de faire goûter aux Abaquis.' Prévost, *Cleveland*, liv. 4, in *Œuvres*, V, 137.

[41] 'Je m'attendois de leur voir dresser quelque autel, et accompagner leur serment de quelques pratiques idolâtres et superstitieuses ; mais je remarquai avec joie que rien n'étoit plus simple que le culte qu'ils rendoient au soleil. Ils n'avoient ni prêtres, ni appareil de religion. Tout consistoit à le reconnoître pour leur divinité, et chacun étoit libre de l'honorer à sa manière, sans s'assujetir à aucune méthode. . . . Je jugeai plus avantageusement que jamais du caractère d'un peuple si religieux, et je ne doutai point que je ne pusse réussir à le civiliser et à le gouverner heureusement.' *Ibid.*, pp. 115–16.

very savages, who did not blush for their nudity and to whom this practice was a matter of indifference.'[42]

'They [the savages] abhor adultery and disapprove of polygamy. Theft is unknown among them. Murder is looked upon as an abominable crime, except when an enemy is involved, in which case it is considered a necessary and virtuous act.'[43]

It is easy to see, given the above observations, why primitive peoples seemed attractive to the sophisticated and why writers questioned the generally accepted thesis that civilization represents a superior way of life. The closing sentences of the following quotation are reminiscent, both in word and in spirit, of Montaigne's 'Des coches' (*Essais*, Bk. III, ch. vi), in which the supposed superiority of the European over the savage is characterized as 'mechanical [which also meant "contemptible"] victory'.

'An Englishman recently from Jamaica has published, in London, a speech which he attributes to the chief of the Negro rebels of that island. . . :

". . . it is not any difference in talent, but education and mere chance, which give the whites that superiority that is their excuse for looking down upon the blacks and trampling them under foot.

"Oh, by that mysterious God that our persecutors claim to

---

[42] 'C'est quelque chose de si choquant pour un européen, que de les voir nuds, hommes et femmes, presque sans aucun égard pour la pudeur . . . ils étoient pourvus d'une multitude incroyable de peaux de tigres, de léopards et d'autres animaux qu'ils tuoient à la chasse . . . mais ils étoient accoutumés à s'en revêtir pendant l'hiver . . . il n'étoit question que de leur faire conserver cet usage pendant l'été. . . . Le motif de la pudeur, qui étoit le seul que j'eusse de souhaiter qu'ils fussent couverts, ne me parut pas aussi fort que les inconvéniens inévitables qui suivroient bientôt l'établissement des habits. A le bien prendre, la honte d'être nud n'est point un sentiment naturel. C'est un préjugé de l'éducation et un simple effet de l'habitude. J'en avois une preuve certaine et présente dans mes sauvages mêmes, qui ne rougissoient point de leur nudité, et qui regardoient cet usage comme une chose indifférente.' *Ibid.*, pp. 124–25.

[43] 'Ils abhorrent l'adultere, et ils n'approuvent point la pluralité des femmes. Le vol n'est point connu parmi eux. Le meurtre y est regardé comme un crime abominable, excepté néanmoins lorsqu'il est question d'un ennemi ; car il passe alors pour une action vertueuse et nécessaire.' Prévost, *Pour et Contre*, II, No. 19 (1733), 75, translation of a letter of Oglethorpe, Governor of Georgia.

worship, what really is that superiority of which their pride boasts? What advantage do they think they derive from their disgusting, colourless whiteness, over the noble, majestic colour that nature has given us? . . .

"The only advantage of these haughty tyrants is that they are indeed happier than we. It is not that they are wiser; but they have more art and industry. They are not braver, but they have more cleverness and ingenuity." '[44]

The savages of the New World are generally praised in this literature; the first quotation below is a classic example of a widespread type. Even when our writers turn critical, the savages almost always end up better and happier than the Europeans, as in the letter of Père Cauchetière, or in the verse of J.-B. Rousseau. The Indians, of course, serve these writers as a vehicle to express their scorn for European luxury and immorality, without much regard for accuracy. The unflattering picture of the Indians that we get in the last passage below rings more true than the idealizations of the preceding quotations.

'These savage peoples seemed to have preserved their original innocence: they are guided by a straight and wise instinct that never leaves them, and the whole function of their reason is limited to providing themselves, in the easiest way possible, the things necessary for living, to avoiding accumulation for a future that they may never enjoy, and to preserving their good health, without which other things are meaningless. On the seventh day after their children are born, they imprint on their left arms, in letters which cannot be effaced, these two words:

[44] 'Un Anglois arrivé récemment de la Jamaïque, a fait imprimer à Londres un Discours qu'il attribuë au Chef des Nègres révoltez de cette Isle. . . .

' ". . . ce n'est point la différence du génie, mais l'éducation et le seul hazard, qui donnent aux Blancs cette supériorité dont ils abusent pour mépriser les Noirs et pour les fouler aux pieds.

' "Eh! par ce Dieu mystérieux, que nos Persécuteurs prétendent adorer, quelle est donc cette supériorité dont leur orguëil se vante? Quel avantage croyent-ils tirer de leur fade et dégoûtante blancheur, sur la couleur noble et majestueuse que nous avons reçûë de la nature? . . .

' "L'unique avantage de ces fiers Tyrans est d'être en effet plus heureux que nous. Ce n'est pas qu'ils soient plus sages ; mais ils ont plus d'art et d'industrie. Ils ne sont pas plus braves, mais ils ont plus de finesse et d'artifice." ' Prévost, *Pour et Contre*, VI, No. 90 (1735), 340–43.

"Adore God", and on their right arms these: "Love your fellowman". Such are their laws; a hundred thousand volumes of moral philosophy contain more phrases but not any more substance.'[45]

'The men went about nude and hid very poorly their parts that should not be seen. The women wore a kind of petticoat . . . the girls wore nothing at all. . . . These were the simplest, sweetest, most humane people in the world; and they had – or at any rate showed – the least wit and memory, malice, bitterness, ambition, and even passion of any people imaginable; they were children rather than men. . . . Besides, they had no system of writing, or anything that took its place, except songs. . . . These fables show that this island folk felt sure that humanity had originated on their island; indeed, there are few nations in America in which so strong a feeling for their country has been observed.'[46]

'We see in these savages the fine qualities of human nature which are entirely corrupted in civilized nations. Of all the eleven passions they experience two only; anger is the chief one, but they are not carried away to excess by it, even in war.

[45] 'Ces Peuples sauvages semblent avoir conservé la primitive innocence : ils se conduisent par un instinct droit et sage qui ne les abandonne jamais, et tout l'office de leur raison se réduit à se procurer par les voyes les plus douces, les choses nécessaires à la vie, à ne point amasser pour un avenir dont on ne jouïra peut-être pas, et à se conserver une bonne santé, sans laquelle on ne possède rien.
'Le septième jour après que leurs enfans sont nés, on leur grave sur le bras gauche, en lettres ineffaçables ces deux mots : *Adore Dieu*; et sur le bras droit, ceux-ci : *Aime ton semblable*. Voilà toutes leurs Loix. Cent mille Volumes de Morale contiennent plus de phrases et ne renferment pas plus de choses.' L.C.D., *Les Femmes Militaires. Relation Historique d'une Isle nouvellement découverte* (Paris : Claude Simon et Pierre de Batz, 1735), quoted in *Journal des Sçavans*, June, 1736, pp. 197–98.
[46] 'Les hommes alloient tout nuds et cachoient assés mal ce qui ne doit point être vû. Les femmes portoient une espèce de jupon . . . les filles ne portoient absolument rien. . . . C'étoit les hommes du monde les plus simples, les plus doux, les plus humains, qui avoient, ou du moins qui montroient le moins d'esprit et de mémoire, sans fiel, sans aigreur, sans ambition, et presque sans passions : des enfans, plûtôt que des hommes. . . . D'ailleurs ils n'avoient ni écriture, ni rien qui supléât à ce défaut, que des chansons. . . . Ces fables font voir que ces Insulaires ne doutoient point que la terre n'eut commencé par leur Isle à se peupler, et il est peu de nations dans l'Amérique en qui l'on n'ait trouvé la même prévention pour leur pays.' R. P. François-Xavier Charlevoix, *Histoire de l'Isle Espagnole ou de S. Domingue* (2 vols; Paris : Hippolyte–Louis Guerin, 1730), I, 37–38.

Living in common, without disputes, content with little, guiltless of avarice, and assiduous at work, it is impossible to find people more patient, more hospitable, more affable, more liberal, more moderate in their language. In fine, all our fathers and the French who have lived with the savages consider that life flows on more gently among them than among us.'[47]

> 'He lives without disturbance or trouble,
> And if his climate refuses him
> Some of the riches that are abused in Europe,
> Those are no longer riches for him.
> Lying in a rustic cave,
> He braves the rigors of the northern cold;
> Our Asiatic luxury
> Has not sapped his strength;
> He does not lament the lack
> Of those arts the discovery of which
> Has cost man so many pains
> And which, having become necessary,
> Have but increased our poverty
> By multiplying our needs.'[48]

'What is heard every day in Europe of those immense reaches of country studded with towns and villages, in which an innumerable multitude of idolaters present themselves in crowds to the zeal of the missionaries, would give room to

[47] 'Nous voyons dans ces sauvages les beaux restes de la nature humaine qui sont entièrement corrompus dans les peuples policés ; de toutes les 11 passions ils n'en ont que deux ; la colère est la plus grande ; mais encore en ont-ils peu dans l'excès lors de la guerre. Vivre en commun sans procès, se contenter de peu sans avarice, estre assidus au travail, on ne peut rien voir de plus patient, hospitaliers, affables, libéraux, modérés dans le parler ; enfin tous nos PP. et les François qui ont fréquenté les sauvages estiment que la vie se passe plus doucement parmy eux que parmy nous.' Letter from R. P. Cauchetière to his brother, August 7, 1694, in *Jesuit Relations and Allied Documents*, ed. Reuben Gold Thwaites (73 vols ; Cleveland, Ohio : Burrows Brothers Company, 1896–1901), LXIV, 130–31.

[48] 'Il vit sans trouble et sans ennui ;/Et si son climat lui refuse/Quelques biens dont l'Europe abuse,/Ce ne sont plus des biens pour lui./Couché dans un antre rustique,/Du nord il brave la rigeur,/Et notre luxe asiatique/N'a point énervé sa vigueur :/Il ne regrette point la perte/De ces arts dont la découverte/A l'homme a coûté tant de soins,/Et qui, devenus nécessaires,/N'ont fait qu'augmenter nos misères,/En multipliant nos besoins.' Jean-Baptiste Rousseau, 'A M. le marquis de La Fare', in *Œuvres* (Paris : Garnier, 1869), pp. 131–32.

believe that things here are exactly thus. The facts are far different, Reverend Father. In a great extent of country, scarcely three or four villages exist. Our lives are spent in threading dense forests, in climbing mountains, in crossing lakes and rivers in canoes, in order to overtake some poor savage who is fleeing from us, and whom we cannot render less savage by either our words or our attentions. Nothing is more difficult than the conversion of these savages. It is a miracle of the Lord's mercy: we must first make men of them, and afterward work to make them Christians. As they are absolute masters of themselves without being subjected to any law, the independence in which they live enslaves them to the most brutal passions. . . . From this independence springs every sort of vice that rules them. They are indolent, traitorous, and fickle and inconstant; deceitful and naturally thievish . . . brutal, and without honour; taciturn; capable of doing everything when you are liberal towards them, but at the same time thankless and ungrateful. . . . Gluttony and the love of pleasures are, above all, the vices most dominant. . . .'[49]

The maxims of the primitives of 1700 were the same as those of other times: the good in men is equated with the natural; men are by nature good, as well as free, but become corrupted by society; country life is infinitely better than city life for bringing out the best in men; and we should follow

[49] 'Ce qu'on apprend tous les jours en Europe, de ces vastes Pays semés de Villes et Bourgades, où une multitude innombrable d'Idolâtres se présente en foule au zèle des Missionnaires, donnerait lieu de croire que les choses sont ici sur le même pied : il s'en faut bien, mon Révérend Père ; dans une grande étendue de Pays, à peine trouve-t-on trois ou quatre Villages : notre vie se passe à parcourir d'épaisses forêts, à grimper sur les montagnes, à traverser en canot des lacs et des rivières pour atteindre un pauvre Sauvage qui nous fuit, et que nous ne saurions apprivoiser ni par nos discours, ni par nos caresses. Rien de plus difficile que la conversion de ces Sauvages ; c'est un miracle de la miséricorde du Seigneur : il faut d'abord en faire des hommes, et travailler ensuite à en faire des Chrétiens. Comme ils sont maîtres absolus d'eux-mêmes, sans être assujétis à aucune Loi, l'indépendance dans laquelle ils vivent, les asservit aux passions les plus brutales. . . . C'est de cette indépendance que naissent toute sorte de vices qui les dominent. Ils sont lâches, traîtres, légers et inconstans, fourbes, naturellement voleurs . . . brutaux, sans honneur, sans parole, capables de tout faire quand on est libéral à leur égard, mais en même-temps ingrats et sans reconnaissance. . . . La gourmandise et l'amour du plaisir sont surtout les vices qui règnent le plus. . . .' Letter from R. P. Gabriel Marest, S.J., to R. P. Germon, S.J., November 9, 1712, *Jesuit Relations*, LXVI, 218–21.

nature rather than resist its urges (this last often applied to
love, as we saw in Chapter 1). The praise of the Golden Age
which runs through much of this literature and of which the
penultimate quotation below is a sample, leads us to include
a passage from Boethius, the uncle if not the father of these
primitives.

'We are the work of God; we therefore have no reason to
think that our nature is evil. We may abuse it; but when we
follow its true impulses, if there is any evil, the cause would
be our nature itself; so, since error is an evil, we cannot err
in refusing to yield to it except when we feel forced to; for the
cause of our error would be our creator, which is not possible.
. . . Men, therefore, are made in such a way that the good
attracts them, and a clear understanding of it carries them
along and forces them to consent to it. And then they are
not mistaken; nature, which is good, cannot force them to
consent to what is false. By nature I mean either the Creator
of all things, or the things themselves as he created them.'[50]

'It is in this way that these peoples, natural and good, show
their zeal and affection for their rulers.'[51]

'But since man lost his place and his dignity, the understanding of what is good for him also was lost, and in the
disorder in which we find ourselves we do not know what our
place and dignity is. . . . I think that there is but one way of
restoring order; that is to follow our instinct, that instinct

[50] 'Nous sommes l'ouvrage de Dieu; nous n'avons donc pas sujet de croire
que notre nature soit mauvaise. Nous pouvons en abuser; mais lorsque nous
suivons ses véritables mouvemens, s'il y avoit du mal, elle en seroit elle-même
la cause; ainsi comme l'erreur est un mal nous ne pouvons pas nous tromper en
ne consentant que lorsque nous nous sentons comme contraints de le faire; car
ce seroit celui qui nous a faits qui seroit la cause de cette erreur, ce qui ne peut
pas être. . . . Les Hommes sont donc faits de manière que comme le bien les attire,
une connoissance claire les entraîne, et les oblige de consentir. Et alors ils ne sont
point trompés; la nature, qui est bonne, ne pouvant les obliger à consentir à ce
qui seroit faux. J'entends ici par nature, ou l'Auteur de toutes choses, ou les
choses mêmes telles qu'il les a faites.' Bernard Lamy, *Entretiens sur les sciences* (1964).
ed. F. Girbal and P. Clair (Paris: Presses universitaires de France, 1966), pp.
79–80.
[51] 'C'est ainsi que ces peuples, bons et naturels, donnent des témoignages de
leur zèle et de leur attachement pour leurs princes.' Prévost, *Mém. d'un homme de
qualité*, liv. 3, in *Œuvres*, I, 138.

which is perhaps all that we have left of the original state of
man; and we have some vestige of it so that it may lead us
back . . . that instinct is our conscience, in which the Divinity
makes itself known to us and speaks to us.'[52]

'Where shall we find Faith in Man? Can neither the Tyes
of Blood, Friendship, Interest, nor Religion, bind Men to be
just: but alas! he lived too long in that curs'd Town, where
Vice takes place of Virtue, where Men rise by Villany and
Fraud, where the lustful Appetite has all Opportunities of
being gratify'd; where Oaths and Promises are only Jests, and
all Religion but Pretence. . . .'[53]

'. . . you seem to me a decent fellow,' [said Mlle Habert.
And Jacob answered:] '. . . it is only three or four months
since I left my village, and so I have not yet had time to
become wicked or bad.'[54]

'When luxury and money are in esteem, true honour is
not.'[55]

'Man in his innocence was destined from the start to till the
soil; we have not lost the feeling of our original nobility. On
the contrary, it seems that any other occupation enslaves or
degrades us. As soon as we can free ourselves, or can breathe
freely for a moment, a hidden inclination leads us back to our
garden. The merchant thinks himself lucky to be able to leave
his counter for his flowers. The artisan, glued by hard necessity

[52] 'Mais depuis que l'Homme a perdu son Occupation et sa Dignité, la Connoissance de ce qui le regarde s'est perduë de même, et dans le Desordre où nous
sommes, nous ne sçavons pas seulement en quoi nôtre Occupation et nôtre Dignité
consistent . . . je pense qu'il y a un seul moien de rentrer dans l'Ordre : c'est
de suivre l'Instinct qui est en nous, l'Instinct qui est peut-être tout ce qui nous
reste du premier Etat de l'Homme, et qui nous est laissé pour nous y ramener . . .
et cet Instinct est la voix de la Conscience, où la Divinité se fait connoître à nous
et nous parle.' Muralt, 'Lettre sur les Voyages', in *Lettres sur les Anglois et les
François*, p. 288.
[53] Pénélope Aubin, *The Life of Madam de Beaumont* (London : E. Bell, J. Darby,
and A. Bettesworth, 1721), pp. 101–2.
[54] '. . . vous me paraîssez un honnête garçon, [dit Mlle Habert. Et Jacob lui
repond :] . . . il n'y a que trois ou quatre mois que je suis sorti de mon village, et
je n'ai pas encore eu le temps d'empirer et de devenir méchant.' Marivaux, *Le
Paysan parvenu*, Part I, in *Romans*, p. 599.
[55] 'Quand le luxe et l'argent sont en crédit, le véritable honneur perd le sien.'
Lambert, *Réflexions sur les femmes*, in *Œuvres morales*, p. 150.

to a single spot, adorns his window with a box of greenery. The soldier and the magistrate sigh for life in the country.'[56]

'Slavery does not derive its origin from nature, for by nature all men are born free.'[57]

'Weary of the world's woes, and tired out by the hurt I had suffered, I left its noise and emptiness without regret. . . . Withdrawing deeply within myself, my serious thoughts have shown me plainly the meaninglessness of a multitude of things held in esteem among the inhabitants of this unhappy earth; this earth, where art almost always destroys nature, on the pretext of beautifying it; where artifice, worse than art, and hypocrisy, fraud, superstition, and depradation hold undisputed sway; where virtually all is error, vanity, disorder, corruption, malice, and misery.'[58]

'What is that Golden Age so much sung by the poets? Did men, under the laws of Saturn or Astraea, combine happiness and innocence? . . . A little reason and an even more assured instinct served them as Code and Digest. . . . The only dependence among them was that based on the heart, established on the loving recognition of favours received, or founded on

[56] 'L'homme innocent avoit été destiné dès le commencement à cultiver la terre : nous n'avons point perdu le sentiment de notre ancienne noblesse. Il semble au contraire que tout autre état nous asservisse ou nous dégrade. Dès que nous pouvons nous affranchir, ou respirer quelque moment en liberté, une pente secrette nous ramène tous au jardinage. Le marchand se croit heureux de pouvoir passer du comptoir à ses fleurs. L'artisan qu'une dure nécessité attache toûjours au même endroit, orne sa fenêtre d'une caisse de verdure. L'homme d'épée et le magistrat soupirent après la vie champêtre.' Abbé Noël-Antoine Pluche, *Le Spectacle de la nature* (1732–33) (9 vols ; Paris : Frèrcs Etienne, 1764), Vol. II, Entretien V.

[57] 'L'Esclavage ne tire point son origine de la Nature, puisque naturellement tous les hommes naissent libres.' N. Gurtler, *Les Origines du monde* (1708–9), quoted in *Nouvelles de la République des Lettres*, April, 1709.

[58] 'Las du tracas du monde, et fatigué des peines que j'y avais souffertes, j'en quittai la vanité et le tumulte sans aucun regret. . . . Recueilli très profondément en moi-même, mes sérieuses réflexions m'ont fait voir là, comme au doigt et à l'œil, le néant d'une infinité de choses qui sont en grand-vogue parmi les habitants de cette malheureuse Terre, où l'Art détruit presque toujours la Nature, sous prétexte de l'embellir : où l'Artifice, pire que l'Art, l'Hypocrisie, la Fraude, la Superstition, la Rapine exercent un tyrannique Empire : où tout, pour ainsi dire, n'est qu'Erreur, Vanité, Désordre, Corruption, Malice, et Misère.' Maximilien Misson, *Les Voyages et Avantures de François Leguat* (2 vols ; London : David Mortier, 1708), p. xxiii.

that gentle soul union that forms the bonds of friendship or
the chains of love. . . . People found pleasure in virtue, and
virtue did not rule out pleasure.'[59]

'Ah, how happy was the first age of men ! They were content
with their fields, which did not fail to nourish them. They did
not ruin themselves piling up wealth which weakens mortals. . . .
They knew neither the gifts of Bacchus, nor honey to add to
wine. They did not possess the art of tinting silk from China
with dye from Tyre. They found healthy sleep on reeds, or on
the grass; they drank from the brook which flowed nearby
and had the shade of pines to protect them from the sun. . . .
Why cannot we alter the ways of our time and go back to
those of former days ! No, the desire of gain and the ambition
to maintain what we have gained burn us more than the
fires of Mount Aetna would burn us. Ah ! who was that wicked
man who first withdrew a mass of gold from the earth, or who
took from it the precious stones which asked nothing better
than to remain buried?'[60]

In at least some of the writings of our period there are ways
of overcoming the ills of civilization, and this without either
returning to a mythical Golden Age or being born an Indian.
Thus Prévost, whose primitivism was not entirely confined to
theoretical descriptions of New World innocence, considered
it possible to leave the evils of civilized society and begin anew.
In a story too long to detail here, he tells of a middle-class
Englishman and his family who left London to live happily in
the country. The account ends as follows:

'He used the money he had left to buy wool and linen to

[59] 'Qu'est-ce que cet âge d'or tant chanté par les Poetes? Sous les Loix de
Saturne ou d'*Astrée* les hommes ont-ils uni la félicité à l'innocence? . . . "Un peu
de raison et un instinct plus sûr encore, leur tenoit lieu de Code et de Digeste. . . .
Il n'y avoit entr'eux d'autre dépendance que celle du cœur, établie sur la tendre
reconnoissance des services reçus, ou fondée sur cette douce sympathie des ames
qui forme les nœuds de l'amitié, ou les chaînes de l'amour. . . . On trouvoit des
plaisirs dans la vertu ; et la vertu ne défendoit pas les plaisirs. . . .' Anon., *Lettres
Philosophiques sur l'Age d'or et sur le bonheur* (London, 1738), quoted in *Journal des
Sçavans*, May, 1739, pp. 44-45.
[60] Boethius, *De Consolatione Philosophiae*, Book 2, in Boethius, *The Theological
Tractates*, trans. H. F. Stewart, Loeb Classical Library (Cambridge, Mass. : Har-
vard University Press, 1946), pp. 205-7.

occupy his daughters, and tools for cultivating the ground for
his sons and himself. He took a farmer into his household to
show them how to use them. A few days' practise sufficed for
them to learn. . . . They live together in wonderful peace and
harmony. . . . The money they make is just enough for the
sober life which has become their habit. They take walks on
holidays; they read, they entertain themselves harmlessly. The
father has several times suggested to his two sons, who are both
over thirty, that they enter the army or seek their fortune some
other way. They protest that nothing can induce them to leave
their cottage, as long as their father, mother, and sisters might
need their help.'[61]

EDUCATION AND INSTRUCTION

Our period precedes the time of great changes in educational
thought, but as usual there were many stirrings. The years
just before and just after 1700 saw the introduction of Locke
into France (original, 1693; translation, 1694 – one of many
signs of a kind of intellectual union which made France and
England almost one nation in intellectual matters), the
development of a new psychology which was to lay the ground-
work for later reform, and generally a wide speculation in
ideas, many of which were to take root in the middle of the
century and after.

Though there was variety in educational thinking, we have
been more struck by the uniformity than by the diversity
among the writers we have examined. Thus, the idea of man
as naturally wicked is exceptional as a basis for educational

[61] 'Il employa ce qui lui restoit d'argent à se pourvoir de laine et de toile,
pour occuper ses filles; et d'instrumens propres à cultiver la terre, pour ses fils
et pour lui-même. Il prit un Paysan dans la maison pour leur en montrer l'usage.
Quelques jours d'exercice leur firent surmonter toutes les difficultez. . . . Ils vivent
entr'eux dans une paix et dans une union admirables. . . . Le profit qu'ils en tirent
suffiroit seul pour la vie sobre dont ils ont formé l'habitude. Ils se promènent les
jours de Fêtes; ils lisent, ils s'amusent innocemment. Le Pere a proposé plusieurs
fois à ses deux fils, qui ont tous deux plus de trente ans, de prendre le parti des
armes, ou de chercher quelqu'autre voye de fortune. Ils protestent que rien n'est
capable de leur faire quitter leur cabane, aussi longtems que leur Pere, leur Mere
et leurs Sœurs peuvent avoir besoin de leurs secours.' Prévost, *Pour et Contre*, VI,
No. 84 (1735), 198–99.

thought, though we shall note it; so is the emphasis on the training of teachers, or 'professionalization', as we might call it, and on the separate types of schooling needed by the different classes in society. Some of these matters, of course, were to become topics of considerable discussion many years later.

'There has been an unfortunate genius for evil in man ever since his fall, and this quickly spoils the small number of good inclinations left in children, unless teachers and parents work hard to nourish and augment those small seeds of virtue, those precious vestiges of original innocence, and unless they tirelessly remove the thorns and brambles that constantly grow from that wretched soil.'[62]

'When one learns an art, no matter how lowly, one goes as apprentice to a master to learn his trade. To what academy, to what school, does one go to learn to be a tutor or govenor to a child? It is a very difficult profession, and yet no one teaches it. We do not even have any books which teach that great art.'[63]

'In my *Educational Plans* . . . each social class will have its own system of education. There is a difference between educating a prince, a petty nobleman, and a child of the lower classes. Girls must be brought up differently from boys in each social class. I have given due attention to all these differences of rank in my *Educational Plans* . . . governesses are no less important than tutors.'[64]

---

[62] 'Il y a dans le cœur de l'homme, depuis sa corruption, une malheureuse fécondité pour le mal, qui altére [*sic*] bientôt dans les enfans le peu de bonnes dispositions qui y reste, si les parens et les maîtres ne travaillent continuellement à nourrir et à faire croître ces foibles semences du bien, restes précieux de l'ancienne innocence, et s'ils n'arrachent avec soin infatigable les ronces et les épines qu'un si mauvais fonds pousse sans cesse.' Charles Rollin, *De la manière d'enseigner et d'étudier les belles-lettres* (Paris: Vve Estienne, 1740), p. xvii.

[63] 'Quand on apprend un Art, quelque vil qu'il soit, on va chez un Maître en apprentissage pour apprendre son Métier. En quelle Académie, en quel Collège va-t-on pour apprendre à être Gouverneur ou Précepteur? C'est une profession très-difficile, et cependant personne ne l'enseigne. Nous n'avons pas même de Livres qui enseignent ce grand Art.' Vallange, *Nouveaux Systèmes ou nouveaux plans de méthodes . . . pour parvenir en peu de tems et facilement à la connoissance des Langues et des Sciences* (Paris: Jombert et Lamesle, 1719), p. 269.

[64] 'Dans mes Plans d'Education . . . chaque condition aura son système par-

H

There is a widespread feeling evident in the writings of
this time, not invented but surely reinforced by Fénelon's
Télémaque of 1699, that education is the key to a good or a
wicked society as well as to the individual's life and character.
The idea that mothers should nurse their babies, as advocated
in the *Spectator* papers in England, gained momentum during
our period and was to become an important ingredient in the
raising of children for Jean-Jacques Rousseau later. Education
of girls, growing opposition to the study of Latin, and attempts
to make learning attractive, in a way reminiscent of Montaigne,
are further points typical of our period in matters of education
and schooling.

'All the disorders that prevail in a state and all the misfortunes that follow in their wake usually arise from the poor
education given to children.'[65]

'Give me leave then to tell you, that of all the abuses that
ever you have as yet endeavoured to reform, certainly not one
wanted so much your assistance as the abuse in nursing of
children.'[66]

'The author points out at the beginning of the third project
that it is in the public interest for girls to be well brought up . . .
for them to acquire . . . Christian prudence, avoid injustice,
get the habit of "doing good", and learn to reason clearly on
the basis of obvious principles. . . .'[67]

---

ticulier d'Education. Autre chose est d'élever un Prince ou un simple Gentilhomme,
ou un enfant du petit peuple. Les Filles doivent être élevées autrement que les
Garçons dans chaque condition. J'ai eu égard à toutes ces différences d'états
dans mes Plans d'Education . . . des Gouvernantes qui ne sont pas moins importantes que les Gouverneurs.' *Ibid.*, pp. 270–71.

[65] 'Tous les désordres qui règnent dans un Etat, et tous les malheurs qui les
suivent, procèdent ordinairement de la mauvaise éducation qu'on a donnée
aux enfans.' Review of T. Staynoe, *Instructions* (London, 1717), in *Nouvelles de la
République des Lettres*, March–April, 1718.

[66] Richard Steele, *Spectator*, No. 246, December 12, 1711, cited in *Nouvelles
de la République des Lettres*, January–February, 1718, Article V, review of Vol. III
of the *Spectator*.

[67] 'L'Auteur fait voir au commencement du troisième Projet qu'il est de l'interêt
public que les filles soient bien élevées . . . leur donner . . . l'habitude à la prudence
Chrétienne, à éviter les injustices, aux œuvres de *bienfaisance*, à raisonner juste sur
des principes évidens. . . .' Review of Abbé de Saint-Pierre, *Œuvres* (Paris, 1730),
in *Journal des Sçavans*, June, 1730, p. 240.

'I know of but one school in France devoted exclusively to the education of girls. . . . It is true that a few convents take girls to bring up, but . . . when they leave these religious institutions, they are so ignorant of the commonest and most important things . . . in a word, so lacking in any feeling of justice and beneficence. . . .'[68]

'The education of girls has in all ages been neglected; attention has been only upon men, and, as if women were a different species, they are left to themselves, without help and without any realization that they make up half of the world's population . . . that they are responsible for the happiness or unhappiness of men, who always feel the need of having reasonable women'[69]

'Nothing, then, is so poorly understood as the education given to young people. They are trained to please: they are taught no more than amenities; their ego is built up . . . they are never taught virtue or strength'[70]

'I did not learn Latin. It is a language, my mother said, which today is needed only by critics and schoolteachers. All its beauties have been communicated in the living languages through translations. The time that a child wastes in learning it may be used more profitably for the acquisition of more substantial knowledge.'[71]

[68] 'Je ne connais en France qu'un Collège uniquement destiné à l'Education des Filles. . . . Il est vrai que plusieurs Couvents prennent des Pensionnaires à élever, mais . . . au sortir de ces maisons Religieuses, elles sont si ignorantes des choses les plus communes et les plus importantes . . . en un mot si peu justes et si peu bienfaisantes. . . .' Saint-Pierre, *Ouvrajes de Politique* (16 vols; Rotterdam: J. D. Bemen; Paris: Briasson, 1733–41), IV, 269–70.

[69] 'On a dans tous les temps négligé l'éducation des filles; l'on n'a d'attention que pour les hommes; et, comme si les femmes étoient une espèce à part, on les abandonne à elles-mêmes, sans secours; sans penser qu'elles composent la moitié du monde; . . . qu'elles font le bonheur ou le malheur des hommes, qui toujours sentent le besoin de les avoir raisonnables. . . .' Lambert, *Avis d'une mère à sa fille*, in *Œuvres morales*, p. 47.

[70] 'Rien n'est donc si mal entendu que l'éducation qu'on donne aux jeunes personnes. On les destine à plaire; on ne leur donne des leçons que pour les agrémens; on fortifie leur amour-propre . . . on ne leur donne jamais de leçons de vertu ni de force.' *Ibid.*, p. 48.

[71] 'Je n'appris point le latin; c'est une langue, disoit ma mère, qui n'est nécessaire à présent qu'aux critiques ou aux maîtres d'école: toutes ses beautés ont été transmises dans les langues vivantes par le moyen des traductions. Le tems

'The only way to induce children of the nobility to turn to the sciences is to make the study of them pleasant and easy; it is that which I claim fortunately to have discovered.'[72]

'In brief, our aim is to take from nature what may stimulate the useful application of reason, without ever touching those things that are apt to tire it out, let alone those that are beyond its power. As for the form of this book, we have tried to eschew the dreary tone, and in place of a continuous discourse or a succession of disquisitions, which often produce distaste or boredom, we have from the start adopted the style of dialogue, which is the most natural of all and the closest to the thought processes of young readers.'[73]

'In the education of youth, my advice is to change everything. . . .
'Since Latin, by my system, is a very easy subject for children, I advise you to offer it to girls as well as boys. . . .
'Since, by my system, languages and sciences are but games, they should also have the form of games.'[74]

---

qu'un enfant perd à l'apprendre peut être employé plus utilement à l'acquisition des connoissances solides.' Prévost, *Cleveland*, liv. 1, in *Œuvres*, IV, 9.

[72] 'Le seul moyen d'engager les Enfans de Qualité de s'attacher aux Sciences, est d'en rendre l'étude agréable et facile ; c'est ce que je prétens avoir heureusement rencontré.' Vallange, *Les Sciences dévoilées* (Paris : Jombert et Gandouin, 1729), p. 38.

[73] 'En un mot, notre objet est de prendre dans la scène de la nature, ce qui peut frapper vivement, à exercer utilement la raison, sans jamais toucher, non seulement à ce qui nous paroît au-dessus de ses forces, mais même à ce qui pourroit aisément lasser ses efforts. Quant à la forme de l'ouvrage, nous avons essayé d'en écarter la tristesse : et au lieu d'un discours suivi ou d'un enchaînement de dissertations qui amènent souvent le dégoût et l'ennui, nous avons pris, dans les commencemens, le style de Dialogue, qui est de tous le plus naturel, et celui qui s'éloigne le moins de la façon de penser des jeunes Lecteurs.' Pluche, *Le Spectacle de la nature*, I, x.

[74] 'Dans ce qui concerne l'éducation de la Jeunesse, je conseille de tout changer.' 'Comme le Latin, selon mon Système, est une étude très léger pour les enfans, je vous conseille d'en faire part aux filles aussi bien qu'aux garçons.' 'Puisque, selon mon Système, les Langues et les Sciences ne sont que des jeux, ils doivent aussi en avoir la forme.' Vallange, *L'Art d'enseigner le Latin aux petits enfans, en les divertissant et sans qu'ils s'en apperçoivent* (Paris, 1730), quoted in *Journal des Sçavans*, January, 1731.

NATURE, THE OUT-OF-DOORS, AND THE SIMPLE LIFE

The 'classical tradition', because of its emphasis on psychological understanding, was a large factor in postponing the
appreciation of nature among French writers. The glorification
of the out-of-doors was a phenomenon which occurred throughout Europe, and in the long run the French joined it, but
during our period other countries were far ahead. There were
no Thomsons or Miltons in France, and if Defoe wrote *Moll
Flanders* with virtually no descriptions of nature, it was, as
we know from his other books, not because of a lack of sensitivity on his part but because of a lack of interest on Moll's:
she was too much taken up with the quality of the watches
she was stealing and the clothes of her prospective victims
In France the omission of nature seldom had such palpable
literary reasons. It is not difficult, however, to find examples
of praise of the out-of-doors and of lyrical descriptions of
nature in French writings, for the French, though belatedly,
did produce them. We shall present examples of these in our
first group of quotations, ending with a statement of the
perspective which an appreciation of nature can give man. If,
in the opening quotation, nature seems to serve as a mere
backdrop for a sex scene, it must be remembered that the
lovers' awareness of the out-of-doors (weather, vegetation, and
generally nature's invitation to love) was by no means com-
monplace at this time.

'It was the finest season of the year. All the countryside was
covered with grain ready to be cut. A light rain that had
fallen that morning had settled the dust and made the ground
firm. The sun was behind a cloud, and a gentle wind tempered the heat of the season. I have told you that my wife
was courageous, even bold, in the execution of what she
embarked upon. You will see. The tall rye, which was up to
our heads and even higher, the solitude in which we found
ourselves, and my love for her gave me a renewed pleasure in
the idea of making love to her on the grass. I asked her to
walk with me into the rye; she objected a good deal; but when
I told her that I absolutely insisted, she came. That was not
the only occasion which proved to me that she wanted me to

be satisfied, no matter how repugnant the thing might be to her. Indeed, it was as though she had foreseen what was going to happen to us. We entered the field of rye, thinking that no one had seen us. I set to work satisfying my whim. We were in the act, when . . .'[75]

'However, I must admit that the country is very beautiful: large streams water it, there are vast, thick forests, pleasant fields, and hills covered with thick woods; all this creates a delightful variety. Though this country is further south than Provence, the winter here is longer; but the cold is not extreme. And in summer the heat is less scorching, for the air is cooled by the forests and the many streams, lakes, and ponds which dot the countryside.'[76]

'As soon as day broke, the Marquis said: "Let us take advantage of the fresh morning air; let us not sleep away the most beautiful hours of the day. Yesterday we imitated those birds that you hear; we began our sleep with the setting of the sun. Let us again follow their example and not use up half of the time that the fates allot us in a state resembling death . . .

[75] 'C'étoit dans les plus beaux jours de l'année. Toute la compagne étoit couverte de grains prêts d'être coupez. Une petite pluie qu'il avoit fait le matin avoit abaissé la poussière, et rendoit la terre ferme. Le soleil étoit couvert, et un petit vent qu'il faisoit temperoit l'ardeur de la saison. Je vous ai dit que ma femme étoit courageuse, hardie dans l'exécution de ce qu'elle avoit entrepris : vous allez le voir. La hauteur des seigles qui venoient jusques à la tête, et qui même le passoient, la solitude où nous étions, et l'amour que j'avois pour elle, m'offrirent un nouveau plaisir à la caresser sur l'herbe. Je la priai d'entrer dans ces seigles, elle en fit mille difficultez ; mais lui ayant dit que je le voulois absolument, elle y entra. Ce n'est pas là le seul endroit qui m'a persaudé qu'elle ne cherchoit que ma satisfaction, quelque répugnance qu'elle en eût. En effet, il sembloit qu'elle prévît ce qui nous alloit arriver. Nous y entrâmes donc, croyant bien n'avoir point été aperçus.

'Je me mis en devoir de satisfaire ma fantaisie. Nous étions dans l'action, lorsque. . . .' Chasles, 'Histoire de Monsieur des Prez et de Mademoiselle de l'Epine', *Illustres Françoises*, I, 250.

[76] 'Il faut couvenir pourtant que le Pays est très-beau : de grandes rivières qui l'arrosent, de vastes et épaisses forêts, des prairies agréables, des collines chargées de bois fort touffus, tout cela fait une variété charmante. Quoique ce Pays soit plus au Sud que la Provence, l'hiver y est plus grand : les froids y sont pourtant assez modérés. Pendant l'été, la chaleur y est moins brûlante : l'air est rafraîchi par les forêts, et par la quantité de rivières, de lacs, et d'étangs dont le Pays est coupé.' Letter from Marest to Germon, November 9, 1712, *Jesuit Relations*, LXVI, 222–25.

do you prefer – contrary to the natural order of things – to stay awake nights and sleep in the daytime? . . . The animals seem to want us to learn from them how to live; their instincts guide them better. . . ." '[77]

'The third day we came to a castle built close by the Pyrenees. All around one sees pines and cypresses and dry, craggy rocks; and the only sound is that of the rushing water racing among the rocks. This wilderness home pleased me, for the very reason that it added to my melancholy. I spent whole days in the woods and upon my return wrote letters in which I expressed all my feelings.'[78]

'The whole countryside gave me the impression of an enchanted garden. Nature and art seemed to have joined hands to make it beautiful. There were arbors stretching as far as the eye could reach, small wooded areas, a planned conjuncture of open prairie and cultivated fields, houses symmetrically placed at corresponding intervals on both sides – and these were as pleasing to the eye as, probably, they were to live in. . . . The sun, which was beginning to spread its rays, gave all parts of the landscape so smiling an aspect that I felt as though I had been transported to another world.'[79]

[77] 'Dès que le jour parut : Allons, dit le Marquis, profitons de la fraîcheur du matin, ne perdons pas dans le sommeil le plus beau de la journée. Nous imitâmes hier ces oiseaux que vous entendez ; dès que le soleil eut quitté notre Hemisphère, nous nous livrâmes au repos : suivons de même leur exemple, et ne consumons point la moitié des jours que la Parque nous file dans une espèce de trépas . . . aimez-vous mieux, en renversant l'ordre des choses, veiller la nuit, dormir le jour? . . . Les bêtes semblent vouloir nous apprendre à vivre, et leur Instinct les conduit mieux. . . .' Boyer d'Argens, *Le Solitaire philosophe, ou Mémoires de Mr. le Marquis de Mirmon* (Amsterdam : Wetstein et Smith, 1739), p. 97.

[78] 'Nous arrivâmes le troisième jour dans un château bâti auprès des Pyrénées ; on voit à l'entour des pins, des cyprès, des rochers escarpés et arides, et on n'entend que le bruit des torrents qui se précipitent entre les rochers. Cette demeure si sauvage me plaisoit, par cela même qu'elle ajoutoit encore à ma mélancolie ; je passois les journées entières dans les bois, j'écrivois quand j'étois revenu des lettres où j'exprimois tous mes sentiments.' Tencin, *Mémoires du Comte de Comminge* (1735), (Paris : Sansot, 1908), p. 44.

[79] 'Toute la campagne me parut un jardin enchanté. L'art et la nature sembloient réunis pour l'embellir. C'étoit des allées d'arbres à perte de vue, de petits bois, un mélange bien ordonné de prairies et de terres cultivées, des maisons d'un côté et de l'autre qui se répondoient avec symétrie, et qui paroissoient aussi bien disposées pour le plaisir des yeux que pour la commodité des habitans. . . . Le

'We could not weary of looking at the small mountains that make up almost the whole [isle], so richly covered were they with beautiful, tall trees. The brooks that we saw flowing down the hillsides fell into small valleys, whose fertility was thus assured, and, after spreading over an area that I shall call neither forest nor plain, though it could be called either, emptied into the sea before our eyes.'[80]

'*Knight:* . . . But nothing pleases me more than this multitude of small live animals. . . . What a pleasure to live in the country ! It daily provides us something new.'

'*Count:* Everyone has his own way of thinking things through. I learned the value of withdrawal in the service and in the hustle-bustle of society. I love the country and have been comfortable in it for a long time.'

. . . .

'*Count:* Since you agree with me, I shall speak to you frankly. The spectacle of nature delights me, and I daily find new pleasure in it, even to the smallest things. . . . The scene before us is magnificent. But what our eyes cannot take in at one sweep we can divide into parts and enjoy in instalments.'[81]

---

soleil qui commençoit à répandre ses rayons donnoit un air si riant à toutes les parties de cette belle campagne, que je me crus transporté dans un nouveau monde.' Prévost, *Cleveland*, liv. 3, in *Œuvres*, IV, 290–91.

[80] 'Nous ne pouvions nous lasser de regarder les petites montagnes dont elle [cette île] est presque toute composée, tant elles étaient richement couvertes de grands et beaux arbres. Les ruisseaux que nous en voyions découler, tombaient dans des vallons, de la fertilité desquels il nous était impossible de douter ; et après s'être répandus dans quelques espaces de terrain uni, auquel je ne donnerai le nom ni de forêt ni de plaine, quoi qu'ils pussent recevoir l'un et l'autre, ils se venaient jeter à nos yeux dans la mer.' Misson, *Les Voyages de François Leguat*, I, 61.

[81] '*Le Chevalier:* . . . Mais rien ne me divertit davantage que cette multitude de petits animaux en vie. . . . Qu'on a de plaisir à vivre à la campagne ! elle fournit tous les jours quelques nouveautés.'

'*Le Comte:* Chacun a sa façon de penser. J'ai appris dans le service et dans le fracas du monde ce que vaut la retraite. Je l'aime et m'en trouve bien depuis lontemps.' . . .

'*Le Comte:* Puisque vous prenez si bien ma pensée, je vous parlerai sans détour. Le spectacle de la nature m'enchante, et j'y trouve tous les jours des plaisirs nouveaux, jusques dans les moindres objets. . . . La scène que nous voyons, est magnifique. Mais ce que notre vûe ne peut saisir à la fois, nous le pouvons diviser et en jouir par partie.' Pluche, *Le Spectacle de la nature*, Vol. I, Entretien I.

'As we were strolling on a terrace, he stopped for a time and pointed out the beauty of the landscape. "If these peaceful spots," he said, "do not offer social pleasures, they compensate by allowing us to breathe a pure air and to enjoy a precious tranquillity; but above all, here one learns to throw off all human views, to take no stock in the world's vanities, to see objectively the empty, meaningless, and illusory nature of the things it prizes, to reflect fully on the hazard of high office, on the utter folly of tormenting oneself for the phantasm of honour, rank, and position, or for false benefits which make one lose the real and lasting benefits of eternity." '[82]

Our second group of quotations will present several examples of the attitude which is more often associated with the intellectuals of the Enlightenment. Sometimes, as in the first of these passages, it is merely a case of the metropolis being so miraculously beautiful as to leave little room for the out-of-doors. In part, such rhapsodical praise of Paris is an expression of the enthusiasm for material progress, comfort, and luxury which we know increased in the course of the eighteenth century. While it should have been possible to admire both Paris and the out-of-doors, more commonly our writers leaned to the one or the other; if Voltaire enjoyed the country and Rousseau often thrived in the city, still we have no doubt as to where they were truly happy. In our second and third quotations the beauty of the landscape impresses the writer deeply, but it is so closely linked to the presence of human habitation and cultivated land that we cannot help wondering whether there could be any beauty in nature all by itself. The last quotation in this group shows perhaps less a lack of sensitivity to wild nature than a realistic appraisal of it. The disgust for

[82] 'Comme nous nous promenions sur une terrasse, il s'arrêta quelque temps à me faire remarquer la beauté du païsage : si ces paisibles lieux, dit-il, ne présentent pas de plaisirs vifs, à ce défaut on a celui d'y respirer un air pur, et de joüir d'un précieux calme ; mais l'essentiel est qu'on y apprend à se dépouiller de toutes les vües humaines, à mépriser de plus en plus les vanitez du monde, à considérer de sang froid le vuide, le néant et l'illusion de ses grandeurs, à réfléchir pleinement sur les dangers des places éminentes, sur l'extrême folie de se tourmenter pour des fantômes d'honneur, de rang et de prééminence, pour de faux biens qui font perdre les biens réels et permanens de l'éternité.' Jacques Ignace de Latouche, *Le Militaire en solitude* (2 vols ; The Hague : Hondt, 1736), I, 50–51.

lakes, rocks, forests, and wild animals is expressed by a man who has suffered from them, for whom nature – meaning, often, swarms of mosquitoes or vast stretches of forbidding country to traverse – is harshly inimical to humanity. The assumption that 'civilization' is superior to 'nature', or more important, or more interesting, or more desirable, seems common to the authors quoted here. It represents an attitude which was more common in France than elsewhere during this period, we feel sure without counting cases.[83]

'The sun does not embellish the heavens more than Paris does the earth; and that fair star does not add more light to the brilliance of the firmament than that great city gives to earth below. It is as though her riches have made the rest of the world poor, for she has brought together all that was most precious in the Orient. . . . The buildings are so beautiful and comfortable that passers-by, as well as occupants, have difficulty knowing which are the finest. The panelling and the gilding are not their most beautiful or most precious feature: the ingenuity of amateurs and the cleverness of craftsmen have created something of extraordinary value and have raised the commonest materials to a rank with the most beautiful and to a value equal to that of rare treasures.'[84]

'One cannot find a more pleasant road than the one from Geneva to Lausanne: it is a slope which is cultivated and inhabited all the way. The lake is hardly ever out of sight, and at some places on the other side there are banks of mountains, their horned peaks always white with snow.'[85]

[83] For a fuller treatment of this subject, with copious quotations from the literature of the period, see G. Atkinson, *Le Sentiment de la nature et le retour a la vie simple (1690-1740)* (Geneva : Droz, 1960).

[84] 'Le Soleil n'embellit pas plus les Cieux, que Paris orne la terre ; et ce bel Astre ne contribue pas plus à l'esclat de ces belles voûtes, que cette grande Ville donne de lustre à ce bas Element. Ses richesses semblent avoir appauvry le reste du monde, et avoir assemblé tout ce que l'Orient a de plus prétieux. . . . Les superbes et commodes bâtiments se disputent à qui les regardent, ou qui les habitent. Les lambris et la dorure n'en est ny le plus beau, ny le plus prétieux. L'esprit des curieux et l'adresse des ouvriers ont donné un prix extraordinaire, et ont élevé les plus communes matières au rang des plus belles, et au prix des plus rares.' Michel de Pure, *La Prétieuse* (1666), ed. E. Magne (Paris : Droz, 1938), p. 183.

[85] 'Il ne se peut pas voir une plus agréable route que celle de Genève à Lausanne : c'est un costeau toujours bien cultivé, et bien habité. On ne perd que très rarement

'If we look in another direction and follow the shore, the winding coastline with small capes washed by the quiet waters, and pretty villages dotting the coast offer an extremely pleasant view. A little farther on, the air becomes thick with the awful fumes of Mt Vesuvius, and one gets a full view of that frightful mountain.'[86]

'From Lake Superior to St Charles, where I have the honour of writing this to you, it is three hundred leagues . . . so long a trip taken in any other country would furnish many things of interest or capable of arousing one's curiosity, but in these vast stretches all that one sees is lakes, rocks, immense forests, savages, and a few wild animals.'[87]

Praise of the simple life, which reached a high point with Rousseau and his school, was anticipated during our period. Since the first volume of this series of studies on the period of 1690–1740 dealt in some detail with the simple life,[88] it is not necessary to give many quotations here. It is enough to point out that the adoration of the simple life which was to flower in the Romantic authors thrived alongside the opposite attitude – that is, praise of city life and 'civilization' – which is associated with Voltaire and the majority of the encyclopaedists.

The Swiss traveller and writer Muralt, writing about London, deplored the poverty and prostitution which he saw and approved of the withdrawal practised by those who could afford it:

---

la veûe du Lac, et en quelques endroits de l'autre costé, ce sont des montagnes amoncelées, dont les cimes cornües sont toujours brillantes de neige.' Misson, *Nouveau Voyage d'Italie* (3 vols; The Hague: H. van Bulderen, 1702), III, 89.

[86] 'Si l'on jette les yeux d'un autre costé, en suivant le rivage, les sinüositez qui se meslent réciproquement avec les petits caps que cette paisible Mer arrose, et les jolis villages dont cette coste est parsemée, sont un objet tout-à-fait agréable. Un peu plus loin, l'air s'épaissit des horribles fumées du Vésuve, et l'on voit tout-à-plein cette affreuse montagne.' *Ibid.*, II, 33.

[87] 'On compte du haut du lac supérieure au fort Saint Charle d'où j'ay l'honneur de vous escrire, trois cent lieues . . . une si longue route faite en tout autre pays, aurait fourny bien des objets divertissants et capables de piquer la curiosité, mais tout ce qu'on voit dans ces vastes contrées se termine a des lacs, des rochers, des forests immenses, des sauvages et quelques bestes feroces.' Letter from R.P. Aulneau to R.P. Bonin, April 30, 1736, *Jesuit Relations*, LXVIII, 288.

[88] Atkinson, *Le Sentiment de la nature.*

'Unable to remain calm spectators of the disarray of their country, when they are expected to do something to improve the situation, they leave their positions and withdraw. Thus, unable to be useful through their regular functions, what better course could they choose as their portion than to do some good in some village?'[89]

His comments on Bussy Rabutin, a nobleman who had been banished from Paris, show us the more accepted attitude of the French nobility:

'If it happens to a man of the Court, to a noble, that he displeases the king and is ordered by the latter to leave the Court, that is, to live on his lands, on those very same lands which he has taken pains to beautify and which he has made a delightful place to spend time – that is an exile which he cannot endure; as soon as he regains his self-control, he begins to languish, and his freedom and leisure make him unhappy.

'Count Bussi, known for his writings, may serve to demonstrate what I am saying. Some mischievous light tales that he wrote caused him to be banished from Court, and though one would think that a writer ought not to be afraid of withdrawing from society, this man did not get used to it; he became unable to write, except as a means of trying to be reinstated. We have his letters addressed to the king; Lord, what self-abasement one sees, what extreme efforts to be reinstated!'[90]

---

[89] '. . . ne pouvant se resoudre d'être Spectateurs paisibles du Désordre de leur Patrie, lors qu'on attend d'eux qu'ils y aportent du reméde, ils laissent là les Emplois et se retirent. Ne pouvant donc lui être utiles par cette voïe, que peuvent-ils faire de meilleur que de choisir, comme pour leur Portion, l'Emploi de faire du bien à quelque Village?' Muralt, *Lettres sur les Anglois et les François*, p. 139.

[90] 'S'il arrive à un homme de la Cour, à un Grand, de déplaire au Roi, et que le Roi lui ordonne de se retirer, c'est-à-dire, d'aller vivre sur ses Terres, sur ces mêmes Terres qu'il a pris soin d'embellir et dont il a rendu le séjour délicieux; c'est un Exil qu'il ne sçauroit supporter: dès qu'il se voit maître de soi-même, il languit, le Loisir et la Liberté le rendent malheureux. *Le Comte de Bussi*, connu par ses Ecrits, peut servir de preuve à ce que je dis. Quelques Historiettes écrites malignement, le firent bannir de la Cour, et quoi qu'il semble qu'un Ecrivain ne doive pas craindre la Retraite, celui-ci ne s'en accommoda pas; il ne sçut plus écrire que pour tâcher d'en sortir. On a ses Lettres écrites au Roi. Eh! quelles soumissions, quels efforts pour rentrer en grâce, n'y voit-on pas?' *Ibid.*, pp. 171–72.

In contrast to Muralt's study, a book expressing the attitude of men like Bussy Rabutin, a book not available to us, was reviewed in the *Journal des Sçavans* of February, 1727. The lesson of this book is 'that a recluse, who has given up the company of men to depend on none but himself and God and who no longer has any contact with society, cannot be happy in this life.'[91]

It will perhaps already have occurred to readers who are acquainted with Marivaux that in him the two attitudes merge in a manner befitting the leading author of the period. Marivaux, and his characters, often show awareness of the corruption of society and the moral superiority of the simple, rustic life; but their practical bent leads them to yield to the blandishments of the elegant life – without, however, losing perspective, which is what gives much of Marivaux's writing its unique and winning quality. The following passage is illustrative:

'Imagine' [said Jacob], 'what it means for a country bumpkin like me . . . to have become the husband of a wealthy girl and the lover of two noble ladies . . . I who was called Jacob ten or twelve days earlier; imagine the amorous flirtations of those two ladies, and especially the charming, though immoral, artfulness that Mme de Ferval used to seduce me; that fine, provocative, stockinged leg, which I looked at a great deal . . . what a school for softness, pleasure, and corruption, and consequently for feeling! For the refinement and the corruption of the soul go hand in hand.'[92]

---

[91] '. . . qu'un Solitaire qui a renoncé a la Societé des hommes, pour ne dépendre que de Dieu et de lui-même, et qui n'a plus aucun commerce avec le monde, ne sçauroit être heureux en cette vie.' Review of Claude Buffier, *Traité de la Société civile, et du moyen de se rendre heureux* (1726), in *Journal des Sçavans*, February, 1727, pp. 263–64.

[92] 'Figurez-vous ce que c'est qu'un jeune rustre comme moi . . . devenu le mari d'une fille riche, et l'amant de deux femmes de condition . . . moi qu'on appelait Jacob dix ou douze jours auparavant; les amoureuses agaceries de ces deux dames, et surtout cet art charmant, quoique impur, que Mme de Ferval avait employé pour me séduire; cette jambe si bien chaussée, si galante, que j'avais tant regardée . . . quelle école de mollesse, de volupté, de corruption, et par conséquent de sentiment! car l'âme se raffine à mesure qu'elle se gâte.' Marivaux, *Le Paysan parvenu*, Part IV, in *Romans*, p. 722.

RELIGION

The literature of our period contains a wide spectrum of opinion and sentiment concerning religion. Traditional Christianity persisted unchanged among pious men and among some writers, but doubts and hesitations, as well as outright attacks, occurred with increasing frequency. As progress, material wealth, and social values became the dominant interests of more and more people, and as this came to be more openly expressed than in the preceding aristocratic age, men of religious bent went on the defensive, and the writers who scoffed at religion, whether at its substance or at its form, wrote with a confidence typical of those who expect the future to go their way.

A statement on this subject which appeared in an English magazine in 1731 was probably applicable to France as well. 'It is a matter of melancholy Observation, that Men are now-a-days afraid of being thought Religious, as if it was a real Reproach; which seems owing to the ill Conduct of the Professors of it.'[93] Marivaux's peasant, Jacob, it will be recalled, progressed from mild doubt about the sincerity of a few priests to a general belief that the whole devout crowd was a mass of hypocrites. The minor writer, Le Noble, put the most widespread objection to the clergy in plain terms in 1700, in a set of conversations between a father and son:

'*The Father:* Whatever pains, whatever labours a man performs in other professions, tell me if there is a single one in which you can overnight gain twenty, thirty, even a hundred thousand pounds of income with one stroke of the pen; and that is what we see happening every day in the Church. A man goes to bed penniless and the next morning wakes up rich for the rest of his life. Another, a poor priest or abbot in the morning, has become a rich prelate or holder of a fat benefice by nightfall. It is in that profession that we see fortune performing her greatest miracles.'[94]

---

[93] *Gentlemen's Magazine*, December 4, 1731.

[94] '*Le Père:* Quelques peines, quelques travaux qu'un homme se donne dans les autres Professions, dites-moy, s'il y en a une seule qui puisse du soir au matin vous donner vingt, trente, et cent mil livres de rente d'un trait de plume, et c'est ce qu'on voit tous les jours arriver dans l'Eglise. Tel se couche sans un sou, qui

Marivaux, in his *Spectateur*, attacked the priests as show-offs, a milder criticism of their motives than the foregoing: 'Frankly, I am not surprised at the lack of effectiveness of sermons; most are but exercises in eloquence, in which the preacher is working less to make us penitent than to make us admire his cleverness.'[95]

Opposition to what was widely considered empty form in religion, or worse, outright abuse, finds expression in a growing admiration of the Quakers, whose rejection of ritual became well known in France. The ideal practice of religion, for the critics of both Catholicism and Protestantism, is portrayed, among others, by Prévost in *Cleveland*, in his description of the purity and simplicity of an Indian religious rite quoted above in this chapter.[96]

The use of religion for private ends is exposed by Chasles, in a discussion of an Indian maharajah, but the application to Christian lands is not left to the reader's imagination: 'Ramraja . . . thought, as do many other noblemen, that religion should yield to private interest. How many Christian rulers, how many popes even, have shared that feeling!'[97]

Were attacks that associated religion with power and oppression justified? Historically, we know that they were. What is perhaps of greater interest is the fact that many writers, including some who must be regarded as 'liberals' in their time, were quite willing (without putting the matter in these terms) to see religion play such a role. Here, for example, is Marivaux rationalizing social inequality on religious

---

le lendemain est enrichi pour le reste de ses jours. Tel se lève petit Capelan ou médiocre abbé, qui se couche gros Bénéficier ou riche Prelat. Et c'est dans cette Profession qu'on voit les plus grands miracles de la Fortune.' Eustache Le Noble, 'Des Moyens particuliers d'arriver à la Fortune dans l'Eglise', *L'Ecole du monde* (4 vols; Paris : Jouvenel, 1700), III, 5–6.

[95] 'A vous parler franchement, je ne suis pas étonné du peu d'effet des prédications : la plupart ne sont que des pièces d'éloquence, où le prédicateur nous exhorte bien moins à devenir pénitents, qu'à le trouver habile.' Marivaux, *Spectateur françois*, No. 5, p. 184.

[96] For the quotation and translation, see p. 102. See also Prévost, *Cleveland*, liv. 6, in *Œuvres*, V, 448–49.

[97] 'Remraja . . . s'imagina, aussi bien que quantité d'autres Grands, que la Religion doit céder à l'intérêt. Que de Princes Chrétiens, que de Papes même, ont été de ce sentiment !' Chasles, *Journal d'un voyage*, III, 21–22.

grounds, and d'Argens accepting religion as a kind of 'opium of the people'.

'. . . there is a superior being that presides over us whose wisdom apparently permits the unequal distribution that we see in the things of life; indeed, it is because of inequality that men do not reject one another, that they draw together, seek one another's society, and offer one another assistance. So, let the fortunate of the world peaceably enjoy their abundance and the benefit of the laws, but let their compassion for the man who is indigent and wretched make provision for the difficulty that he feels in observing those laws; it is he who has all the hardship. . . .'[98]

'I admit – and this is a matter on which there can be no doubt – that the belief in the immortality of the soul is necessary to keep the common people and lower classes down. Born wicked by nature, these people act more like slaves than like free men endowed with that reason which makes us love virtue for its own sake, as the most perfect benefit that can be acquired. But I also think – and experience daily confirms my opinion – that among men of a certain rank, belief in the immortality of the soul is not an attribute which is necessary for them to become, or to be, good men.'[99]

As the last sentence in the Marivaux passage indicates, this

[98] '. . . il est un être supérieur qui préside sur nous, et dont la sagesse permet sans doute cette inégale distribution que l'on voit dans les choses de la vie; c'est même à cause qu'elle est inégale que les hommes ne se rebutent pas les uns des autres, qu'ils se rapprochent, se vont chercher et s'entr'aident. Ainsi, que les heureux de ce monde jouissent en paix de leur abondance et du bénéfice des lois; mais que leur pitié pour l'homme indigent, pour le misérable, aille au-devant de la peine qu'il pourrait sentir à observer ces lois, tout l'embarras en est de son côté. . . .' Marivaux, *Spectateur français*, feuille 25, pp. 317–18.

[99] 'Je conviens, et c'est une chose qu'on ne sauroit mettre en doute, que la croiance de l'immortalité de l'âme est nécessaire pour contenir le bas peuple et les personnes vulgaires, qui, nées naturellement mauvaises, agissent plutôt en esclaves qu'en hommes libres et doués de la raison, qui nous fait aimer la vertu par rapport à elle-même, comme étant le bien le plus parfait qu'on puisse acquérir. Mais je pense aussi, et l'expérience certifie tous les jours mon sentiment, que parmi les gens d'un certain rang, la croiance de l'immortalité de l'âme n'est point un attribut qui leur soit nécessaire pour devenir, ou pour être honnête homme.' Du Boyer d'Argens, *La Philosophie du bon sens* (2 vols; The Hague: P. Paupie, 1740), II, 126–27.

attitude was not devoid of its compassionate side. Religion, according to Marivaux and many other writers of our period, should teach kindness to one's fellow man.[100]

Positive statements on religion, in our writers, are seldom interesting or original. They range from an identification of piety with goodness (Blanchard and Huber), through feelings of the presence of God in nature and of infinity as evidence of God's existence (Pluche), to blind acceptance of traditional religious dogma (Tanevot), and in fiction, to the view that God watches over the virtuous and stage-manages many a melodramatic scene, in order to preserve the innocence of a maiden, for example (Mme Méheust).

'True, solid piety always inspires feelings of compassion for those who suffer, and there is no greater affliction than to be both poor and sick.'[101]

'Divine justice is thus very different from the conception that people ordinarily have of it. It is often thought of as hatred, vengeance, anger, wrath. . . . It is obvious that kindness and wrath, mercy and vengeance cannot exist together.'[102]

'The plants that he [man] cultivates have been proportioned to his smallness. They rise but little, in order to be within easy reach of the hand that planted them. But God has kept for himself the trees of the forests. . . . The forests are properly His garden; He alone has planted them, He alone maintains them. . . . It is He who has given wings to most of their seeds so that they may the more easily be carried through the air and spread in many places. To look at the seed of the linden

[100] For a discussion of the role of compassion in the literature of the age, see Chapter IV of the second volume of this series of studies, *The Sentimental Revolution: French Writers of 1690–1740* (Seattle: University of Washington Press, 1965).

[101] 'La véritable et solide piété inspire toujours des sentimens de compassion pour ceux qui sont dans l'affliction: il n'en est pas de plus grande que d'être pauvre et malade tout ensemble.' A. Blanchard, *Secours spirituels* (Paris: Pralard, 1722), Preface.

[102] 'La Justice Divine est donc bien différente de l'idée qu'on s'en forme communément. On se la représente comme une Haine, une Vengeance, une Colère, une Fureur. . . . Il est évident que la Bonté et la Fureur, la Miséricorde et la Vengeance ne peuvent subsister ensemble.' Marie Huber, *Sentimens différens de quelques théologiens* (Rouen: Prévost, 1728), p. 13.

I

tree, the maple, or the elm is to become convinced of this truth.'[103]

'*The Countess:* Not long ago there was a man of great intelligence here who made a study of the number of seeds on one branch of a twelve-year-old elm tree. Judging its eight other large branches by that one, and calculating the seeds to be produced in a hundred years on the basis of one year, he found millions and billions of millions of seeds . . . he arrived at a figure which staggered us all, and he wisely concluded that the character, not only of wisdom and power, but also, if we dare say so, the very character of infinity, was imprinted on all the works of God. . . .'

'*The Prior:* These truths are worthy of all our admiration and respect; they overwhelm us because we are limited. . . . God has deliberately tried to overwhelm us with this kind of infinity which we feel on every hand, even in the smallest creatures, in order to put our minds under the dominion of the infinity which is in His essence, in His attributes, in His providence, in His operations, and in His mysteries.'[104]

'Imperilled child of Lucretius' thought,
Shun the vagaries of human reason.

[103] 'Les plantes qu'il cultive ont été proportionnées à sa petitesse. Elles montent peu pour ne pas refuser un accès facile à la main qui les façonne. Mais Dieu s'est réservé les arbres de forêts. . . . Elles sont proprement son Jardin, lui seul les a plantées, lui seul les entretient. . . . C'est lui qui a donné des ailes à la plupart des graines pour être plus aisément emportées par l'air et répandues en plus de lieux. Il suffit pour s'en convaincre de jetter les yeux sur la graine du tilleul, de l'érable, et de l'orme.' Pluche, *Le Spectacle de la nature,* quoted in *Journal des Sçavans,* September, 1735.

[104] '*La Comtesse:* Il y avoit ici, il n'y a pas fort longtems, un homme de beaucoup d'esprit qui fit sur une des branches d'un jeune orme de douze ans l'essai de compter ce qu'il s'y trouveroit de graines. Jugeant des huit autres maîtresses branches par celle-là, et du produit de cent ans par celui d'un an, il trouvoit des millions et des milliards de millions de graines . . . il formoit un calcul qui nous effraya tous, et conclut fort sagement que le caractère non seulement de sagesse et de puissance, mais, si on ose le dire, le caractère même d'infini étoit imprimé sur tous les ouvrages de Dieu. . . .'

'*Le Prieur:* Ces vérités sont dignes de toute notre admiration et de tous nos respects : elles nous épouvantent, parce que nous sommes bornés. . . . Dieu a voulu exprès nous accabler par cette espèce d'infinité qui se fait sentir partout, même dans les moindres créatures, pour assujettir nos esprits à l'infinité qui est dans son essence, dans ses attributs, dans sa providence, dans ses opérations, dans ses mystères.' Pluche, *Le Spectacle de la nature,* Vol. I, Entretien XIV.

> Its duty is not to understand
> What God has revealed to us,
> But to yield and keep silent.'[105]

' "This event," said the Marquise to us, "clearly proves that Providence is on our side. Thank God, dear Julie; it is He who has delivered you from the hands of your cruel ravishers. Do not credit chance or cleverness for our Knight's success: the Supreme Being guided his blows. He refused to allow your innocence and virtue to be so unjustly violated." '[106]

---

[105] 'De Lucrece aujourd'hui dangereux nourrisson,/Sauves-toi de l'écart de l'humaine raison,/Son devoir n'est pas de comprendre/Ce que Dieu nous a revelé,/ Mais de se taire et de se rendre. . . .' Tanevot, *Poësies diverses* (1732), in *Journal des Sçavans*, May, 1733, p. 63.

[106] 'Cet événement, nous dit la Marquise, prouve visiblement que la Providence s'est intéressée pour nous : remerciez Dieu, ma chère Julie, c'est lui qui vous a délivrée des mains de vos cruels ravisseurs : n'imputez point au hazard, ni à l'adresse l'heureux succès de Monsieur le Chevalier ; le souverain Etre conduisoit les coups. Il n'a pas voulu permettre que votre innocence, et votre vertu fussent si injustement opprimées.' Mme Méheust, *Les Mémoires du Chevalier de* —— (Paris : Dupuis, 1734), p. 67.

PART II

The Broadening World of 1700

CHAPTER 3

The Expression of the Real World

LIKE any masterpieces, those of the age of Louis XIV had their limitations. The ability of subsequent writers to identify these limitations is never, and was not in this case, any guarantee of improvement, except in equally limited ways. Thus it is that the changes wrought by the authors of our period, while frequently adding one dimension, sacrificed another. If the tragedies of the eighteenth century (some critics would put 'tragedies' in quotes) dealt with more 'real' people, places, and ideas – that is, more readily identifiable – than did the tragedies of Racine, they were utterly lacking in the sublimity that even today moves readers and audiences. But the bourgeois of the early eighteenth century were not to be appealed to in terms or in a framework intended for the aristocracy of the seventeenth, no matter how beautiful or profound the treatment.

The poverty of some works of the high period of French literature in certain respects cannot be doubted, nor can the superiority of the works of 1690–1740 over their predecessors, in those specific respects. Principally, the distinction between the two periods in matters of expression lies in a different kind of interest in people and things. A comparison of a few sentences from Mme de Lafayette and from Robert Chasles will illustrate the difference immediately, and though these are admittedly extreme rather than random examples, and therefore other cases will not show as much variance, the change from one period to the other is unmistakable. The separate tendencies – of Mme de Lafayette to write in general terms and of Chasles to give a wealth of specific detail – are visible on every hand in the two periods.

'Never has a woman possessed so much grace and charm in appearance and in manner . . . there was something curious and animated about her face. She bore no resemblance to other beautiful English ladies.'[1]

'Passion has never been as fond and furious as it was at this time in the Prince [de Nemours]. He went out under the willows alongside a small stream which flowed behind the house where he was hidden. He went as far away as possible so as not to be seen or heard by anyone; he gave himself over to the rapture of his love, and his heart was so touched that he was forced to weep.'[2]

'Mlle Fenoüil was tall and well proportioned, with a pleasant figure and a delicate white complexion; she had black eyes, eyebrows, and hair, large, deep-set, animated eyes which the least sorrow left languid, asking for the heart of all she looked upon. A wide and smooth forehead, a well-formed nose, the face oval-shaped, a dimple on the chin, a small and rosy mouth, white, well-set teeth, a narrow and slightly aquiline nose, a finely formed neck, a high and ample bosom, well-formed arms, and the most beautiful hand that ever a woman might possess. You see from her portrait that I may be excused for loving her to the extent of risking everything for her.'[3]

Reasons for the difference lie, in great part, in the history and sociology of the time, though it may also be observed that 'general' and 'specific' have a way of alternating in the history of literatures independently of social developments. In our case, the growing importance of bourgeois taste would suffice

[1] 'Jamais femme n'a eu tant de charmes et tant d'agréments dans sa personne et dans son humeur . . . son visage avoit quelque chose de vif et de singulier, et elle n'avoit aucune ressemblance avec les autres beautés angloises.' Mme Marie-Madeleine de Lafayette, *La Princesse de Clèves* (Paris : Georges Crès et Cie ; London : J. M. Dent & Sons ; n.d.), pp. 89–90.

[2] 'La passion n'a jamais été si tendre et si violente qu'elle étoit alors en ce prince. Il s'en alla sous des saules, le long d'un petit ruisseau qui couloit derrière la maison où il étoit caché. Il s'éloigna le plus qu'il lui fut possible, pour n'être vu ni entendu de personne ; il s'abandonna aux transports de son amour, et son cœur en fut tellement pressé, qu'il fut contraint de laisser couler quelques larmes.' *Ibid.*, p. 194.

[3] Chasles, 'M. de Jussy et Mlle Fenoüil', *Illustres Françoises*, I, 174. For French original, see Ch. I, Note 91.

to explain the new interest in realistic detail. An additional
factor, travel, shows its importance in the works of numerous
writers of the eighteenth century. Our period witnessed a
great increase in travel, and this was, if not a cause, surely
a stimulus to an intensified interest in people and places on the
part of both writers and public. We shall quote several sentences from Prévost, who was generally devoted to detailed
accounts and descriptions and who had a close acquaintance
with England, where he lived for a number of years:

'I have seen nothing, in all of my travels, which approaches
the beauty of this spectacle. The Thames from London to the
sea is not only one of the widest rivers of Europe but one of the
most pleasant and most suitable to navigation. . . . Its banks
are lined with shops and arsenals. . . . In places where one can
see beyond the banks, one sees a great number of beautiful
houses, scattered in all directions on the flat country and on
the slopes of the hills, and colourful gardens . . . in short, one
cannot open one's eyes on this happy island without getting
an idea of its abundance and the happiness of its inhabitants.'[4]

It may be noted that, in contrast to this passage, Prévost's
accounts of travels in Hungary, Portugal, Spain, and Holland,
in the same book, are so lacking in detail that they could as
well have been written by any of the classic writers of the
seventeenth century. The heroes spend three days in the
Escurial without noticing or describing the building, and
several weeks in and around Lisbon without commenting on
the beauty of the city and its environs. The explanation is
that Prévost had never been in these places and apparently
had not bothered to read much about them. One cannot but
recall the similar case of Defoe, whose Colonel Jack and Moll
Flanders spent time in Virginia without seeing a river, a wood,

[4] 'Je n'ai rien vu, dans tous mes voyages, qui approche de la beauté de ce
spectacle. La Tamise, depuis Londres jusqu'à la mer, est non-seulement une des
plus larges rivières de l'Europe, mais une des plus agréables, et des plus propres
à la navigation. . . . Ses bords sont remplis de magasins, d'arsenaux. . . . Dans les
endroits où la vue peut s'étendre davantage, on aperçoit un grand nombre de
belles maisons, répandues de tous côtés dans les plaines ou sur le penchant des
collines, des jardins ornés . . . enfin l'on ne peut ouvrir les yeux dans cette heureuse
île, sans prendre une idée de l'abondance qui y règne et du bonheur de ses habitans.'
Prévost, *Mém. d'un homme de qualité*, liv. 10, in *Œuvres*, II, 234-35.

or any other landscape, as far as the reader can tell, whereas in London they regale us with a staggering wealth of picturesque detail.

Interestingly, travel did not have the effect of favouring aristocratic tastes, even though one might expect aristocrats to have travelled more than bourgeois did. Actually, if we believe Rousseau, who was himself a hearty and hardy traveller, not only did the French travel more than any other Europeans, but the appetite for travel reached down the social ladder to the bourgeois and the common people in a way that was quite unknown in England or other countries. Even more important than the fact that bourgeois were numerous among Frenchmen who travelled is the question of where they went. Frenchmen of no matter what class journeyed much less to aristocratic Spain than to Italy, Switzerland, Holland, and England, all heavily bourgeoisified countries. England particularly became the mecca of travelling Frenchmen, and what impressed them there were bourgeois practices and institutions – the triumph and prestige of business and of merchants, widespread literacy and participation in the country's cultural and intellectual life, the growth of democratic political institutions, and religious pluralism. The success of these bourgeois developments in England inevitably bolstered those men in France who had such innovations as their dream, and shook the faith in the old order held by even staunch supporters of aristocratic society. An assessment of some of France's aristocratic and bourgeois neighbours which fairly represents the opinion of perceptive Frenchmen in the early eighteenth century appears in the following statement by Vauban, which clearly links France with Spain as declining powers, and England with Holland as those which were on the rise:

'At the present time, who can shake two strong powers which border upon each other, which have so much advantage in being closely united and so many ways of helping each other? The trouble in all this is that Spain is quite depopulated and that France, for its part, has lost a third of its population, because of the low estate to which it has fallen or for other reasons; and, since I do not see any inclination – or ability – to repair these losses, and since on the other hand the populations of England and Holland are increasing, the situation might well become dangerous.'[5]

Literary men of the time were conscious of the down-to-earth quality of their writings and often made a point of it; there came to be a premium on commonness. One noble hero, in the *Mémoires du Comte de Comminge* by Mme de Tencin, in order to see his beloved, disguises himself as a house painter and joins the work crew in her husband's château, as we have seen before. We can get some of the impact of this if we recall that even a century or more later, a figure like Armand Duval, in *La Dame aux camélias*, would go no further than to suggest, in a moment of extreme passion: '*S'il le faut, je travaillerai.*' The following passages may give the reader a notion of the tone of our literature. We shall then examine several specific aspects of the realism of the period.

'. . . since the subject matter with which I was dealing was usually open to ridicule, I was led to a manner of writing which was far from the sublime. It seems to me that one should use a sublime style only as a last resort; it is so unnatural! I confess that a base style is even worse; but there is a style in between, perhaps several; this is what is difficult; one has a hard time choosing just the tone that one wishes and not deviating from it.'[6]

---

[5] 'Pour lors, qui pourra ébranler deux Puissances formidables qui se touchent, qui ont tant d'intérêt à être parfaitement unies et tant de facilités à s'entre-secourir? Ce qu'il y a de mauvais à tout cela est que l'Espagne est toute dépeuplée et que la France, de son côté, a perdu le tiers de ses peuples, faute de bon appareil ou autrement; et comme il ne me paraît pas qu'on soit dans le dessein de réparer ces pertes, ni même dans le pouvoir, et que, tout au contraire, l'Angleterre et la Hollande augmentent les leurs, cela pourrait bien devenir dangereux.' Vauban to Puyzieulx, Toulon, December 4, 1700, in Vauban, *Lettres intimes (inédites) adressées au marquis de Puyzieulx (1699–1705)*, éd. Hyrvoix de Landosle (Paris: Bossard, 1924), p. 102. For the Rousseau reference earlier in the paragraph, see Paul Lacroix (who quotes Rousseau but uses other sources as well), *France in the Eighteenth Century: Its Institutions, Customs and Costumes*, pp. 434–35.

[6] '. . . les matieres que j'avois en main estant le plus souvent assez susceptibles de ridicule, m'ont invité à une maniere d'écrire fort éloignée du sublime. Il me semble qu'il ne faudroit donner dans le Sublime qu'à son corps défendant. Il est si peu naturel! J'avoüe que le stile bas est encore quelque chose de pis; mais il y a un milieu, et mesme plusieurs. C'est ce qui fait l'embarras; on a bien de

'The author has proposed to provide young people a know-ledge of the commonest and most ordinary things, the ignorance of which is often lamented. . . . This book may enlighten those who think that our language cannot, without degrading itself, describe the details of gardening and agriculture. Perhaps the Romans said the same of the Latin language before Virgil composed his *Georgics*.'[7]

'One will not see here unflinching bravery or surprising incidents, because all will be true and natural. I have made use of the simple truth. If I had wished, I could have em-bellished everything with forced adventures . . . and if there is anything that may appear fantastic, it will be the action of Du Puis, who stabs himself in Mme de Londé's room; however, I could not suppress this since it is true. . . . If I had written stories, I could have turned them as I wished; but these are truths for which the rules run counter to those of novels. I have written as I would have spoken to my friends, in a natural and familiar style. Nevertheless I hope that it will not grate on sensitive ears or bore the reader.'[8]

---

la peine à prendre juste le ton qu'il faut, et à n'en point sortir.' Fontenelle, *Histoire des oracles* (1686), ed. Louis Maigron (Paris : Droz, 1934), p. x.

[7] '. . . l'auteur s'est proposé de procurer à la Jeunesse la connoissance même des choses les plus communes et les plus ordinaires, dont on se reproche tous les jours à soi-même l'ignorance. . . . Ce livre pourra même désabuser les personnes qui s'imaginent que notre Langue ne sçauroit sans s'avilir, descendre dans les détails du Jardinage et de l'Agriculture, peut-être que les Romains en disoient autant de la Langue Latine avant que Virgile eût composé ses Georgiques.' Review of Pluche, *Le Spectacle de la nature*, in *Journal des Sçavans*, September, 1735, p. 107.

[8] 'On ne verra point ici de brave à toute épreuve, ni d'incidens surprenans ; et cela parce que tout, en étant vrai, ne peut être que naturel. J'ai affecté la simple vérité ; si j'avois voulu, j'aurois embelli le tout par des avantures de commande . . . et s'il y a quelque chose qui puisse paroître fabuleux, ce sera l'action de Du Puis qui se perce le corps dans la chambre de Madame de Londé : cependant je n'ai pas dû la taire puisqu'elle est vraie. . . . Si j'avois écrit des fables, j'aurois été maître des incidens que j'aurois tourné comme j'aurois voulu ; mais ce sont des veritez qui ont leurs règles toutes contraires à celles des romans. J'ai écrit comme j'aurois parlé à mes amis, dans un stile purement naturel et familier ; néanmoins j'espère qu'il n'écorchera pas les oreilles délicates, et qu'il n'ennuïera pas le lecteur.' Chasles, *Illustres Françoises*, I, lxi–lxii.

DETAILS: CLOTHES, APPEARANCE,
NATURE, ANIMALS

French writers of the Classical age consciously sought uni-versality. Since concrete detail was often regarded as an enemy of universality, much of the literature of the seventeenth century seems divorced from the life of the time. Contemporary attitudes, as well as all sorts of personal views and inclinations of the authors, appear nevertheless, but usually indirectly. A hierarchy could probably be established in which, from the standpoint of abstraction, tragedy would no doubt head the list and comic novels be at the bottom. Comedies, of course, were richer in detail than tragedies; satirical poetry shows us more about manners of the time than lyric poetry; and so on. But on whatever level, the frankness and fullness of detail compare unfavourably with those of the early eighteenth century. In travel literature, for example, of which the seven-teenth century possessed a great deal, one can read hundreds of accounts and learn less about the life of a sailor aboard a ship than from one book by Robert Chasles, in our period. The same is true of descriptions of the life of peoples en-countered by the travellers; our bourgeois readers seem to have read avidly about the household management, dress, and personal relationships of Indians, Orientals, and various island peoples. The type of writing found in the following paragraph from Lahontan's *Dialogues curieux* would have been unusual in travel accounts of the seventeenth century but is common in the early eighteenth.

'They use, then, a certain headdress of the appearance or form of a hat, and shoes of elk or deer skin which reach halfway up the leg. Their villages are fortified with double palisades of hard wood as thick as one's thigh, 15 feet tall with small squares in the middle of the walls. Their cabins are usually 80 feet long, 25 or 30 feet wide and 20 feet high. They are covered with the bark of young elm or white wood. One sees two platforms, each one foot high and nine feet wide, one on the right and one on the left. They make their fires between the two platforms, and the smoke goes out through the openings cut in the roofs of these cabins.'[9]

Descriptions of persons or things and accounts of events have, in our period, a fullness which is not typically encountered in the classic age. Below is a comparison of Mme de Lafayette's style and that of three eighteenth-century authors; it may be added that Mme de Lafayette's novel takes place in a vague '*désert*' on the coast of Spain.

'One day when the weather was nice, seeing that she did not leave her room, Consalve entered to find out if she did not wish to take a walk. . . .

'It was according to fortune that I was born and placed in a position worthy of the envy of the most ambitious. I was favoured by a prince whom I was by nature impelled to love. I was loved by the most beautiful lady in Spain, whom I adored; and I had a friend whom I thought loyal, and whom I was helping to get ahead.'[10]

'A youthful appearance, thanks to a skin of dazzling white-ness and the softness of a child's after being in a convent, where it does not become sunburnt as in the outside world. She has full, deep-set, black, languid eyes, animated when she wishes; an admirable forehead, wide and smooth; a well-proportioned nose; a small rosy mouth; and teeth like ivory: the sweet face of a maiden. All that beauty supported by a

[9] 'Ils se servent alors de certains Bonnets de la figure ou de la forme d'un Chapeau, et des Souliers de peau d'Elan ou de Cerf qui leur montent jusqu'à la mi-jambe. Leurs villages sont fortifiez de doubles palissades d'un bois très-dur, grosses comme la cuisse, de quinze pieds de hauteur avec de petits quarrez au milieu des Courtines. Leurs Cabanes ont ordinairement 80 pieds de longueur, 25 ou 30 de largeur et 20 de hauteur. Elles sont couvertes d'écorce d'Ormeau, ou de bois blanc. On voit deux estrades l'une à droite et l'autre à gauche, de neuf pieds de largeur, et d'un pied d'élévation. Ils font leurs feux entre ces deux estrades, et la fumée sort par des ouvertures faites sur le sommet de ces Cabanes.' Lahontan, *Dialogues curieux*, p. 94.

[10] 'Un jour qu'il faisoit assez beau, voyant qu'elle ne sortoit point de sa chambre, Consalve y entra pour savoir si elle ne vouloit pas se promener. . . .

'La fortune m'avait fait naître et m'avoit placé dans un rang digne de l'envie des plus ambitieux. J'étois favori d'un prince que j'aimois d'une inclination natur-elle. J'étois aimé de la plus belle personne d'Espagne, que j'adorois; et j'avois un ami que je croyois fidèle, et dont je faisois la fortune.' LaFayette, *Zaïde* (1670), ed. L. S. Auger (Paris : Garnier, n.d.), p. 27.

neck which seemed perfectly fashioned, plump and meaty; a very beautiful hand, arms like her neck; her leg shapely; her step firm and proud; all her actions and words animated but filled with a certain natural modesty which enraptured me. In short she is a perfect beauty.'[11]

'I begged her before my departure to give me her portrait: after some protests she promised it to me and asked me for mine. I promised it to her and gave mine to her first, as she had desired. It lay simply in a gilded rose box with a mirror inside to the right of the portrait. She did not give me hers until the day I left. It was far more elegant, much richer than mine. It was of perfectly fashioned enamel, a miniature bearing a perfect resemblance to her; there was a row of pearls around it on the inside and another around the mirror. The box was also of enamel and on the other side of the portrait showed Dido at the stake, dagger in hand. . . .'[12]

'She wore a dress of wool: her hair, which was the most beautiful in the world, was neither powdered nor curled. She wore a white linen apron which covered her completely in front and put her on a level with the woman who was at her side with the same garb. . . . Around her I saw her materials for work – some linen, some thread, some needles, some pieces

[11] '. . . un air de jeunesse soutenu par une peau d'une blancheur à éblouir, et de la délicatesse de celle d'un enfant, telle qu'on peut l'apporter d'un couvent, où ordinairement on ne se hale point tant que dans le monde. Elle a les yeux plains, bien fendus, noirs et languissans, et vifs lors qu'elle le veut, le front admirable, large et uni, le nez bien fait, la bouche petite et vermeille, et les dents comme de l'ivoire, la phisionomie douce et d'une vierge. Tout cela étoit soutenu par une gorge qui sembloit faite au tour, potelée et charnuë, la main très belle, le bras comme le col, la jambe bien faite, la démarche ferme et fière, et toutes ses actions et ses paroles animées, mais remplies d'une certaine modestie naturelle qui m'enlevoit : En un mot c'est une beauté achevée.' Chasles, 'M. Des Ronais et Mlle Du Puis', *Illustres Françoises*, I, 16–17.

[12] 'Je la priai avant mon départ de me donner son portrait : après quelques petites façons elle me le promit et me demanda le mien. Je le lui promis, et le lui donnai le premier, comme elle l'avoit souhaité. Il étoit simplement dans une boëte de vermeil doré avec un miroir dedans à la droite du portrait. Elle ne me donna le sien que le jour que je partis ; il étoit bien plus galant, et bien plus riche que le mien. Il étoit d'émail parfaitement bien travaillé, d'une mignature fine, et parfaitement ressemblant, il y avoit un rang de perles autour en dedans : et un autre autour du miroir. La boëte étoit aussi d'émail et représentoit d'un côté, au dos du portrait, Didon sur un bûcher, le poignard à la main. . . .' *Ibid.*, p. 28.

begun, others finished; in short, the weapons of a strong woman. I could no longer resist this scene.'[13]

'Her eyes were so large, black, and shiny, that it was difficult to meet them. Her mouth was small and rosy . . . her complexion had all the whiteness and brilliance characteristic of blonde women, without their pallor. Her colouring was animated by the most brilliant and beautiful hues, and her blonde, naturally curled hair enhanced her charm.'[14]

In the following excerpts, which may serve as further examples of the presentation of detail, we shall see some rather surprising, grotesque, and amorous details. In the last category, the amount of bodily detail, especially for women and girls, is enormous in our period; we do not consider it necessary to multiply cases like that of Chasles's young hero being introduced to love by a woman who 'revealed to me among other things a throat and a pair of breasts as beautiful as any I have ever seen in my life'.[15] We will conclude this section with several sentences from *Manon Lescaut* which show another side of 'realism': Prévost, surprisingly, describes his heroine without the details which we might expect. On the opposite side of the ledger, we could show passages from authors of the classic period which are rich in detail. But despite such cases, there is little doubt of the overwhelming drift toward realistic detail, if one reads a large number of the works.

'I cannot without laughing recall the action which I saw

[13] 'Elle étoit vêtue d'un habit de laine. Ses cheveux, qu'elle avoit les plus beaux du modne, étoient sans poudre et sans frisure. Un tablier de toile blanche lui couvroit tout le devant du corps, et la mettoit sur la même ligne que la femme qui étoit auprès d'elle avec le même ornement. . . . Autour d'elle je voyois la matière de son travail, de la toile, du fil, des aiguilles, des ouvrages commencés, d'autres finis ; enfin les armes de la femme forte. Je ne pus résister plus longtems a ce spectacle.' Prévost, *Killerine*, liv. 4, in *Œuvres*, VIII, 361.

[14] 'Ses yeux étoient noirs, et si brillans, qu'il étoit difficile d'en soutenir les regards, sa bouche étoit petite et vermeille . . . son teint avoit toute la blancheur et tout l'éclat des blondes sans en avoir le fade, il étoit animé des plus vives et des plus belles couleurs, et ses cheveux blonds et naturellement frisez augmentoient ses charmes.' Aulnoy, *Histoire d'Hypolite*, p. 27.

[15] '. . . me découvrit entr'autres choses, une gorge et une paire de tétons aussi beaux que j'en aye vû de ma vie.' Chasles, 'M. Dupuis et Mme de Londé', *Illustres Françoises*, II, 414-15.

performed by one of these animals [monkeys of Central America]. After firing several shots which removed a part of its belly, so that all of its entrails came out, I saw it hang by one of its paws (or hands, if one prefers) from the branch of a tree, while with the other paw it picked up its intestines, stuffing them back into what remained of its belly.'[16]

'She [Fanny] gave birth first to a boy. . . . I was somewhat worried about the bad effects that sometimes follow these accidents. They lasted six whole weeks, at the end of which Fanny made me the father of a second son, which had as happy a birth as the first.'[17]

'But what a surprise when he saw that he was not alone [in bed], and when he gathered, from the softness of a foot which came to rest upon him, that he was in bed with a woman; he was young and sensitive. This adventure, of which he understood nothing, had already caused him considerable emotion, when this woman, who was still sleeping, drew near in such a way that he could judge the beauty of her body in some detail.'[18]

'She was in her eighteenth year. Her charms were more than one can describe. She had such a delicate, sweet, and winning way, the way of love itself.'[19]

[16] 'Je ne puis me souvenir sans rire de l'action que je vis faire à un de ces animaux auquel après avoir tiré plusieurs coups de fusil qui lui emportoient une partie du ventre, en sorte que toutes ses tripes sortoient; je le vis se tenir d'une de ses pattes ou mains, si l'on veut, à une branche d'arbre; tandis que de l'autre il ramassoit ses intestins qu'il se refouroit dans ce qui lui restoit de ventre.' Raveneau de Lussan, *Journal du voyage*, p. 25.

[17] 'Elle mit d'abord au monde un garçon . . . j'avois quelque inquiétude sur les fâcheuses suites qui naissent quelquefois de ces accidents. Elles durèrent six semaines entières, au bout desquelles Fanny me fit père d'un second fils, qui naquit aussi heureusement que l'autre.' Prévost, *Cleveland*, liv. 5, in *Œuvres*, V, 272.

[18] 'Mais quelle fut sa surprise quand il s'aperçut qu'il n'étoit pas seul, et qu'il comprit, par la délicatesse d'un pied qui vint s'appuyer sur lui, qu'il étoit couché avec une femme; il étoit jeune et sensible. Cette aventure, où il ne comprenoit rien, lui donnoit déjà beaucoup d'émotion, quand cette femme, qui dormoit toujours, s'approcha de façon à lui faire juger tres avantageusement de son corps.' Tencin, *Le Siège de Calais*, I, 25.

[19] 'Elle étoit dans sa dix-huitième année. Ses charmes surpassoient tout ce qu'on peut décrire. C'étoit un air si fin, si doux, si engageant! l'air de l'amour même.' Prévost, *Manon*, in *Œuvres*, III, 278.

K

THE CONTEMPORARY SCENE

The 'broadening' to which we refer in the title of this part
of our book is perhaps best seen in the fullness with which
all sides of the contemporary scene are portrayed in literature.
If, on first thought, the presentation of details of everyday
life, the here and now, seems to represent the opposite of a
broadening view, it may be answered that the kind of impact
which a movement has depends on accompanying circumstances, and that in 1700 the effect of details of everyday life
upon polite literature was distinctly an enlargement of its
scope and vision.

In the following excerpts we shall give a sampling of the
kinds of contemporary detail that readers of our period were
apt to find in the books they read. Represented will be city
life, which grew greatly in importance during our period,
household details and family life, life in the country, and dress.
Several of our excerpts are from Jean Buvat's *Journal*, and it
may not be amiss here to introduce this little-known but
remarkable writer, for it is in the area with which we are
here concerned that he excelled. Buvat (1660–1729), a petit
bourgeois, that is, a man of no social eminence, worked as a
copyist in the Royal Library in Paris from 1697 to 1729.
Unpretentious in his tastes and education, Buvat recorded
what interested or stirred him in the day-to-day happenings
around him. Since, except for his sharp eye, ear, and nose, he
was a man with no special distinction or high connections, his
interests may well mirror those of many people on his economic
and social level. Thus, in August, 1715, when a group of high-
ranking visitors from Persia, upon their departure from Paris,
left such a frightful stench in the residence which had been
assigned to them that the next occupant, the Portuguese
Ambassador, raised loud objections to staying there, Buvat
explained that 'those infidels, because of their superstitions,
had scruples about exposing themselves in the toilet arrangements of the residence, although these were very clean. They
put their excrement into a barrel which was subsequently
found filled in one corner of the house.'[20] It is typical that while

[20] 'Comme ces infidèles avaient scrupule de s'exposer dans les lieux communs

Buvat dealt with such homely details, the courtly memorialist, Saint-Simon (*Mémoires*, XXVI, 126–35, and XXVII, 179–80), treating the same visit of these ambassadors, devoted his attention to the inadequacy of their presents and their lack of proper clothes and courtly manners. It is very likely that Buvat's concern with waste, mess, and smells reflected the interests of Parisians better than Saint-Simon's discussions of taste, dress, and belles.

Among details which Buvat reveals to us are the strong reactions of people of his class to the inflation of 1719–20, when the prices of commodities like beef, mutton, and tallow skyrocketed beyond all previous experience. Merchants, says Buvat, explained this by crop failures due to drought, but the suffering Parisian populace blamed the merchants, who refused to accept payment in paper money (*Journal*, II, 35), and the newcomers from Protestant countries, whose lack of abstinence on Fridays and during Lent increased the demand for meat and pushed meat prices upward.

We turn now to the matters mentioned previously. Readers of our period were given abundant material relative to ordinary life and its problems and hazards, especially in the big city. Financial dealings among members of the lower and middle classes are among the many details of material existence which, though always present in life and usually present in a certain stratum of literature, in this period made their way into the writings of the best authors.

'The herring-women from the market did not fail to distinguish themselves on this occasion. They got into coaches with violin players and a supply of bottles of wine. Leaving their coaches, they entered the Garden of the Tuileries opposite the King's apartments. There they performed several round dances to the sound of violins, from time to time drinking to the health of the King and shouting: "Long live the King, in spite of the damned Regency." The King, who appeared on the balcony, threw them four louis d'or, which made the

---

de cet hôtel, quoique très-propres et très-commodes pour cet usage, ils jetaient leurs ordures dans un tonneau, qui s'en était trouvé rempli dans un coin de la maison.' Jean Buvat, *Journal de la Régence, 1715–23* (2 vols; Paris: Plon, 1865), I, 38.

women redouble their cries of joy. And they promised to give
him a sturgeon. Madame de Saint-Pierre, delighted by the
good humour of these women, mingled with them and started
to dance. She took them to her residence, where she gave them
dinner, there being plenty of food and excellent Burgundy
wine, which made them sing and tell many yarns which made
the lady almost faint from laughter. They did not spare the
Regency or the bank notes, which they said were only fit to
use for toilet-paper.'[21]

'On the sixth of this month [February, 1716] the ice, having
broken free of the bridges in this city, crushed several boats.
Several washerwomen (on laundry barges moored to the
banks) perished and were cut in two. The heads of some
appeared above the ice, and their bodies were carried below,
without anyone being able to help. This made a sad sight.'[22]

'I have already indicated that large cities do not offer a
habitat suitable to virtue and I had no difficulty taking this
point of view, against Saint-Evremond.'[23]

'Hardly was I seated than I took out some money to pay

[21] 'Les harengères de la halle ne manquèrent pas de se distinguer en cette
occasion. Elles se mirent dans des carrosses avec des violons et avec une provision
de bouteilles de vin. Étant descendues de carrosse, elles entrèrent dans le jardin
des Tuileries, et vis-à-vis de l'appartement du Roi, elles formèrent plusieurs
danses en rond au son des violons, et de temps en temps se mettaient à boire à la
santé du Roi et à crier : *Vive le Roi, malgré la Régence au diable* ! Le Roi, qui parut
au balcon, leur envoya quatre louis d'or, ce qui leur fit redoubler leurs cris de
joie et promirent de lui donner un esturgeon. Madame de Saint-Pierre, charmée
de la bonne humeur de ces femmes, se mêla avec elles et se mit à danser, et les
emmena dans son hôtel où elle leur donna à dîner, leur fit grande chère et leur
fit boire d'excellent vin de Bourgogne, qui les fit chanter et dire bien des contes
qui la faisaient presque pâmer de rire, sans épargner la Régence ni les billets
de banque, qu'elles disaient n'être propres qu'à torcher leurs derrières.' *Ibid.*, II,
280–81.

[22] 'Le 6 de ce mois, les glaces s'étant détachées sur les trois heures après midi
entre les ponts de cette ville, fracassèrent plusieurs bateaux, dont plusieurs blanchis-
seuses périrent et furent coupées en deux ; les têtes de quelques-unes paraissaient
sur des glaçons et leurs corps étaient enfoncés en dessous, sans pouvoir leur donner
aucun secours, ce qui faisait un triste spectacle.' *Ibid.*, I, 119.

[23] 'J'ai déjà fait remarquer que les grandes Villes ne sont point un séjour favor-
able à la vertu, et je n'ai pas fait difficulté de prendre parti là-dessus contre Saint-
Evremond.' Prévost, *Pour et Contre*, II, No. 18, 60.

the coachman; but Mme Dutour, as a woman of experience, considered it her duty to supervise me, thinking me too young to manage that little detail. "Leave it to me," she said, "I will pay. Where did he pick you up?" "Near the parish church," I answered. "Oh, that's right nearby," she said, counting out some small change. "Here, fellow, this is the right amount."

' "The right amount! That?" said the coachman, returning the money to her with brutal contempt. "Oh no, dearie! I don't get paid by the yard."

' "What does he mean, by the yard?" said Mme Dutour earnestly. "You should be satisfied; we know about coaches; don't think this is the first time we've taken one."

' "I don't care if it's the millionth," said the coachman. "Give me my money, and don't shout. What are you getting into it for anyway? Did I bring you? Who asked you anything? What a bag, with her twelve sous! She thinks she's buying a bunch of carrots at the market."

'Mme Dutour was proud, well dressed, and what is more, right good-looking, which gave her additional pride. Women of a certain class fancy that they have more station if they have a pretty face; they look upon that advantage as a matter of rank. Vanity feeds on anything, and fulfils its needs with whatever is at hand. So, Mme Dutour felt offended at the coarse manner in which the coachman had addressed her (I am telling you this for your amusement); the bunch of carrots bothered her. How could anyone who saw her talk to her in those terms? Was there anything in her manner that could make one think of such a thing? "In truth, my man," she said, "you are a boor, and I don't have to listen to your nonsense! Get out now! Here's your money; take it or leave it. What do you mean talking to me like that? If I call a neighbour, he'll teach you to address respectable citizens more politely."

' "Well! What is this rag-lady telling me?" he replied in true coachman style. "Look out! Watch out for her; she has her Sunday kerchief on. Polite talk she wants, does she? I will bow low to your highness. By gum, pay me! You can be four times as respectable as you are for all I care. Don't my horses have to eat? How would you eat, Mme Big Mouth, if

people didn't pay you for your cloth? Would your face be as
fat as it is? Shame! What a disgrace to be so tight!" '24

'The country is not suitable to your tastes. Let those whom
people dislike dislike people, but let those whom people love
live all their lives in society. A cultivated man must live and
die in a capital; and in my opinion Rome, London, and
Paris are the only true capitals. . . . I do not give you six
months [to live] if you live in the country with that bleak
morality which you have adopted.'25

24 'A peine fus-je assise, que je tirai de l'argent pour payer le cocher; mais
Mme Dutour, en femme d'expérience, crut devoir me conduire là-dessus, et me
trouva trop jeune pour m'abandonner ce petit détail. "Laissez-moi faire, me dit-
elle, je vais le payer; où vous a-t-il prise?—Auprès de la paroisse, lui dis-je. —Eh!
c'est tout près d'ici, répliqua-t-elle en comptant quelque monnaie. Tenez, mon
enfant, voilà ce qu'il vous faut.
    '—Ce qu'il me faut! cela! dit le cocher, qui lui rendit sa monnaie avec un
dédain brutal; oh! que nenni: cela ne se mesure pas à l'aune. —Mais que veut-il
dire avec son aune, cet homme? répliqua gravement Mme Dutour: vous devez
être content; on sait peut-être bien ce que c'est qu'un carrosse, ce n'est pas d'aujourd'hui qu'on en paye.
    '—Eh! quand ce serait demain, dit le cocher, qu'est-ce que cela avance?
Donnez-moi mon affaire, et ne crions pas tant; voyez de quoi elle se mêle! Est-ce
vous que j'ai menée? Est-ce qu'on vous demande quelque chose? Quelle diable
de femme avec ses douze sous! Elle marchande cela comme une botte d'herbes."
    'Mme Dutour était fière, parée, et qui plus est assez jolie; ce qui lui donnait
encore une autre espèce de gloire.
    'Les femmes d'un certain état s'imaginent en avoir plus de dignité, quand
elles ont un joli visage; elles regardent cet avantage-là comme un rang. La vanité
s'aide de tout, et remplace ce qui lui manque avec ce qu'elle peut. Mme Dutour
se sentit donc offensée de l'apostrophe ignoble du cocher (je vous raconte cela
pour vous divertir): la *botte d'herbes* sonna mal à ses oreilles. Comment ce jargon-là
pouvait-il venir à la bouche de quelqu'un qui la voyait? Y avait-il rien dans son
air qui fît penser à pareille chose? "En vérité, mon ami, il faut avouer que vous
êtes bien impertinent, et il me convient bien d'écouter vos sottises! dit-elle. Allons,
retirez-vous. Voilà votre argent; prenez ou laissez: qu'est-ce que cela signifie?
Si j'appelle un voisin, on vous apprendra à parler aux bourgeois plus honnêtement
que vous ne faites."
    '—Eh bien! qu'est-ce que me vient conter cette chiffonnière? répliqua l'autre
en vrai fiacre. Gare! prenez garde à elle; elle a son fichu des dimanches. Ne
semble-t-il pas qu'il faille tant de cérémonies pour parler à madame? On parle
bien à Perrette. Eh! palsambleu! payez-moi. Quand vous seriez encore quatre
fois plus bourgeoise que vous n'êtes, qu'est-ce que cela me fait? Faut-il pas que
mes chevaux vivent? Avec quoi dîneriez-vous, vous qui parlez, si on ne vous
payait pas votre toile? Auriez-vous la face si large? Fi! que cela est vilain d'être
crasseuse!" Marivaux, *Marianne*, Part II, in *Romans*, pp. 149–50.
25 'La campagne n'est point faite pour vous. Que celui-là se dégoûte du monde,
dont le monde est dégoûté: mais que ceux qui lui sont chers comme vous y de-
meurent toute leur vie. Un honnête homme doit vivre et mourir dans une capitale;

'A speech in which one speaks only of woods, rivers, meadows, countryside, and gardens has a depressing effect, unless there are new pleasures; but human matters, inclinations, affections, and feelings naturally try to find expression. The same nature produces and receives them; they flow easily from the men who depict them to those who see them depicted.'[26]

'They [the streets of London] should only be cleaner and better paved; they are usually so filthy that it would be impossible to walk on them, if pains had not been taken to arrange, alongside the houses, a small space protected by wooden posts which prevent carriages from approaching; this space serves as a passage for pedestrians. When one wishes to cross the street, one looks for a row of stones a little broader and higher than the rest. . . . It is necessary, in order to keep them clean, to scrub them several times a day.'[27]

Family life was usually depicted in a far more frank and realistic manner than in literature of a corresponding level in the seventeenth century, as were the wicked influences to which people were exposed in the cities. The excerpts dealing with details of dress are a tiny sampling; the reader will by now have observed in other passages how great an interest writers had in the clothing of their characters, perhaps in

---

et à mon avis toutes les capitales se réduisent à Rome, à Londres et à Paris. . . . Je ne vous donne pas six mois si vous demeurez à la campagne avec cette morale noire que vous avez prise ' Saint-Evremond, Letter to M. le comte de Saint-Albans, 1676, *Œuvres de Saint-Evremond*, ed. René Planhol (3 vols; Paris: Cité des Livres, 1927), III, 224.

[26] 'Un discours où l'on ne parle que de bois, de rivières, de prés, de campagnes, de jardins, fait sur nous une impression bien languissante, à moins qu'il n'ait des agrémens tout nouveaux; mais ce qui est de l'humanité, les penchants, les tendresses, les affections, trouvent naturellement au fond de notre âme à se faire sentir : la même nature les produit et les reçoit; ils passent aisément des hommes qu'on représente en des hommes qui voient représenter.' Saint-Evremond, 'De la Poésie', 1671, *ibid.*, I, 138.

[27] 'Il ne leur manque que d'être plus nettes et mieux pavées ; elles sont ordinaire-ment si sales, qu'il seroit impossible d'y marcher à pied, si l'on n'avoit eu soin de ménager, le long des maisons, un petit espace défendu par des poteaux de bois, qui empêchent les carrosses d'en approcher, et qui sert pour le passage des gens de pied. Lorsqu'on veut traverser la rue, on cherche un rang de pavés un peu plus large et plus haut que les autres . . . l'on est obligé, pour les tenir propres, de les nettoyer plusieurs fois le jour.' Prévost, *Mém. d'un homme de qualité*, liv. 10, in *Œuvres*, II, 236.

reaction to the abstract, universal, and almost nondescript dress in the high literature of the seventeenth century.

'. . . often a woman's tenderness is a burden on her husband: let's take my example. I often come home burdened with business. My wife thinks that, being preoccupied, I am in bad humour and comes with extraordinary caresses, which cause me to forget for ever some good idea I had. The same thing occurs when I work in my office. I dare not force her to leave for fear of hurting her feelings; so that . . . I sometimes would like, I do not say to be unmarried, but at least to be far from my wife.'[28]

'In London, like most young men of his age, Glandore had forgotten the noble principles and teachings of virtue that he possessed upon arrival. He had adopted the popular vices which characterize the handsome gentleman: he laughed at marriage, drank a great deal, and deceived people with perfect ease.'[29]

'That day we met more than a hundred carts that were coming from the Bolsane fair: they are almost all drawn by oxen. I noticed that the cloven hoof of these animals is shod with two metal pieces. . . . The clothing of the mountain dwellers is the most delightful in the world; some have green hats, others have hats of yellow and blue. . . .
'Upon entering the valley of Bolsane we were astonished to find the most peaceful atmosphere one could wish: vineyards almost all of which were green, as well as willow trees, rose bushes, mulberry trees, and various other trees. Veritable spring in the middle of winter. This was due to the place

[28] '. . . souvent la tendresse d'une femme est à charge à son époux : suivons toûjours mon exemple. Je rentre assez souvent au logis chargé d'affaires. J'y rêve, ma femme croit que je suis de mauvaise humeur, et vient, par des caresses hors de saison, me faire perdre une idée, que je ne ratrappe plus. La même chose quand je suis à travailler dans mon cabinet. Je n'ose pas la faire retirer, crainte de lui donner du chagrin ; de sorte que . . . je passe assez souvent des momens, où je voudrois, sinon n'être pas marie, du moins être bien loin de ma femme.' Chasles, 'M. des Prez et Mlle de l'Epine', *Illustres Françoises*, I, 278.
[29] Aubin, *Madame de Beaumont*, p. 56.

being sheltered from bad winds, or to some other features of the topography.'[30]

'He [Brissant] had no hat or jacket. His vest was torn in several places and his shirt was no less shredded. His hair, which was ordinarily handsome, was so dishevelled that he looked like a madman or a wild man.'[31]

'I gave her [Manon] my jacket, the overcoat being enough for me to leave [the hospital]. There was nothing lacking in her outfit except the trousers, which unfortunately I had forgotten. The fact that I had forgotten this essential item would surely have made us laugh, if the situation into which it put us had been less serious. I was distressed that a trifle of this nature should be able to stop us. However, I made my decision, which was to leave without trousers myself. I gave them to Manon.'[32]

'The clothing of the women is a covering which extends from the neck to the middle of the leg and which they adjust quite decently. . . . Their leggings reach from the knee only to the ankle. Socks made of elk-skin, and lined inside with hair or with wool, take the place of shoes. This footgear is

---

[30] 'Nous avons rencontré ce mesme jour plus de cent charrettes, qui venoient de la foire de Bolsane : elles sont presque toutes tirées par des bœufs. J'ay remarqué que le pied fourchu de ces animaux est aussi ferré de deux pièces. . . . Les habits des montagnards sont les plus plaisants du monde ; les uns ont des chapeaux verds, les autres en ont de jaunes et de bleus. . . .

'En entrant dans la vallée de Bolsane, nous avons esté étonnez de trouver l'air de la plus grande douceur qu'on puisse souhaitter : Les vignobles presque tous verds, aussi bien que les saules, les rosiers, les meuriers, et quantité d'autres arbres. Un véritable Printemps au milieu de l'Hyver. Cela vient d'un certain abri des mauvais vens, ou de quelque autre circonstance de la disposition du païs.' Misson, *Nouveau Voyage d'Italie*, I, 143, 147.

[31] 'Il étoit sans chapeau et sans justaucorps. Sa veste étoit déchirée en plusieurs endroits, et sa chemise n'étoit pas plus entière. Ses cheveaux, qu'il avoit naturelle- ment fort beaux, étoient si mêlés et si dérangés, que cela lui donnoit un air de fou ou de furieux.' Prévost, *Mém. d'un homme de qualité*, liv. 11, in *Œuvres*, II, 374.

[32] 'Je lui donnai mon justaucourps, le surtout me suffisant pour sortir. Il ne se trouva rien de manqué à son ajustement, excepté la culotte, que j'avois mal- heureusement oubliée. L'oubli de cette pièce nécessaire nous eût sans doute apprêté à rire, si l'embarras où il nous mettoit eût été moins sérieux. J'étois au désespoir qu'une bagatelle de cette nature fût capable de nous arrêter. Cependant je pris mon parti qui fut de sortir moi-même sans culotte. Je laissai la mienne à Manon.' Prévost, *Manon*, in *Œuvres*, III, 357.

absolutely necessary for the purpose of adjusting their snowshoes, by means of which they easily walk on the snow. These
snowshoes, made in lozenge shape, are more than two feet
long and a foot and a half broad. I did not believe that I
could ever walk with such contraptions; but when I tried
them, I suddenly found myself so skilful that the savages
could not believe that that was the first time I had used
them.'[33]

[33] 'L'habillement des femmes est une couverture qui leur pend depuis le
cou jusqu'au milieu des jambes, et qu'elles ajustent assez proprement. . . . Leurs
bas ne vont que depuis le genou jusqu'à la cheville du pied. Des chaussons faits
de peau d'élan, et garnis en dedans de poil ou de laine, leur tiennent lieu de souliers.
Cette chaussure leur est absolument nécessaire pour s'ajuster aux raquettes, par
le moyen desquelles on marche commodément sur la neige. Ces raquettes faites
en figure de losange, ont plus de deux pieds de longueur, et sont large d'un pied
et demi. Je ne croyais pas que je pusse jamais marcher avec de pareilles machines :
lorsque j'en fis l'essai, je me trouvai tout-à-coup si habile, que les Sauvages ne
pouvaient croire que ce fût la première fois que j'en fesais usage.' R.P. Rasles,
1723, in *Jesuit Relations*, LXVII, 134–35.

CHAPTER 4

Intellectual Horizons

THE broadening view of the world which characterizes our period is most obvious, first, in the large number of foreign works which made their way into French thinking, and second, in a growing commitment to tolerance of intellectual and religious pluralism. On the first point, the Quarrel of Ancients and Moderns, which excited many writers in the decade or so before 1700, was symptomatic. Articles and books arguing one side or the other were almost as likely to be answered or refuted in another country as in the one where they were published. It made little difference on which side of the Channel Perrault, Temple, Fontenelle, Wotton, or Swift lived; they were clearly members of a single intellectual community. And if the relations between France and England are the most striking, and were to lead, for example, to Voltaire's fruitful stay in England from 1726 to 1729, the interest of the French in the literary output of the other countries of western Europe was only slightly less marked. Books from abroad were promptly translated and discussed; one has only to look in any of the literary journals to observe the large number of Italian, German, and English books, most of them now forgotten, which became part of the French intellectual baggage. (The fact that German books were less popular than the English and Italian does not affect our basic point.)

Our second point is rather more difficult to prove directly; it will appear in the course of this chapter in several areas. The Enlightenment was to be characterized in part by demands for an untrammelled search for truth, and in our period there is much evidence of a growing freedom from dogmatism. The tone is well set in the Preface to the first volume of the *Journal littéraire*, published at The Hague in 1715, from which we shall quote here. If the attack on dogmatism and the vindication of

freedom of thought are disappointing because they often fail
to extend to Jews or atheists, we can only answer that that
degree of tolerance, which has scarcely been achieved even
now, was perhaps too much to expect in the early eighteenth
century.

We shall close these introductory remarks with a quotation
from the *Journal des Sçavans* of March, 1738, near the end of
our period, in which the editors give their assessment of the
improvement of taste and the increasing breadth of appreciation for the arts and *'lumière'* in the French public.

'It remains to inform the public that we will never give our
opinion on matters of theology or on philosophical ideas that
directly influence religion; we will limit ourselves to presenting
faithful excerpts and to showing different opinions clearly. . . .
Each person thinks himself orthodox in his opinions, and
anything outside of the sphere of his own opinions seems to
him removed from the divine teachings. Therefore, regardless
of what position we were to take, we would not be able to
avoid the odious name of heretic which is so commonly
bestowed in our century. We do not promise to have the same
regard for those people who oppose all religion in general.'[1]

'Never has the taste for the fine arts been more widespread.
Never before have there been so many lovers of painting,
sculpture, music, etc.; in this we might match the Italians
themselves. Everywhere learning, which used to reach only a
few cultivated individuals, is spreading steadily to the multitude. Men are becoming more and more refined, using their
minds more, and becoming more aware of the pleasures in
which intellect has a part.'[2]

[1] 'Il nous reste à avertir le Public, que nous ne dirons jamais notre sentiment
sur les matières de Théologie, ni sur les sujets Philosophiques qui influent directe-
ment sur la Religion ; nous nous contenterons d'en faire des Extraits fidèles, et de
mettre les différentes opinions dans tout leur jour. . . . Chacun se croit Orthodoxe
dans ses sentimens, et tout ce qui est hors de la Sphère de ses opinions lui paroît
éloigné de la Sainte Doctrine. Ainsi quelque parti que nous prissions, nous ne
saurions jamais éviter le titre odieux d'Hérétique, dont on est si prodigue dans
notre Siècle. Nous ne nous engageons pas à avoir les mêmes égards pour ceux
qui se déclarent contre toute Religion en général.' *Journal littéraire*, I (1715),
xv–xvi.
[2] 'Jamais le goût des beaux Arts ne fut plus généralement répandu. Jamais

COSMOPOLITANISM

'Only by seeing other skies, other places, and other men do we expand the sphere of our ideas. Descartes's travels, although limited to a few European lands, taught him much more than books,' says the Continuation of Prévost's vast history of world travel, much in the spirit of the master.[3] Interest in foreign lands and a sympathetic approach to foreign peoples, both very strong in our period, sometimes exceeded actual knowledge in humorous ways, for though the intention of creating a feeling of the oneness of mankind and an ideal of easy communication made considerable progress on the basis of real travel and live contacts, this did not stop writers from engaging in fanciful accounts in which imagination took the place of knowledge. Prévost himself, who made sound use of his European travels, especially in England, sinned conspicuously in his depiction of New World scenes. Pénélope Aubin, rather over-eager in her cosmopolitanism, had her heroes in *The Noble Slaves*, after a shipwreck on the coast of Mexico, encounter a Persian, escape on a Japanese vessel, and fall into the hands of North African pirates. Earlier in the same book she had arranged for the hero to rent horses in Quebec for a trip to Panama in search of his lady love.

For the most part, however, the passages offered below show a serious attempt to acquaint the French public with the ways of other cultures, to engage in meaningful comparisons, and to counteract narrow patriotism by building a respect for all men. Here one finds a suggestion to canonize the distant Confucius, there a study of the nearby Swiss,

---

il n'y eut parmi nous plus d'amateurs de Peinture, de Sculpture, de Musique, etc. et sur ce point nous pourrions le disputer aux Italiens mêmes. . . . Par-tout la lumiere qui n'éclairoit qu'un petit nombre d'habiles gens, se répand de proche en proche jusques sur la multitude. Les hommes se polissent de plus en plus, font plus d'usage de leur esprit, et deviennent plus sensibles aux plaisirs auxquels il a quelque part.' Review of *Eloge Historique de Monsieur Coustou*, in *Journal des Sçavans*, April, 1738, p. 533.

[3] 'Ce n'est qu'en voyant un autre ciel, d'autres lieux, d'autres hommes, que s'étend la sphère de nos idées. Les voyages de Descartes, quoique bornés à quelques contrées de l'Europe, l'avoient bien mieux instruit que les Livres.' Prévost, *Histoire générale des voyages* (20 vols; Paris: Didot; Rozet; Montardier, 1746–1801), Vol. XVIII (Vol. I of *Continuation*, Paris, Rozet, 1768), Discours préliminaire, p. iii.

always to the same effect – tolerance, understanding, brotherhood. The ninety volumes of the *Journal des Sçavans* (which we can boast having read), to take an outstanding example, give the impression of a new internationalism, whether in science, literary theory, or social questions. One feels that France is becoming part of a new Europe in which the nations know and respect one another and in which broad-mindedness regarding European neighbours is not slow to be applied on a bigger, world-wide scale. Patriotic lines such as Gresset's, quoted near the end of our series, continued to be written (and have never ceased to be), but it is the enlightened statement of Pinot Duclos, the last of our group, which epitomizes the contribution of the eighteenth century.

'Those good men (so let me call them, those Followers of Mahomet) came one after the other, offering to serve me, and testifying the greatest Pity and Goodness of Heart. They generally called us Protestants their *Brothers in God*, and testified the utmost Regard to our Opinions. . . . Yet those are they whom Christians call Barbarous! Would to God that Christians would but imitate their Integrity and Virtue; the Wicked can never with Justice be called truly polite, nor the virtuous reproached with barbarity. We are notwithstanding to make a Distinction between Persons of the same Religion, who come from different parts of the World, and who consequently differ in their Manners and Customs. Those from Morocco, Tripoli, and Algiers, are generally the greatest Villains alive; thievish, cruel, false, assassins, and wicked to the last Degree. But the Turks of Asia and Europe seem to be of a different Species. [The latter] are zealous in the observation of their Religion, tenacious of the Truth, and charitable in a supreme Degree. This last Virtue they even carry to excess. I have seen them give all they were possessed of, to purchase the Freedom of a Bird in a Cage.'[4]

---

[4] 'Ces bonnes gens donc, voyant que je serais embarrassé pour ne savoir à qui me fier, vinrent tous, les uns après les autres, me prier de me servir d'eux, me marquant des sentiments si pieux et me témoignant tant d'affection pour ceux de notre religion, qu'ils appelaient leurs frères en Dieu, que j'en fus touché jusqu'aux larmes. . . . Ce sont ces gens que les chrétiens nomment *barbares*, et qui, dans leur morale, le sont si peu, qu'ils font honte à ceux qui leur donnent ce nom.

'The parents succeed in inspiring great respect, love, and politeness in their children. . . . Regarding politeness, it is so great in the Orient even towards foreigners, that a European who has lived there a long time has a great deal of difficulty becoming accustomed to the familiar manner and lack of respect in this part of the world.'[5]

'I know, however, that the Chinese have vices, but they perhaps sin less against their moral standards than we do against ours. How much our morals have degenerated from those of our ancestors! The Chinese, far older than we are, consider it a shame to violate their moral rules publicly, or to fail in respect due one another; or to be guilty of any disobedience towards their parents, or of quarrels with their peers.'[6]

'If all travels were written with as much precision and accuracy as those that have been published on the kingdom of Siam, one would be wrong to call them, as M. de Sorbière has, philosophical novels, or to apply to them a proverb

---

Il faut cependant distinguer ces turcs d'avec ceux qui, quoique de même religion, n'ont pas les mêmes mœurs. Ces derniers sont les turcs de l'Afrique, nommément ceux des royaumes de Maroc, Alger, Tripoli, etc., qui sont en général des gens de sac et de corde, fripons, cruels, parjures, traîtres et scélérats au suprême degré. Aussi n'avions-nous garde de nous y fier. Mais les turcs de l'Asie et de l'Europe . . . sont en général zélés à l'observation de leur religion, gens de parole et d'honneur, et surtout charitables au suprême degré. Ils outrent même la charité. J'en ai vu qui donnaient tout l'argent qu'ils avaient, pour acheter un oiseau privé en cage, afin d'avoir le plaisir et la consolation de lui donner la liberté.' Jean Marteilhe, *Mémoires d'un Protestant condamné aux galères de France pour cause de religion* (Paris : Société des Ecoles du dimanche, 1865), pp. 255-56 ; English trans. by Oliver Goldsmith, *The Memoirs of a Protestant* 2 vols ; (London : Dent, 1895), II, 9-10.

[5] 'Leurs parents savent se faire beaucoup aimer et respecter de leurs enfants et leur inspirer une extrême politesse. . . . Quant à la politesse, elle est si grande par tout l'Orient, même à l'égard des étrangers, qu'un Européan [*sic*] qui y a demeuré long-temps, a bien de la peine à s'accoutumer derechef aux familiaritez et au peu d'égards de ces païs-ci.' Simon de la Loubère, *Du Royaume de Siam* (2 vols ; Amsterdam : A. Wolfgang, 1691), I, 164-65.

[6] 'Je say pourtant que les Chinois ont des vices, mais ils péchent peut-être moins contre leur Morale, que nous ne péchons contre la nôtre. Combien nos mœurs n'ont-elles pas dégénéré de celles de nos ancêtres? et les Chinois incomparablement plus anciens que nous, estiment encore que c'est une honte de violer leurs mœurs en public, et de manquer aux égards qu'ils se doivent les uns aux autres, ou par quelque désobéissance envers leurs parents, ou par quelque querelle avec leurs égaux.' *Ibid.*, II, 296.

which seems to grant the right to lie to those who come from afar.'[7]

'I promise to insert, on every occasion, some interesting peculiarity of the genius of the English, curiosities of London and other regions of the Island, the progress which is daily made in the arts and sciences, and even some translations of the most beautiful scenes from their plays.'[8]

'I intend to make clear the basic and permanent difference between France and England.'[9]

'I particularly admire the progress that freedom of the press has been making daily [in Paris]. . . . But the spirit of satire, which does not submit as easily to a yoke, has found channels other than the press. Everything that they want to use to hurt religion and whatever else is most respectable, to destroy the honour of one's neighbour, to satisfy hatred, envy, and the desire for vengeance, is communicated to the public by manuscript copies, which are soon multiplied endlessly. There is a great effort to procure them. . . . In our country a satirical writer always takes care to spare the reputation of his country and the honour of his own opinions . . . [in England] private feelings never blind an Englishman to the point of forgetting that he is an Englishman – and consequently of worrying about never denouncing publicly things that pertain to the glory of that name.'[10]

[7] 'Si tous les Voyages étoient écrits avec autant d'exactitude et de fidélité que ceux qu'on a publiez du Royaume de *Siam*, on auroit tort de les apeller, [sic] comme a fait M. de *Sorbière*, les Romans des Philosophes, et leur appliquer un Proverbe, qui semble accorder le droit de mentir à ceux qui viennent de loin.' Review of Simon de la Loubère, *Description du royaume de Siam* (new edn; 1713), in *Journal littéraire*, I (July–August, 1713), 325.

[8] 'Je promets d'insérer chaque fois quelque particularité intéressante touchant le génie des Anglois, des curiositez de Londres, et d'autres parties de l'Isle, les progrès qu'on y fait tous les jours dans les Sciences et les Arts et de traduire même quelquefois les plus belles Scènes de leurs Pièces de Théâtre.' Prévost, *Pour et Contre*, I, No. 1 (1733), 11.

[9] 'Je me propose de faire remarquer la différence réelle et constante entre la France et l'Angleterre.' *Ibid.*, V, No. 61 (1734), 6.

[10] 'J'admire en particulier le progrès que la liberté d'écrire y fait [à Paris] de jour en jour. . . . Mais l'esprit de satire qui ne s'accomode pas si aisément du joug, s'est ouvert d'autres voyes que la Presse. Tout ce qu'on veut faire servir à blesser la Religion et ce qu'il y a de plus respectable, à détruire l'honneur du prochain,

'The English have shortcomings, because they are human; but I will always count on an Englishman who tells me that he is my friend.'[11]

'Those who look upon Switzerland as merely a country of mountains, rocks, and precipices, inhabited by half barbaric people, will find that they have had misconceptions when they read the description by M. Kipseller. They will find in the form of government, the natural history, and the description of the cities of this Republic an infinity of things worthy of their attention. And what will perhaps surprise them even more will be the discovery that this country has a person capable of describing, in a simple, natural and pleasant manner, the charm of his native land.'[12]

'. . . my retreat [in Italy] has shown me, moreover, that I have no homeland of my own on earth.'[13]

'The Pope could have freed himself of all these difficulties by canonizing Confucius, thereby making him worthy of the

---

à satisfaire la haine, l'envie, les désirs de vengeance, se communique au Public par des Copies manuscrites, qui se multiplient bientôt à l'infini. L'ardeur est extrême à se les procurer. . . . Chez nous, un auteur satyrique a toujours soin de ménager la réputation de sa Patrie, et l'honneur de son propre jugement . . . [en Angleterre] les ressentimens particuliers n'aveuglent personne jusqu'à lui faire oublier qu'il est Anglois, et par conséquent intéressé à ne jamais dénoncer publiquement ce qui appartient à la gloire de ce nom.' Letter from an Englishman, *ibid.*, No. 85, pp. 217–18.

[11] 'Enfin, les Anglois ont des défauts, parce qu'ils sont hommes ; mais je compterai toujours beaucoup sur un Anglois qui me dira qu'il est de mes amis.' *Ibid.*, p. 225.

[12] 'Ceux qui ne regardent la Suisse que comme un païs plein de montagnes, de rochers et de précipices, habité par des *demi Sauvages*, trouveront dans la description que nous en donne M. Kipseller, de quoi se détromper. Ils verront qu'il y a dans la forme du gouvernement de cette Republique, dans son histoire naturelle, et dans la déscription des villes qui la composent, une infinité de choses qui méritent d'occuper pendant quelque temps leur curiosité. Et ce qui les surprendra peut-être encore davantage, ils connoîtront qu'il y a dans cette Republique une personne capable de décrire d'une maniere simple, mais naturelle et aisée les délices de sa patrie.' Review of Gottlied Kipseller, *Les Delices de la Suisse* (1714), in *Journal des Sçavans*, April, 1715, pp. 400–1.

[13] '. . . le refuge où je suis [en Italie] m'ayant d'ailleurs assez fait connoistre que je n'ay point de patrie particulière icy bas.' Misson, *Nouveau voyage d'Italie*, avis au lecteur.

L

religious honours that are bestowed upon him. This Chinese philosopher was a very decent man, who had great virtue. Why should the Pope, who has canonized saints who never lived, hesitate to canonize Confucius?'[14]

> 'Man by hidden inclination –
> Be it instinct, be it gratitude –
> Cherishes his native nation;
> Loving it is his fixed attitude.'[15]

'Men of merit, regardless of their nation, form but a single body. They are free of childish national vanity; they leave that to the common people, to those who, having no fame themselves, are forced to take advantage of that of their compatriots.'[16]

SCIENCE

The interest in foreign lands which we have observed had its counterpart in a voracious appetite for scientific knowledge. Experiments of any kind attracted great attention; there was a multiplicity of books denouncing sorcery and magic; and among literate men there was a substantial growth of interest and even active participation in science, especially chemistry, paleontology, and entomology. In accounts of extraordinary voyages, a genre long popular in France, new scientific information was used to enhance credibility, and often accuracy. In the successful *Voyages of Glantzby*, supposedly translated from the Danish, the protagonist uses medical science and

[14] 'Le Pape eût pu se tirer de tous ces embarras en canonisant *Confucius* et le rendant digne par ce moyen des honneurs Religieux qu'on lui adresse. Ce philosophe de la Chine a été un très-honnête homme, qui avoit de la vertu; pourquoi le Pape, qui a canonisé des saints qui ne furent jamais, se feroit-il un scrupule de canoniser Confucius?' Anon., 'Réflexions sur le nouveau Décret ... de la Chine', *Nouvelles de la République des Lettres*, September, 1709, Article VII.

[15] 'Soit instinct, soit reconnoissance,/L'homme par un penchant secret,/ Chérit le lieu de sa naissance,/Et ne la quitte qu'à regret.' Jean-Baptiste-Louis Gresset, 'Ode sur l'amour de la Patrie', in *Œuvres* (3 vols; Paris: L. de Bure, 1826), I, 265.

[16] 'Les hommes de mérite, de quelque nation qu'ils soient, n'en forment qu'une entre eux. Ils sont exempts d'une vanité nationale et puérile; ils la laissent au vulgaire, à ceux qui, n'ayant point de gloire personnelle, sont réduits à se prévaloir de celle de leurs compatriotes.' Duclos, *Considérations sur les mœurs*, p. 17.

deism as a dual weapon of enlightenment and service among the backward peoples whom he encounteres, and though the geography is sometimes fanciful, the author seems to be a good amateur scientist:

'I am a botanist, an anatomist, a bit of a chemist – in short, a man fascinated by the secrets of nature; it took little to keep me entertained. It did not rain a drop during my stay in this land. . . . When I was dressed in my laced outfit, more lizards looked at me, and more attentively, and the females visited me with their little ones on their backs. I set up a mirror, and the poor creatures passed back and forth many times in order to look at themselves; and I took advantage of everything that might be amusing in this quiet spot.'[17]

Montesquieu, whether writing history, travel, or fiction, showed frequent signs of scientific preoccupation. Passages like the two that follow are not rare in his works, and if we were to quote his descriptions of pumps, or of machines for removing sand from the port of Venice, or technical descriptions of factories, we should see that he was always trying to understand the phenomena which came before his eyes in terms of the natural sciences.

'On the banks of this same lake is the Cave of the Dog. In just about one minute, the dog collapses from weakness, short of breath as if unable to breathe further. I took a frog from the water; it died after seven or eight minutes. One foot above ground level, a candle goes out; gunpowder will not ignite. Three feet above the ground steam loses its force.'[18]

[17] 'Je suis Botaniste, un peu Chimiste, Anatomiste, en un mot un homme curieux des secrets de la nature ; peu de chose m'amusoit. Il ne plut point pendant mon séjour sur cette terre. . . . Lorsque j'étois en habit galonné, les Lézards me regardoient en plus grand nombre, et avec plus d'attention, les femelles me rendoient visite avec leurs petits sur leur dos ; j'attachois mon miroir à mon coffre, ces pauvres bêtes passoient et repassoient souvent pour se mirer ; et je tirois avantage de tout ce qui pouvoit m'amuser dans ce lieu tranquille.' Glantzby, *Les Voyages de Glantzby . . . Avantures surprenantes des rois Loriman et Osmundan, Princes orientaux, trad. de l'original danois* (Amsterdam : Aux dépens de la Compagnie, 1730), p. 8.
[18] 'Sur les bords de ce même lac est la Grotte du Chien. Dans près d'une minute, le chien se laisse tomber de foiblesse, et l'haleine lui manque, comme ne pouvant respirer. J'ai tiré une grenouille de l'eau, qui est morte dans un demi-quart

'I went today, Saturday the thirtieth, to see the liquefaction of Saint Janvier's blood. I think that I saw this liquefaction take place – although it is difficult to see it clearly, because they only show you the reliquary momentarily, and its glass is smudged by everyone's kisses. But, however the case may be, I think that it is very definitely a thermometer, that this blood, or liquid, which comes from a cool place, entering this place heated by the multitude of people and a great number of candles, must be liquefied. . . . Moreover, the priest holds the reliquary in his two hands, which warms the metal.'[19]

Evidence of a sophisticated awareness of the need for scientific progress is abundant in our period, along with an appreciation of both the richness of its possible contribution to humanity and the obstacles that stood in its way. The extent to which the scientific attitude shows itself in writings of all sorts is sure to surprise anyone who reads widely in the literature of this time. Scepticism with regard to historical and religious tales, the beginning of the emergence of the man of science as a recognizable type, a feeling of an international brotherhood in science, and actual personal interest or involvement in scientific projects and observations on the part of writers are among the impressions left upon us by our perusal of many books and articles, of which the quotations which follow are fairly representative. A note of caution, a warning that scientific discovery has its limitations, was audible in the early eighteenth century, as it has been in every period before and since.

'They are working in Bordeaux to give to the public the history of the earth and all the changes that have occurred

---

d'heure. A 1 pied de la terre, la chandelle s'éteint; la poudre ne prend point à un fusil. A 3 pieds de terre, la vapeur n'est plus nuisible.' *Voyages de Montesquieu, publiés par le baron Albert de Montesquieu* (2 vols; Bordeaux: G. Gounouilhou, 1894–96), II, 18.

[19] 'J'ai été, aujourd'hui, samedi 30, voir la liquéfaction du sang de saint Janvier. Je crois avoir vu que cette liquéfaction s'est faite; quoiqu'il soit difficile de s'en bien apercevoir, parce que l'on ne fait que vous montrer un moment un reliquaire, dont le verre est fané par les baisers de tout le monde. Mais, quoi qu'il en soit, je crois que c'est précisément un thermomètre; que ce sang ou cette liqueur, qui vient d'un lieu frais, entrant dans un lieu échauffé par la multitude du peuple et un grand nombre de bougies, doit se liquifier. . . . De plus, le prêtre tient le reliquaire de ses deux mains; ce qui chauffe le métal.' *Ibid.*, II, 18–19.

on it . . . of wastelands caused by plagues, wars, and other scourges. . . . They are asking the scholars in the countries where such events occur to give information about them. . . . Address communications to Monsieur de Montesquieu, Chairman of the Parlement of Guyenne in Bordeaux, who will pay the postage.'[20]

'As this work is portable, one may compare the plant in nature with the pictures of it and thus recognize the original in the copy. Then one may, by diligent study, impress on the mind what direct observation in the field only gave a sketchy idea of; this advantage should not be scorned . . . for those who are beginning to apply themselves to this activity.'[21]

'As I had seen by looking through my field glasses that on the other side of the bay the country was far less mountainous and more beautiful, I persuaded some of my fellow travellers to make some excursions there with me. . . . [We found] twenty-five or thirty leaves which were very narrow at the bottom and which became much wider at the top . . . they were of a very lovely pale green, striped with long veins of the most beautiful golden-yellow that one might imagine. We picked some of them with considerable difficulty, as the leaves had many thorns.'[22]

[20] 'On travaille à Bordeaux à donner au public l'*Histoire de la Terre*, et de tous les changemens qui y sont arrivez . . . des Deserts causez par les Pestes, les Guerres et autres fleaux. . . . On prie les Sçavans dans les païs desquels pareils évenemens seront arrivez d'en donner connoissance. . . . Il faut adresser les memoires à Monsieur de Montesquieu Président au Mortier au Parlement de Guyenne à Bordeaux, ruë Margaux, qui en payera le port.' 'Avis aux Savans' [*sic*], *Journal des Sçavans*, April, 1719, pp. 475-76.
[21] 'Cet ouvrage étant portatif, on peut au pied de la plante conférer les figures qu'on y donne avec le naturel, reconnoître dans la copie la vérité de l'original; et ensuite graver fortement dans l'Esprit par l'étude sérieuse du cabinet, ce que la simple vûë n'auroit fait qu'y ébaucher dans les campagnes; cet avantage n'est point à mépriser . . . pour ceux qui commencent à s'appliquer à cet exercice.' Nicolas de Ville et Montesquieu, *Histoire des Plantes* (2 vols; Lyon: Nicolas de Ville, 1726), 'Au Lecteur'.
[22] 'Comme j'avois vu par le moyen de mes Lunettes d'approche, que de l'autre côté du Golfe le païs étoit beaucoup moins montagneux et plus beau, j'engageai quelques-uns de mes Compagnons de voyage à y faire quelques courses avec moi. . . . [Nous trouvâmes] 25 ou 30 feuilles fort serrées par le bas, mais qui s'élargissent considérablement par en haut . . . d'un très-beau verd pâle, et pleines de grandes veines du plus bel aurore qu'on puisse voir. Nous en arrachâmes quelques-

Title of a speech which Simon Tyssot was to give on his inauguration as Rector of Deventer:

'Address by M. Simon Tyssot, Sr Patot, in which, with a view to establishing consistency among different nations in matters of chronology, he claims to prove philosophically, without involving Holy Scripture, that the earth and the heavens, which he thinks incredibly ancient, were not created in six normal days; that animals also have existed since time immemorial; and that the world will probably exist for millions of years. . . .'[23]

'The two marvellous varieties of birds in America are the flamingo and the hummingbird; the first one is the largest and the second is the smallest of all creatures that fly, except insects. . . . The flamingoes are found in large flocks in the marshlands; . . . people claim that there are always some perched as sentinels while the others look for food. . . . The feathers of the flamingo are of a very beautiful flesh colour, with some black and white colouring. . . . The hummingbird, which is called the fly-bird in Canada . . . with its nest weighs about as much as two peas and is called *Tominos* in Spain. . . . Its colours are red, black, green, and white, with shades of gold over the green and red. It has a tiny black crest on its head, and its throat is a brilliant red; its breast is of a lovely white, and the rest of its body is roseleaf green. Of all of these colours the female has only the white breast, all the rest of its plumage being ash-coloured.'[24]

---

unes, mais avec assez de peine, à cause des pointes dont elles sont armées.' Anon., *Relation d'un voyage du pôle arctique au pôle antarctique* (Paris : G. Amaulry, 1723), Ch. viii.

[23] 'Discours de M. Simon Tyssot, Sr. Patot, où dans la vuë de concillier les différentes Nations au sujet de la Chronologie, il prétend démontrer Philosophiquement, et sans intéresser l'Ecriture Sainte, que le Ciel et la Terre, qu'il croit d'une ancienneté inexprimable, n'ont point été créez en six jours naturels ; que les animaux ont aussi été produits depuis un tems immémorial ; que le monde doit vraisemblablement encore durer des millions d'années. . . .' *Journal littéraire*, Vol. XII (1722–23), Article 6.

[24] 'Mais les deux merveilles de l'Amérique en genre d'oiseaux, sont le Flamand et le Colibry, un des plus grands, et le plus petit de tous les animaux qui volent, et ne sont point insectes. . . . Les Flamands se trouvent par grandes troupes dans les marais ; . . . l'on prétend qu'il y en a toujours quelques-uns en sentinelles,

'A blade of grass that we trample underfoot is the stumbling-block of the whole proud structure of philosophy. A peasant sees as much of it as a physicist does after thirty years of study and contemplation, except that perhaps the physicist with the help of his good microscope will speculate more carefully about the surface of the blade of grass. . . . The formal cause, which is the essence and nature of any body, is not within the reach of optical equipment, nor within the jurisdiction of the senses.'[25]

'God did not create the world so that it might be the object of our research. He created it so that we might seek Him in it, so that we might recognize in the silence of religious contemplation His divinity, His eternal power.'[26]

'He was a perfect philosopher, a contemplative Male-branchist, who had never seen a naked sword and who knew gunpowder only because of the experiments which he had performed on the elasticity of the air which it contains. . . . We all listened to him with pleasure, particularly when he spoke about physics and explained the cause of eclipses, of winds, of the tide's ebb and flow – in other words, the most interesting

---

tandis que les autres sont occupés à chercher leur vie. . . . Les plumes du Flamand sont d'un très-bel incarnat, mêlé d'un peu de blanc et de noir. . . . Le Colibry, qu'on appelle Oiseau-Mouche en Canada . . . avec son nid il ne pèse qu'environ deux de ces petits pois, qu'on appelle en Espagne *Tominos*. . . . Ses couleurs sont le rouge, le noir, le verd, et le blanc, avec des nuances d'or sur le verd et le rouge. Il a sur la tête une petite aigrette noire, sa gorge est d'un rouge très-vif; son ventre est d'un beau blanc, et tout le reste d'un verd de feuille de rosier. La femelle n'a de toutes ces couleurs que le blanc sous le ventre, tout le reste de son plumage est d'un cendré clair.' Charlevoix, *Histoire de l'Isle Espagnole ou de S. Domingue*, I, 30–31.

[25] 'Un brin d'herbe, que nous foulons sous nos pieds, est l'écueil de tout le superbe apareil [*sic*] de la Philosophie. Un paysan en voit autant par ses yeux, qu'un Physicien en fait après trente années d'étude, et de contemplation : si ce n'est peut-être, que ce Physicien par le secours d'un bon microscope spéculera plus intimement la surface de ce brin d'herbe. . . . La cause formelle, qui fait l'essence, et la nature de quelque corps que ce soit, n'est point à la portée des machines de l'Optique, ni de la jurisdiction des sens.' Biron, *Curiositez de la Nature et de l'Art*, pp. v–vi.

[26] 'Dieu n'a point fait l'Univers pour être l'objet de nos recherches. Il l'a fait, afin que nous l'y cherchassions lui-même ; et que nous y reconnussions dans le silence d'une contemplation Religieuse sa Divinité, sa Puissance éternelle.' *Ibid.*, p. xiii.

phenomena of nature – which he did in clear and easy language appropriate to his listeners.'[27]

THE SENSE OF HISTORY

Eighteenth-century thought is perhaps best known for its belief in tolerance, which it made a part of Western tradition. Though geographical perspective – a knowledge of manners of life in other parts of the world – played a major role in the development of attitudes of tolerance, historical perspective was no less important a part of the base on which relativism and tolerance were built, and our period is as rich in the one as it is in the other. The leading spirit in the battle for tolerance was Pierre Bayle. Sometimes fighting for greater faithfulness to tradition, sometimes for freedom from the past, Bayle helped create the modern habit of understanding institutions in the light of history. His iconoclasm *vis-à-vis* the ancients and his belief in the idea of progress were usually supported by documents and represented an attempt at free investigation in which a knowledge and understanding of history were paramount. The quotations from Bayle presented below should give the reader a fair indication of the place that history occupied in his thought.

Writers of the eighteenth century generally believed in progress. Our period, being more than a half century before Condorcet, who stood at the apex of the belief in progress, did not yet venture to proclaim the perpetual and inevitable improvement of humanity, but the location of the Golden Age in the future rather than in the prehistoric past was a step in the direction of Condorcet. In historical outlook, certainly the writers of the early eighteenth century are not comparable to Condorcet with his passion or to those of the

[27] 'C'était un parfait philosophe, un méditatif malebranchiste, qui n'avoit jamais vu d'épées nues, et ne connoissoit la poudre à canon que par les expériences qu'il avoit faites sur le ressort de l'air qu'elle contient. . . . Nous l'écoutions tous avec plaisir, surtout lorsqu'il parloit physique, et nous expliquoit la cause des éclipses, des vents, du flux et reflux de la mer, enfin les effets les plus surprenants de la nature, ce qu'il faisoit en s'assujettissant aux expressions simples et convenables à la portée de ses auditeurs.' Alain-René Lesage, *Aventures du chevalier de Beauchêne* (1732), in *Œuvres* (4 vols; Paris: A. A. Renouard, 1821), IV, 91.

nineteenth century with their documents; yet the standards of truth and accuracy in our period were excellent, and the aims of many of the writers can only be judged admirable.

'The spirit of our century is totally opposed to the spirit of fables and miracles. . . . The earth, formerly static in men's opinion, now turns in our opinion, and nothing equals the speed of its movement. Everything has changed: the gods, nature, politics, customs, taste, and manners. Will not so many changes produce change in our works?'[28]

'The best histories are those that are written by authors who are contemporary, faithful, precise, and truthful. Those are monuments for posterity.'[29]

'The great erudition with which this book is filled deserves the attention of those who like that sort of thing. It is unfortunate that the learning displayed is not accompanied by that philosophic spirit which alone can give full value to the treasures unearthed by reading.'[30]

'There is no prescription against truth: errors are not the better for being old.'[31]

'Now, it is no less glorious to discover something that was formerly known [in this case, circulation of the blood] but not discussed, than to find out something that has never before

[28] 'Le génie de notre siècle est tout opposé à cet esprit de fables et de faux mystères. . . . La terre immobile autrefois, dans l'opinion des hommes, tourne aujourd'hui dans la nôtre, et rien n'est égal à la rapidité de son mouvement. Tout est changé: les Dieux, la nature, la politique, les mœurs, le goût, les manières. Tant de changemens n'en produiront-ils point dans nos ouvrages?' Saint-Evremond, 'Sur les Poèmes des Anciens' (1685), in *Œuvres*, ed. Planhol, I, 279–80.
[29] 'Les meilleures Histoires sont celles qui sont écrites par les Auteurs contemporains, fidèles, exacts et véridiques. Ce sont là des monumens pour la postérité.' (Not by Prévost) ; *Pour et Contre*, III, No. 31 (1734), 7.
[30] 'La grande érudition, dont cet Ouvrage est chargé, mérite l'attention de ceux, qui se plaisent à ces sortes de matiéres. C'est dommage qu'on n'y voie pas le savoir accompagné de cet esprit Philosophique, qui seul fait mettre en œuvre comme il faut les thrésors, que la Lecture fournit à la mémoire.' Review of Pierre Petit, *Traité historique sur les Amazones pour prouver qu'elles ont existé* (1718), in *Journal littéraire*, X (1718), 105.
[31] 'Il n'y a pas de prescription contre la vérité: les erreurs pour être vieilles, n'en sont pas meilleures.' Pierre Bayle, review of Van Dale, *Oracles*, in *Nouvelles de la République des Lettres*, March, 1684, Article 1.

been discovered. . . . Less than forty years ago almost all doctors were protesting that they were being driven off ground which they had occupied for two thousand years and that doctors of three days' standing were not going to insult ancient doctrine. And now one learns that it was they who had abandoned it. . . . One may be regarded as an innovator for establishing something that has been hidden for a long time.'[32]

'It is certain that France lost a good third of her population and that the two-thirds that remain are not the equal of the third that was lost. The upper class, although small in number, crushes the lower in France and always will, for I can see no other possibility. However, there is an enormous difference between the usefulness of the one and the other: the one, which is large, cultivates the earth and does not profit from it; the other reaps the fruit and works hard only at finding ways to get more; one possesses all of the wealth, devours it, and dissipates it on luxuries, while the other dies of hunger and poverty. What means is there to change this? I know of none; for far from helping the common people, one is daily contriving something new to their disadvantage.'[33]

'Luxury is the result of wealth and of the stability of a government. It is a necessary consequence of a well-governed

[32] 'Or il n'est pas moins glorieux de découvrir une chose qui a été autrefois connue, mais dont néanmoins l'on n'a pas ouï parler, que d'en découvrir une qui n'avait jamais été trouvée. . . . Il n'y a pas encore quarante ans que presque tous les Médecins se récrioient, qu'on les venoit chasser d'une possession de deux mille ans, et qu'il ne falloit pas souffrir que des Docteurs de trois jours insultassent l'ancienne Doctrine. Et présentement il se trouve que c'étoient eux qui l'avoient abandonnée. . . . On passe pour Novateur lorsqu'on établit une chose qui a demeuré longtemps cachée.' Bayle, review of *Traité de l'origine et du progrès de la Médicine*, in *ibid.*, June, 1684, Article 2.

[33] 'Il est certain que la France a perdu un grand tiers des siens et que les deux tiers qui restent ne valent pas le tiers perdu. La partie supérieure, quoique peu nombreuse, écrase l'inférieure en France et l'écrasera toujours parce que je ne vois pas d'apparence que cela puisse être autrement. Cependant il y a une différence infinie de l'utilité de l'une à celle de l'autre : l'une, qui est la grande, cultive la terre et n'en profite pas et l'autre s'en approprie les fruits et ne s'applique qu'à trouver moyen de les avoir ; l'une possède tous les biens, les mange et dissipe en superfluités et l'autre meurt de faim et de misère. Quel moyen de remédier à cela? Je n'en sais aucun ; car loin de soulager les peuples, on invente tous les jours quelque chose de nouveau à leur préjudice.' Letter from Vauban to Puyzieulx, from Toulon, December 4, 1700, in Vauban, *Lettres intimes*, pp. 102–3.

society. . . . What was luxury for our fathers is now widespread, and what is luxury for us . . . will not be luxury for our descendants. . . . The peasant considers that the bourgeois of his village possesses luxury, while the latter thinks the same of his counterpart in the nearby town. . . . The word luxury is an empty term, which ought to be eliminated from all matters of government and commerce, because its meaning is vague, confused, and misleading, and its misuse can discourage industry before it gets started.'[34]

'The present does not satisfy me, and the future even less. If God does not look upon us with that eye of mercy which so many times has saved us, I do not know what will become of us. . . .'[35]

The treatment of antiquity, in matters of both history and literature, shows an independence of mind and a determination to submit everything to critical examination which can only command the respect of modern readers. Moreover, the early centuries of Christian history, like the older pagan epochs, are often subjected to scholarly scrutiny. A few examples will demonstrate the tone of this category of historical writing.

'One can gather from this work that the Roman Church imperceptibly departed from the customs of antiquity and that it accuses the Eastern Church of innovation only because the latter has more carefully preserved ancient usage. From which it appears that tradition is deceptive and that one may often be fooled by the term "antiquity".'[36]

[34] 'Le Luxe résulte des richesses et de la sécurité d'un gouvernement. C'est une suite nécessaire de toute société bien policée. . . . Ce qui étoit Luxe pour nos pères est à présent commun, et ce qui l'est pour nous ne le sera pas pour nos neveux. . . . Le Paysan trouve du Luxe chez le Bourgeois de son Village, celui-ci chez l'Habitant de la Ville voisine. . . . Le terme de Luxe est un vain nom, qu'il faut bannir de toutes les opérations de Police et de Commerce, parce qu'il ne porte que des idées vagues, confuses, fausses, dont l'abus peut arrêter l'industrie même dans sa source.' Prévost, *Pour et Contre*, VI, No. 83 (1735), 171.
[35] 'Le présent ne me satisfait pas, l'avenir encore moins. Si Dieu ne nous regarde avec cet œil de miséricorde qui nous a tant de fois tirés d'affaire, je ne sais ce que nous deviendrons. . . .' Vauban to Puyzieulx, Bazoche, October 27, 1701, in Vauban, *Lettres intimes*, p. 107.
[36] 'On peut recueillir de cet Ouvrage que l'Eglise Latine s'est insensiblement écartée des coûtumes de l'Antiquité, et qu'elle n'accuse les Orientaux d'innovation,

'The corruption and the avarice of the clergymen of the fourth century would be hard to believe if they were not attested by St Jerome, St Hilary, St Gregory of Nazianze, St Basil, St Ambrose, and generally all the saints of that era, and if we did not find a law in the Theodosian Code that forbids ecclesiastics from asking anything of widows and orphans, and from accepting any gift from women to whom they attached themselves under religious pretences.'[37]

'Juvenal and Horace are far removed from that degree of perfection: the epigrams of Martial, even further removed . . . those ancient times that are so greatly venerated had no trace of true *urbanity*.'[38]

'One of the principal objections to Homer is based on the ideas that that poet gave us of his gods, ideas which seem false and ridiculous. But we must remember that Homer spoke to us of his gods according to the theology of his day. Therefore, it would be as unjust to regard him as the inventor of these ideas or to attribute their repulsiveness to him, as to condemn today a painter who reproduced the adventures of the *Iliad* or the *Metamorphoses* of Ovid. . . . Virgil, it will be said, wrote about the same divinities as Homer and treated them in a more tasteful and appropriate manner. Yes, but each one presented these gods in accordance with the assumptions of

---

que parce qu'ils ont plus soigneusement conservé l'ancient usage. D'où il paroit que la Tradition est une voye trompeuse, et que le terme d'*antiquité* est souvent fort illusoire.' Bayle, review of *L'Histoire critique de la créance . . . des Nations du Levant*, in *Nouvelle de la République des Lettres*, May, 1684, Article 2.

[37] 'On auroit de la peine à croire la corruption, et l'avarice des Ecclésiastiques du quatrième siècle, si elle n'étoit attestée par S. Jérôme, par S. Hilaire, par S. Grégoire de Nazianze, par S. Basile, par S. Ambroise, et en général par tous les Saints de ce temps-là, et si l'on ne trouvoit encore une Loi dans le Code Théodosien, qui défend aux Ecclésiastiques d'obséder les Veuves et les Orphelins, et de recevoir aucune libéralité des femmes auxquelles ils s'attachent sous prétexte de Religion.' Bayle, review of *Histoire de l'origine du progrès des Revenus Ecclésiastiques*, in *ibid.*, Article 3.

[38] 'Juvenal et Horace sont bien éloignez de ce degré de perfection : les Epigrammes de Martial en sont encore plus éloignées . . . ces anciens temps pour lesquels on témoigne une si grande vénération, n'avoient aucune teinture de la véritable *urbanité*.' Bayle, *ibid.*, June, 1684, Article 4.

his time, and these were perhaps more refined in Virgil's age than in Homer's.'[39]

'But where did he [Father Buffier] find those things in Homer that we are incapable of judging because of the centuries that separate Homer from us? He ought to cite a few, for as soon as we are informed of the customs of the period Homer described – as we are by many books, one being the Holy Scriptures – then we are able to judge whether or not he portrayed those customs faithfully.'[40]

As we stated earlier, the growth of the idea of progress required the destruction of the myth of a Golden Age. If there must be a Golden Age, said our writers, it is better located in the present or in the future than in the past. A thorough-going doctrine of progress – that is, a belief in inevitable and indefinite perfectibility – will, of course, recognize no age as perfect, because of the static quality which perfection implies. From this standpoint the writers in our part of the eighteenth century may be said to have blazed the trail for Condorcet and the nineteenth-century faith in progress, rather than to have quite expressed it themselves. However, few if any contributions to the idea of progress, in its long development, had as liberating an effect on historical

[39] 'Une des principales objections contre Homère est fondée sur les idées que ce poète nous a données de ses Dieux, idées qui paraissent fausses et ridicules. Mais il faut se souvenir qu'Homère nous a parlé de ses Dieux suivant la théologie de son temps. Ainsi, il y aurait autant d'injustice à le regarder comme l'inventeur de ces mêmes idées et à le charger de ce qu'elles peuvent avoir de rebutant qu'il y en aurait à condamner un peintre qui représenterait aujourd'hui les aventures de l'*Iliade* ou *les Métamorphoses* d'Ovide. . . . Virgile, dira-t-on, a parlé des mêmes divinités qu'Homère a employés et il en a parlé d'une manière plus décente et plus convenable. Soit. Mais l'un et l'autre nous ont représenté ces Dieux suivant les idées reçues de leur temps, et ces idées étaient peut-être plus épurées du temps de Virgile que du temps d'Homère.' Letter from Brossette to J.-B. Rousseau, June 26, 1715, *Correspondance de J.-B. Rousseau et de Brossette*, ed. P. Bonnefon (2 vols; Paris: Société des Textes français modernes, 1910), I, 8–9.

[40] 'Mais où a-t-il pris ces choses dans Homère dont nous ne sommes point à portée de juger à cause de l'éloignement des siècles? Il faudrait qu'il prît la peine d'en citer quelques-unes, car dès que nous sommes informés des mœurs du siècle qu'Homère a décrit, comme nous le sommes par une infinité de livres à commencer par l'Ecriture Sainte, nous sommes à portée de juger si Homère a bien ou mal représenté ces mœurs.' Letter from Rousseau to Brossette, January 29, 1716, *ibid.*, I, 33.

thinking as this attack on the obstacle to progressivist history represented by the legend of the Golden Age.

'It is far less appropriate to place the Golden Age at the beginning of the world than it is the Iron Age. Rather than give our age that title, we might very reasonably call it the age of silver, which will perhaps be followed, at least in France, by a happy era which until now has unfortunately existed only in the minds of poets and orators. What would it take to bring such an age to reality? Three things that are very possible and not far from realization: a free and universal commerce, a lasting peace, and new Colberts and Fleurys.'[41]

At this point, the editor of the *Journal des Sçavans*, from which the preceding passage is quoted, adds the following remarks:

'. . . the difference between our world and that of our ancestors is more than one of degree. We may go further: without deluding ourselves, we can easily imagine a world happier than ours. That will be the Golden Age. . . . It is certain that manners are becoming more genteel, that society is changing for the better, and that the progress of Reason and of the Arts and Sciences is a source of happiness for many men. More people are happy in our century than in preceding centuries, and above all there are happier people.

'However, one always complains of the present, and one always praises the past. This is an accepted pattern. Even if the illusory Golden Age were to reveal itself, people would still say "the good old days". Some say this only out of prejudice and narrow-mindedness, while others speak out of pride, spite, ill will, or personal discontent. . . . The innocence of the Golden Age is as fanciful as its happiness. The author has stated this already; however, he thought it his duty to prove it at greater length in his second letter. He admits that justice,

41 'C'est bien moins l'âge d'or qu'il faut placer dans ces premiers tems du Monde, que l'âge de fer. Au lieu de donner ce nom à notre siècle, nous pourrions très-raisonnablement l'appeler l'âge d'argent, auquel succèdera peut-être après nous, du moins en France, un âge fortuné, qui n'a malheureusement encore existé que dans les idées des Poëtes et des déclamateurs. Que faudroit-il pour assurer la supposition? Trois choses très possibles, et dont nous ne sommes pas fort éloignés, un commerce libre et universel, une paix durable, et toujours des Colbert ou des Fleury.' Anon., *Lettres philosophiques sur l'âge d'or et le bonheur* (London, 1738), quoted in *Journal des Sçavans*, May, 1739, pp. 46–47.

good faith, and other virtues with which men have adorned
the fable of the golden age may have existed in isolation in
some corner of the world; but, he says, it was without these
things constituting virtue. Here is the explanation of the
paradox: Imagine men wandering in the forests, like the
savages of America, living off hunting and fishing; they can
scarcely sin against justice. All wealth is almost as much common property as the air they breathe. They all have the same
right to this wealth. There is no fear that they will trick one
another or strip one another of a piece of land, or of a house,
nor that they will steal money or furniture from one another;
they have none of these things. In short, their way of living
makes it virtually impossible for them to be unjust. They
are therefore not really virtuous, for virtue consists in avoiding
evil which one could do. This is the idea presented in the
Bible in praise of the virtuous rich man, *potuit facere mala et
non fecit*. Thus, what is termed innocence and virtue in savages
is only ignorance and inevitability. Furthermore, there are no
crimes where there are no laws; and that – if one believes
the poets – was one of the great advantages of the Golden
Age. . . .'[42]

[42] '. . . la différence de notre état à celui de nos premiers Ancêtres est de plus
d'un degré. Nous pouvons aller encore plus loin ; et sans se livrer à des chimères,
on conçoit aisément la possibilité d'un état plus heureux que celui où nous sommes.
Ce sera l'âge d'or. . . . Il est certain que les mœurs s'adoucissent, que la société
se perfectionne, et que le progrès de la Raison, des Sciences et des Arts est pour
un grand nombre d'hommes une source de bonheur. Il y a plus d'heureux dans
notre siècle que dans les siècles précédens, et surtout il y a des gens plus heureux.
'Cependant on se plaint toujours du temps présent, et on vante toujours le
temps passé. C'est la formule reçue. La chimère de l'âge d'or se réaliseroit, qu'on
diroit encore, *le bon vieux tems*. Les uns ne le disent que par prévention et par
petitesse d'esprit. Mais dans plusieurs autres, c'est orgueil, malignité et mauvais
cœur, ou mécontentement personnel. . . . L'innocence de l'âge d'or est aussi
chimérique que sa félicité ; l'Auteur l'a déjà dit ; mais il a cru devoir le prouver
plus au long dans sa seconde Lettre. Il convient cependant que la justice, la bonne
foi, et d'autres vertus dont on a orné la Fable de l'âge d'or ont pu absolument
subsister dans quelque coin du Monde ; mais dit-il, c'est sans être vertu. Voici
l'explication du paradoxe. Qu'on se représente les hommes errans dans les forêts,
comme les Sauvages de l'Amérique, vivans de la chasse et de la pêche, ils ne peuvent guère pécher contre la justice. Tous les biens sont presque aussi communs
chez eux que l'air qu'ils respirent. Ils ont tous le même droit sur ces biens. Il
n'est point à craindre qu'ils se chicanent et se dépouillent les uns les autres d'un
champ, d'une maison, ni qu'ils se volent de l'argent ou des meubles ; ils n'ont
rien de tout cela. Enfin leur état les met presque dans l'impossibilité d'être in-

LITERATURE AND CRITICISM

The critical spirit, which was nourished by a growing acquaintance with foreign lands and by the development of scientific and historical perspective, is abundantly evident in the literature of the period and in writings about literature. The openness with which writers discussed various aspects of French literary tradition, their interest in making comparisons with other literatures, and their freedom from dogmatism as they searched for standards of 'truth' in fiction (sometimes called 'reality' or 'naturalness') all are indications of an atmosphere in which the critical spirit thrived. It may be doubted whether France had ever before experienced such intense and many-sided discussion for so extended a period of time. The Quarrel of Ancients and Moderns, which occurred at the threshold of our period, undoubtedly opened floodgates of criticism, within the stream of literature itself, for the progress of that quarrel, as well as of that which followed, regarding Homer, proved nothing so much as the power of the questioning mind. Convinced of the value and the possibility of independent thought – a notion richly supported from fields other than literature, such as history and science – writers displayed an adventurousness in their thinking which must strike anyone who reads them as a most appropriate introduction to the Enlightenment.

Though the literature and literary criticism of our period touched on every facet of life and learning, a visible drift occurred, during our fifty years, away from theology and towards ethics, foreign countries, and, after 1725, education of children. In novels – and to some extent in drama and poetry – the period of 1715–30 saw a distinct decline in the popularity of imaginary tales in favour of those in which '*le véritable*' was at the fore. This, at least, is the conclusion that one must draw after comparing the methods of Prévost, Marivaux, Defoe,

justes. Ils ne sont donc pas vertueux, à proprement parler. Car la vertu consiste à éviter le mal que l'on pourroit faire. C'est l'idée qu'en donne l'Ecriture en louant le riche vertueux, *potuit facere mala et non fecit.* Ainsi ce qu'on appelle innocence et vertu dans les Sauvages, n'est qu'ignorance et nécessité. D'ailleurs il n'y a point de crimes où il n'y a point de Loix ; et c'étoit là, si l'on en croit les Poëtes, un des principaux avantages de l'âge d'or. . . .' *Ibid.*, pp. 47–48.

and the minor novelists of the 1730s and 1740s to those of the inventors of the hundreds of wildly imaginary novels that dominated the closing years of Louis XIV's reign.

The passages which we give below are not always easy to categorize, but because of the large number of them, we have none the less thought it wise to present them under separate rubrics as follows: (1) formal literary questions, (2) literary history and comparative literature, and (3) truth and realism.

FORMAL LITERARY QUESTIONS

As we might expect, writings on formal literary subjects, such as the place of rhyme in French poetry, and comments on specific authors – Montaigne, in the excerpts quoted here – showed much the same refreshing independence from tradition that we have seen in numerous other contexts. The fact that, as these passages will indicate, there was no unanimity in these discussions is but a mark of the freedom with which writers approached their craft. There was distinctly not, in our period, a dominant school of prominent writers who held one set of views, as against lesser writers forming a dissenting group.

'The author [of *Rash Reasonings on French Poetry*] states that the search for rhymes does not stimulate genius, does not reinforce it, but rather stupefies and freezes it; that it is surprising that in this most rigid of tyrannies – for it enslaves the mind, whose freedom is proof against all the world's tyrants – French poets can still keep so much vitality, or rather, our author says, they can be excused if they have so little of it left. Imagine what they would be like if they were to break their bonds !'[43]

'One would not succeed in doing in France [what Milton

[43] 'L'auteur [dit] que la recherche des rimes n'échauffe pas le génie, qu'elle ne le soûtient pas, qu'elle l'abrutit plutôt et le glace, Qu'il est surprenant que dans le plus dur des esclavages, tel qu'est celui-ci *puisqu'il captive l'esprit auquel tous les Tyrans du monde ne sçauroient ôter la liberté*, les Poëtes François puissent conserver encore tant de feu, ou plutôt, dit notre Auteur, ils sont excusables s'il leur en reste si peu, et que ne seroient-ils pas s'ils brisoient leurs liens. . . ?' Review of *Raisonnemens hazardés sur la Poësie Françoise* (1737), in *Journal des Sçavans*, February, 1738, p. 185.

M

did in England]. Our verse freed of rhyme does not appear
different in any way from prose. . . . We have grown accustomed
to it, and habit makes this little embellishment, however
Gothic and barbaric, seem pleasant to us. . . . It is therefore
because of the impossibility of doing otherwise that the French
continue and always will continue, to rhyme.'[44]

'Rhyme is not a mark of perfection in poetry. Indeed, it
should be looked upon as a flaw. . . .
'Our greatest poets (Boileau among others) confuse poetry
with the art of rhyming.'[45]

'Most of them [the English] feel that the French language
does not have the strength necessary for poetry. They are not
entirely mistaken; refining by the purists has impoverished
this language; many expressive old words have been eliminated,
and new terms have been permitted only to the extent that
need has demanded them . . . very often the only way to achieve
any variety is through circumlocutions, which by replacing a
single word with an entire phrase, leave a gap in the meaning
and inevitably enervate the diction. It is true that this sterility
is difficult for a poet; but there is nothing that a superior
mind cannot overcome. . . . It remains certain, however,
that the same degree of genius would show far more energy
of style in a less limited language. Such is the English language,
surely; never has a language been less reluctant to adopt
foreign expressions; it appropriates not only words but also
phrases; everything which is expressive and which helps
make speech direct, receives immediate acceptance and
legitimacy in the English language.'[46]

[44] 'On essayeroit sans succès de faire la même chose en France. Nos vers affran-
chis de la rime ne paroissent différer en rien de la Prose. . . . Nous y sommes
accoutumez, et l'habitude nous rend agréable ce petit ornement, quoique gothique
et barbare. . . . C'est donc par impossibilité de faire autrement, que les François
continuent, et qu'ils continueront toujours de rimer.' Prévost, *Pour et Contre*, II,
No. 29 (1733), 327–28.
[45] 'La Rime n'est pas une perfection dans la Poësie, et elle doit même être
regardée comme un défaut. . . .
'Nos plus grands Poëtes (*Boileau entre autres*) confondent la Poësie avec l'*Art de
rimer*.' *Ibid.*, VI, No. 79 (1735), 75, 78.
[46] 'La plûpart d'entr'eux sont du sentiment, que la langue Françoise n'a pas
la force necessaire pour la Poësie. Ils ne se trompent pas tout-à-fait; le rafinement
[*sic*] des Puristes a appauvri cette langue; beaucoup de vieux mots expressifs

'Any man of middling education who has read Montaigne, Charron, and a few other authors of similar bent, could compose a book like this one . . . Montaigne, speaking constantly of himself. . . . Nor would we want to assert that this method greatly pleased those who lived in his time. What is certain is that a man who always focuses on himself could become unbearable. . . . Perhaps some day people will be pleased to know all this [what our author feels and what he thinks], and perhaps the years will augment the value of this work.'[47]

'Listen to Montaigne. A delight, a havoc. It is not a question of seeing. Do our eyes, whether opened wide or tightly shut, see the splendour of a flash of lightning? They feel. To have taste is to feel through the eyes, through the ears, etc. Define it better.'[48]

'We are warned in a preliminary letter that this translation is "an amusement undertaken during holidays in the country", and that the author spent just six weeks working on it. I do

---

en ont été retranchez, et on n'a admis de termes nouveaux qu'autant que la necessité l'exigeoit . . . on ne sauroit bien souvent varier le stile, que par des circonlocutions, qui remplaçant un seul mot par tout une phrase, causent du vuide dans le sens, et doivent absolument énerver la diction. Il est vrai que cette sterilité est incommode pour un Poëte, mais il n'y a rien dont un Esprit superieur ne vienne à bout. . . . Il reste pourtant certain, que le même degré d'esprit donneroit beaucoup plus d'énergie à son stile dans une langue moins bornée. Telle est l'Angloise à coup seur ; jamais langue ne fut moins scrupuleuse à adopter des expressions étrangeres, elle s'approprie non seulement des mots, mais des tours de phrases ; tout ce qui est expressif et propre à abreger le discours obtient d'abord droit de bourgeoisie chez elle.' 'Dissertation sur la Poësie Angloise', *Journal littéraire*, IX, (1717), 160–61.

[47] 'Tout homme médiocrement éclairé, qui auroit lû Montaigne, Charron, et quelques autres Auteurs de même goût, pourroit composer un livre comme celui-ci . . . Montaigne, en parlant perpétuellement de soi-même. . . . Encore ne voudrions-nous pas assurer que cette méthode ait fait fort grand plaisir à ceux qui vivoient de son temps. Ce qui est certain, c'est qu'un homme qui se mettroit toujours en jeu, deviendroit insupportable. . . . Peut-être que l'on sera un jour fort aise de savoir tout cela, et peut-être que les années augmenteront le prix de cet Ouvrage.' Review of Anon., *Le Génie, la Politesse, l'Esprit et la Delicatesse de la Langue Françoise* (1705), in *Journal des Sçavans*, August 17, 1705, p. 974.

[48] 'Ecoutez Montagne. Un ravissement, un ravage. Il n'est pas question de voir. Les yeux les plus ouverts et les plus fermes, voyent-ils la splendeur d'un éclair? Ils sentent. Avoir du goût, c'est sentir par la vûë, par l'oüie, etc. Définissez-le mieux.' Prévost, *Pour et Contre*, IV, No. 54 (1734), 213–14.

not know whether the reader will be satisfied with this excuse.
. . . Who stopped him from doing his translation in town, and
less hurriedly? If he had taken this wise precaution, perhaps
he would more successfully have preserved the finesse and
animation of the original.'[49]

'. . . those frivolous works born of ignorance and love, which
seem to have no purpose but to make virtues of weaknesses; in
which common sense and reason are usually neglected and
propriety scorned. . . .'[50]

'Moreover, why are pirates rejected so scornfully in works of
the imagination? A novel is a poem. All poems (at least the
good ones) are the same in outline. Ulysses plays the same role
with Circe as Aeneas with Dido . . . can we not give, as justification of pirates, the same reason as that which makes us
accept the invocations and the sorceresses in the epic poems?'[51]

LITERARY HISTORY AND COMPARATIVE LITERATURE

If the quotations given below create the impression that, in
the years covered by this study, the French had a particularly
great interest in England and English literature, that impression is accurate. This was due in part to the sojourns in England
of Voltaire and Prévost, to mention two of the most prominent
and the most articulate on the subject, in part to the fact that

[49] 'On nous avertit dans une lettre préliminaire, que cette traduction est *un
amusement pris à la campagne, pendant les vacances*, et que l'Auteur *n'a mis que six
semaines à la faire*. Je ne sais si l'on se contentera de cette excuse. . . . Qui l'empêchoit de traduire à la Ville, et de le faire avec plus de loisir? S'il avoit pris
cette sage précaution, peut-être auroit-il mieux conservé toute la délicatesse et
toute la vivacité de son Original.' Review of *Epigrammes d'Owen*, in *Nouvelles de
la République des Lettres*, April, 1709.

[50] '. . . ces Ouvrages frivoles, que l'ignorance et l'amour ont enfantez; qui ne
semblent faits que pour ériger en vertus des foiblesses; où le bon sens et la Raison
sont assez souvent negligez, et les bienseances méprisées. . . .' Review of *L'Iliade
d'Homère, traduite par Madame Dacier*, in *Journal des Sçavans*, June, 1711, p. 624.

[51] 'D'ailleurs pourquoi rejette-t-on avec tant de mépris les Corsaires dans les
Ouvrages d'imagination? Un Roman est un Poëme. Tous les Poëmes (au moins
les bons) se ressemblent par le plan. Ulisse chez Circé joue le même rôle qu'Enée
avec Didon . . . et ne peut-on pas donner, pour excuser les Corsaires, la même
raison qui fait regarder comme une chose nécessaire les Je chante, et les
Magiciennes dans les Poëmes Epiques?' Auvigny, *Mémoires de Comminville*, Preface,
p. 2.

the two countries found themselves involved in many common social and intellectual problems. From the French standpoint, there is no doubt that there was much to be learned from the English, who were widely thought to be at a superior stage of development in many respects. Older literature, of France itself, was not utterly neglected, however. Thus, the *Journal des Sçavans* of September to November, 1724, announced new editions of the following sixteenth-century works: a three-volume *Histoire du Petit Jehan de Saintre* (1523); *Œuvres d'Étienne Pasquier*; and a ten-volume *Mémoires de Brantôme*.

'In town, in country, indoors and out-of-doors, seated and standing, the English write verse. They write it on the walls; they print it on the windowpanes. There is no cabaret or other public place which does not offer epigrams, and madrigals without number. . . . In short, the windowpanes and walls of England are annals of love.'[52]

The following statement comes after a list of thirty-five books published in London in January, 1734: 'If we add approximately twenty weekly sheets, and a far greater number of leaflets . . . we must judge the English a nation of writers and men of letters.'[53]

'It is not for us to decide . . . whether one finds in this work that absolute clarity which readers rigidly demand of French authors. . . . One feels no shame in openly confessing that one has understood nothing in it. It is the author's fault, not ours. The acceptable obscurity of certain English books would be pompous nonsense in a French book.'[54]

[52] 'A la Ville, à la Campagne, dans leurs Maisons et dehors, assis et debout, les Anglois composent des Vers. Ils les écrivent sur les murs, ils les gravent sur les vitres. On ne trouve point de Cabaret ni d'autre lieu public qui n'offre des Epigrammes, et des Madrigaux sans nombre. . . . Enfin, les vitres et les murs d'Angleterre sont des Annales d'amour.' Prévost, *Pour et Contre*, VI, No. 88 (1735), 300.

[53] 'Si l'on ajoute environ vingt feuilles hebdomadaires, et un bien plus grand nombre de petites Pièces fugitives . . . on regardera les Anglois, avec raison, comme un peuple d'Ecrivains et de Gens de Lettres.' *Ibid.*, III, No. 37 (1734), 160.

[54] 'Il ne nous appartient pas de décider . . . si l'on trouve dans cet Ouvrage cette parfaite clarté que les Lecteurs exigent indispensablement d'un Auteur François. . . . On ne croit pas se faire aucun tort en avouant sans façon qu'on n'y a rien compris. C'est la faute de l'Auteur et non pas la nôtre. L'obscurité respectable de certains livres Anglois seroient dans un Livre François un galimatias

'Another form of slavery, which is no less severe or less unjust, is rhyme, for which the rules are so inflexible that the least flaw of rhyming is not excused, no matter how new or right the idea to be expressed may be and even if it were to lose all its force by straining to express itself in richer rhyme. . . .

'In longer works, they [the English] are satisfied with metre without rhyme, which is a relief to both the poet and the reader; it spares the one hardship, and the other boredom. Would that the French could bring themselves to imitate such reasonable forthrightness; it is an error to think that they could not succeed in making this sort of verse attractive.'[55]

'M. Dacier . . . typically presumptuous, has decided that we may expect nothing good from the English in the field of drama.'[56]

[*The Thousand and One Hours, Peruvian Tales*] . . . 'are frivolous books written to amuse certain idle people who have neither the knowledge nor the intelligence to enjoy other more substantial books.'[57]

'Take a look at the books which are esteemed in London, look at our clothing, our houses, our customs, our plays,

---

ridicule.' Review of Ste. Hyacinthe [?], *Recueil de divers Ecrits, sur l'Amour et l'Amitié, la Politesse, la Volupté, les Sentimens agréables, l'Esprit et le Cœur* (1736), in *Journal des Sçavans*, September, 1736, pp. 6–7.

[55] '. . . une autre Esclavage, qui n'est pas moins severe, ni moins injuste ; c'est celui de la Rime, sur laquelle les regles sont d'une telle rigueur, que la moindre défectuosité de ce côté-là n'est pas pardonnée en faveur de la pensée la plus neuve et la plus juste, quand elle perdroit toute la force sous la tyrannie d'une rime plus riche. . . .
'. . . dans des Ouvrages de longue haleine, ils se contentent de la mesure en renonçant à la rime, ce qui soulage et le Poëte et le Lecteur, en épargnant de la peine à l'un, et de l'ennui à l'autre.
'Il seroit à souhaiter que les François voulussent imiter une hardiesse si raisonnable ; c'est un abus de croire qu'ils ne vinssent pas à bout de faire goûter ces sortes de vers. . . .' 'Dissertation sur la Poësie Angloise', *Journal littéraire*, IX (1717), 163–65.

[56] 'M. Dacier . . . par une présomtion digne de lui a décidé, qu'il ne falloit attendre rien de bon des Anglois dans le genre dramatique.' *Ibid.*, p. 215.

[57] '*Les Mille et une heures, Contes Péruviens* . . . sont de ces Livres frivoles faits pour amuser certaines personnes oisives, qui n'ont ni assez de lumieres, ni assez d'esprit, pour goûter d'autres Livres plus solides.' Prévost, *Pour et Contre*, II, No. 26 (1733), 256.

even our ideas on matters as serious as religion and government, and everywhere you will recognize our scorn for antiquity.' [After quoting the preceding sentence from an English
writer in *The Weekly Miscellany*, No. 126, Prévost continues]:
'The French, after long vacillating between the Ancients and
the Moderns, have made what is surely the most reasonable
decision. . . . Since their taste moves less toward time than
toward things . . . one can say, with a meaning different from
M. LaMotte's, that they are "contemporaries of all men and
citizens of all places".'[58]

'*The Spectacle of Nature* [by Abbé Pluche], which is so successful in Paris, and the second volume of which is impatiently
awaited, has been translated into English and much appreciated in London.'[59]

'While admitting that it [*Zaïre*] contains some touching
situations, the English have not recognized in it the trademark
of Voltaire; I mean, that noble and gracious poetic style . . . of
the "Poem of the Ligue".'[60]

'M. V[oltaire] will also allow me to say that his plays smack
a little too much of epic poetry. They suffer from the principal
talent of the author.'[61]

'. . . all his plays [Molière's] have just been published in

[58] ' "Voyez nos Livres, dit un Auteur, estimez à Londres, nos Habits, nos
Maisons, nos Usages, nos Spectacles, nos Opinions mêmes sur des matieres aussi
sérieuses que la Religion et le Gouvernement, et vous reconnoîtrez partout notre
mépris pour l'Antiquité."
'Les François après avoir paru balancer longtems entre les Anciens et les
Modernes, ont pris sans doute le seul parti raisonnable . . . leur goût portant moins
sur les tems que sur les choses . . . l'on peut dire dans un autre sens que M. de la
Motte, qu'ils sont *Contemporains de tous les hommes, Et Citoyens de tous les lieux*.' *Ibid.*,
VI, No. 88 (1735), 292–93.
[59] 'Le Spectacle de la Nature, qui a eu tant de succès à Paris, et dont on attend
avec impatience le second Volume, a été traduit en Anglois, et a été goûté à
Londres.' *Ibid.*, II, No. 23 (1733), 192.
[60] 'En confessant qu'il s'y trouve [i.e., dans *Zaïre*] quelques situations touchantes,
les Anglois n'y ont pas reconnu le sceau de M. de Voltaire ; je veux dire ce tour
de Poësie noble et gracieux . . . du Poëme de la Ligue.' *Ibid.*, I, No. 2 (1733), 37.
[61] 'M. de V—— me permettra de remarquer encore, que ses Pièces de Théâtre
sentent un peu trop le Poëme Épique. Elles souffrent du talent principal de
l'Auteur.' *Ibid.*, No. 5, p. 111.

London with notes and the English translation facing the French.'[62]

'Villon overshadowed all of his rivals. . . . In truth, he was the first to seize the genius of our language. . . . He was the inventor of that banter which is something between the pleasant and the comic.'[63]

TRUTH AND REALISM

'If we speak of this book it is only to warn readers not to believe all the fables with which it is filled. . . .

'Hardly was that great event [the siege of Vienna] over, than it was appropriated in Paris as the basis of an amorous tale. In truth, such liberties ought not to be allowed. It would be well to require all novelists either to create imaginary heroes or to take those that antiquity furnishes them. . . . Why so blatantly poison modern history? Why say so seriously that the last war in Hungary was caused only by the love of the Grand Vizier for the wife of the Pasha of Buda?'[64]

'The reading of a good novel is not unworthy of a sensible man. A novel sometimes has more basic truth than history has. The details of both are often imagined. But the former does not offend verisimilitude, whereas the latter offends it on

[62] '. . . toutes ses Piéces viennent d'être imprimées à Londres avec des Notes, et la traduction Angloise placée à côté du François.' *Ibid.*, No. 4, p. 79. In this same article Prévost reports that in 1733 *L'Avare* was performed thirty-five times in three months.

[63] 'Villon effaça tous ses concurrens . . . en effet, il est le premier qui soit bien entré dans le génie de notre Langue. . . . Il fut l'inventeur de ce badinage qui tient le milieu entre l'agréable et le bouffon.' Abbé Massieu, *Histoire de la Poësie Françoise*, quoted in review in *Journal des Sçavans*, December, 1739, p. 521.

[64] 'Si nous parlons de ce livre ce n'est que pour avertir les Lecteurs de n'ajouter point foi à toutes les Fables dont il est plein . . .' 'A peine ce grand événement [siege of Vienna] étoit achevé, que l'on commença de s'en saisir à Paris pour en faire une Historiette amoureuse. En vérité on ne devroit pas souffrir cette licence. On feroit fort bien d'obliger tous les Faiseurs de Romans ou à forger des Héros imaginaires, ou à prendre ceux que l'Antiquité leur fournit. . . . Pourquoi empoisonner si hardiment l'Histoire Moderne? Pourquoi dire si sérieusement, que la dernière guerre de Hongrie n'a eu pour cause que l'amour du Grand Vizir pour la Femme du Bacha de Bude?' Bayle, review of *Cara Mustapha Grand Vizir . . . Siège de Vienne* (Paris, 1684), in *Nouvelles de la République des Lettres*, October, 1684, Article 8.

many occasions and is moreover filled with obscurity and contradictions.'[65]

'If Homer were alive now, he would write some admirable poems, appropriate to the century in which he would be writing. Our poets write poor poetry which is modelled on that of antiquity and governed by rules which lost their meaning when time destroyed the things with which they were associated.'[66]

'Poetry is good only to the extent that it expresses thoughts appropriate to the subject treated; and all thought, whether comic or heroic, must always be expressed in a natural manner.'[67]

'Perhaps after the brilliant and the beautiful style of today, fashion will bring Frenchmen to a simple and sensible style, which some of them, who have ventured to take the lead, have already attained.'[68]

> '. . . the wise man
> Must make noble use
> Of his studious leisure
> And, justly charmed
> By fair Antiquity,
> Must search his generous heart

[65] 'La lecture d'un bon Roman . . . n'est point indigne d'un homme sensé. Un Roman a quelquefois plus de fond de vérité que l'Histoire. Les détails de l'un et de l'autre sont souvent imaginés. Mais le premier ne blesse point la vraisemblance, lorsque la dernière la choque en mille endroits, et d'ailleurs est pleine d'obscurité et de contradictions.' Review of M. de Seré, *Maximes et Reflexions morales, traduites de l'Anglois*, in *Journal des Sçavans*, May, 1739, p. 135.

[66] 'Si Homère vivoit présentement, il feroit des poèmes admirables, accommodé au siècle où il écriroit. Nos poètes en font de mauvais, ajustés à ceux des anciens et conduits par des règles qui sont tombées avec les choses que le temps a fait tomber.' Saint-Evremond, 'Sur les Poèmes des Anciens' (1685) in *Œuvres*, I, 279–80.

[67] 'La Poësie n'est bonne qu'autant qu'elle renferme des pensées convenables au sujet que l'on traite; et toute pensée, soit héroïque, soit comique, doit toûjours être rendue d'une maniere naturelle.' Saint-Jory, *Œuvres mêlées* (1735), quoted in *Journal des Sçavans*, August, 1735, p. 471.

[68] 'Peut-être qu'après le Brillant et le Beau stile d'aprésent, la Mode amenera les François au Simple et au Sensé, où quelques-uns d'entre eux, qui ont osé prendre le devant, sont déjà arrivez.' Muralt, *Lettres sur les Anglois et les François*, p. 208.

For solid pleasure,
Truth, honesty, and utility.'⁶⁹

'Few people before me have thought of giving their heroes
French names. And it is to be feared that some romantic
souls, seeing a name like the Marquis of Riberville, or Mirestan, or Franlieu or others, rather than Tiridate or Cléante,
may jump to conclusions about my book. I ask those gentle
souls to excuse me, if to please them I do not make Greeks or
Arabs of those whom I wish to present as rather gallant
Frenchmen.'⁷⁰

'The Clélies, the Cyruses, the Polexandres, and so many
other fanciful heroes and heroines. . . . The true, and consequently the useful, are banished from these works . . . those
syrupy heroes, those straying heroines, repel and disgust a
reasonable mind.'⁷¹

'No one could fail to see that one must not look for truth in
this narration [*Robinson Crusoe*]. One must be satisfied to find
in it some verisimilitude which the author has tried to render
interesting with the aid of novelty.'⁷²

'The public has read with a great deal of pleasure the last
volume of the *Memoirs of a Gentleman*, which contains the
adventures of the knight Des Grieux and Manon Lescot . . . in

---

⁶⁹ '. . . le sage/De son loisir studieux/Doit faire un plus noble usage,/Et juste-
ment enchanté/De la belle antiquité,/Chercher dans son sein fertile/La solide
volupté,/Le vrai, l'honnete, et l'utile.' J.-B. Rousseau, 'A M. l'abbé Courtin', in
Œuvres, ed. Antoine de Latour (Paris: Garnier, 1869), p. 97.

⁷⁰ 'Peu de gens avant moy s'étoient avisez de donner des noms François à leurs
Héros. Et il est à craindre que quelques esprits Romanesques voyant un nom de
Marquis de Riberville, de Mirestan, de Franlieu, et d'autres, au lieu de celui d'un
Tiridate ou d'un Cléante, ne fassent d'abord le procez à mon Livre. Mais je
demande pardon à ces esprits délicats, si pour leur plaire je ne fais pas des Grecs ou
des Arabes, de ceux que je veux faire passer pour des François un peu galans.'
Chasles, *Histoires françoises galantes et comiques* (Amsterdam, 1710), Preface.

⁷¹ 'Les Clélie, les Cyrus, les Polexandre et tant d'autres Héros ou Héroïnes
chimériques. . . . Le vrai, et par conséquent l'utile, en sont bannis . . . ces Héros
doucereux, ces Héroïnes errantes, révoltent un esprit solide, et le rebutent.'
Prévost, *Pour et Contre*, II, No. 17 (1733), 47.

⁷² '. . . il n'y a personne qui ne voye qu'on ne doit point rechercher la vérité
dans ce récit, et qu'on doit se contenter d'y trouver quelque vraisemblance que
l'Auteur a tâché de rendre intéressante par la nouveauté.' Review of translation of
Robinson Crusoe, in *Journal des Sçavans*, October, 1720, pp. 387–88.

short, a young man at once wicked and virtuous, thinking good thoughts and acting evilly; likeable for his feelings, detestable for his actions. . . . I say nothing about the style of this work. There is neither jargon, nor affectation, and no sophistic reflections: it is nature herself that speaks. How pathetic a stiff, unnatural author appears in comparison! The author [of *Manon Lescaut*] does not run after witty language, or what people refer to as such. . . . Throughout he gives us merely descriptions and feelings, but true descriptions and natural feelings.'[73]

'[*Memoirs of a Gentleman* is] a book which has had as warm a reception in London as in Paris. . . .
'Whatever opinion one may have of this long story, it will be pleasing at least because of its veracity.'[74]

'Nothing is more opposed to true poetry than methodical reasoning, and a geometrical poet will always be a cold and insipid poet.'[75]

'Only eleven years ago this miracle took place in the kingdom of Peru. Ordinarily these things happen in the New World, either because they are more necessary there than elsewhere (since Christianity is not yet well established) or because one believes them more readily when they come from afar.'[76]

[73] 'Le Public a lu avec beaucoup de plaisir le dernier Volume des *Mémoires d'un Homme de qualité*, qui contient les Avantures du Chevalier Des Grieux et de Manon Lescot . . . enfin un jeune homme vicieux et vertueux tout ensemble, pensant bien et agissant mal ; aimable par ses sentimens, détestable par ses actions. . . . Je ne dis rien du stile de cet Ouvrage. Il n'y a ni jargon, ni affectation, ni réflexions sophistiques : c'est la nature même qui écrit. Qu'un Auteur empesé et fardé paroît pitoyable en comparaison ! Celui-ci ne court pas après l'esprit, ou plutôt après ce qu'on appelle ainsi. . . . Ce n'est partout que peintures et sentimens, mais des peintures vrayes et des sentimens naturels.' Prévost, *Pour et Contre*, III, No. 36 (1734), 137–39.
[74] '. . . un livre que Londres a reçu avec autant d'indulgence que Paris. . . .'
'Quelque jugement qu'on porte de cette longue Histoire, elle mérite de plaire à titre du moins de vérité.' *Ibid.*, V, No. 69 (1734), 203, 214.
[75] 'Rien n'est plus opposé à la vraye Poësie que le raisonnement méthodique, et un Poëte Géometre sera toujours un Poëte froid et insipide.' *Ibid.*, No. 31 (this passage not by Prévost).
[76] 'Il n'y a que onze ans que ce Miracle s'est fait au Royaume du Pérou. C'est ordinairement dans le Nouveau Monde qu'arrivent ces choses, soit parce qu'elles y sont plus nécessaires qu'ailleurs, à cause que le Christianisme n'y est pas encore bien établi, soit parce qu'on les croit plus aisément, quand elles viennent de loin.' Bayle, *Nouvelles de la République des Lettres*, October, 1684, Article 2.

'In these matters [saints' lives] the farther one is removed from the source, the more one knows. Father Ribadeneira, who has written the life of his contemporary, St Ignatius, confesses honestly that this founder of the Jesuits performed no miracles, and he even examines why not; but modern historians of the same saint are far better informed, for they report a great number of his miracles.'[77]

'Instead of having Descartes, Malebranche, Newton, Gassendi, Goedaert, Grew, Leeuwenhoek, and Swammerdam speak, [I shall attempt] increasingly and as far as possible, to substitute the appeal of beautiful nature and the love of truth, for the false wonders in the tales and novels which are re-appearing in a hundred new forms, in spite of the disrepute to which they were assigned by the good taste of the last century.'[78]

'Only in the country are we in our natural setting; in the country we are delightfully between isolation and sociability, as well as between rest and work, which we can alternate. It frees us from dependency, giving us the freedom without which we could not live happily. Here are found the paths which conceal us from the crowd and which allow us agreeably to follow the course of life. Custom, which is the plague of sensible people and which reigns sovereign in the cities, has so little power here that it is scarcely noticeable; and opinion, on which one depends when one depends on custom, also ceases to disturb us here. The happiness which we seek without

[77] 'En ces matières plus on est éloigné de la source, plus on en sçait. Le P. Ribadeneira qui a fait la vie de S. Ignace son Contemporain, avouë de bonne foi que ce Fondateur des Jésuites n'a point fait de Miracles, et il en cherche même les raisons, mais les Historiens modernes du même Saint sont incomparablement mieux instruits, car ils rapportent un grand nombre de ses miracles.' *Ibid.*, September, 1684, Article 2.

[78] 'Au lieu de faire parler Descartes, Malebranche, Newton, Gassendi, Goedaert, Grew, Leeuwenhoek et Swammerdam de plus en plus selon notre portée, à substituer le goût de la belle nature et l'amour du vrai, au faux merveilleux des fables et des romans qui se remontrent sous cent formes nouvelles, malgré le décri où le bon goût du dernier siècle les avoit fait tomber.' Pluche, *Le Spectacle de la nature*, Preface.

knowing what it consists of and which, therefore, we seek in vain, reveals itself here and offers itself to us.'[79]

'*Dorinda*: But pray, madam, how came the poets and philosophers, that laboured so much in hunting after pleasure, to place it at last in a country life?

'*Mrs Sullen*: Because they wanted money, child, to find out the pleasures of the town.'[80]

POLITICAL AND SOCIAL IDEAS

Political and social ideas associated with the broadening intellectual horizons which are the subject of this chapter bear principally on tolerance and equality – tolerance above all in a religious sense, equality both social and racial. Some of the excerpts given below will show a high degree of political sophistication or awareness; but the expressions of democratic or egalitarian sentiments motivated by personal feeling are no less impressive than those based on theory. The distinction is difficult to determine in many cases, such as Chasles's lament on the death of a sailor. The sentiment expressed there comes from personal feeling in the face of an event, not from any *a priori* theoretical position; yet one cannot resist the impression that the first led to the second – which would not be surprising, since it very much represents the historical process that led to the French Revolution. Rather inconsistently, we open this series of quotations with a sentence from the sixteenth-century writer Sébastien Châteillon (Castellio), because his statement, which moreover was well known in

---

[79] 'Je comprens que la Campagne seule nous met dans nôtre situation naturelle. Elle nous place agréablement entre la Retraite et la Societé, aussi bien qu'entre le Repos et le Travail, que nous y pouvons faire succeder l'un à l'autre; elle nous tire de la Dépendance et nous met en liberté, sans quoi nous ne saurions vivre heureux. Ici se trouvent les Sentiers qui nous dérobent à la Foule, et nous font faire agréablement le passage de la vie. La Coûtume, qui est le fléau des Gens sensés, et qui regne souverainement dans les Villes, conserve ici à peine des droits qui la fassent remarquer, et l'Opinion, dont on dépend dès que l'on dépend de la Coûtume, cesse de même de nous tourmenter ici. Le Bonheur que nous cherchons, sans sçavoir en quoi il consiste, et qu'à cause de cela nous cherchons en vain, se fait connoître ici et s'offre à nous.' Muralt, 'Lettre sur les Voyages', in *Lettres sur les Anglois et les François*, p. 283.

[80] George Farquhar, *Beau-Stratagem* (London: B. Lintott, 1707), II. i.

our period, seems a perfect definition of tolerance as it was conceived by liberal writers of the eighteenth century.

'If anyone disturbs the commonwealth by an assault under colour of religion, the magistrate may punish such an one not on the score of religion, but because he has done damage . . . like any other criminal.'[81]

'Those good men (so let me call them, those Followers of Mahomet) came one after the other, offering to serve me, and testifying the greatest Pity and Goodness of Heart. They generally called us Protestants their *Brothers in God*; and testified the utmost Regard to our Opinions. . . . Yet those are they whom Christians call Barbarous! Would to God that Christians would but imitate their Integrity and Virtue; the Wicked can never with Justice be called truly polite, nor the virtuous reproached with barbarity.'[82]

'[Robert Chasles is] fair-minded enough to give due credit to all nations and even to all faiths, except for the English and the Reformers, against whom he is sometimes a little harsh. As completely Roman Catholic as he was, he could not tolerate persecution: he wanted everyone to be allowed the freedom to follow the dictates of his conscience; and this fact alone no doubt will cause him to be respected by cultivated men.'[83]

[81] 'Si quelqu'un trouble la République en battant, ou frappant aucun sous couleur de religion, le bon Magistrat le peut punir, comme celui qui fait mal au corps et biens, comme les autres malfaiteurs, mais non pour sa religion.' Sébastien Châteillon, *Traité des hérétiques, à savoir, si on les doit persécuter* (Rouen [?]: Pierre Freneau, 1554), p. 4; English translation by Roland H. Bainton, *Concerning Heretics* (New York: Columbia University Press, 1935), p. 137.

[82] 'Ces bonnes gens donc, voyant que je serais embarrassé pour ne savoir à qui me fier, vinrent tous, les uns après les autres, me prier de me servir d'eux, me marquant des sentiments si pieux et me témoignant tant d'affection pour ceux de notre religion, qu'ils appelaient leurs frères en Dieu, que j'en fus touché jusqu'aux larmes. . . . Ce sont ces gens que les chrétiens nomment *barbares*, et qui, dans leur morale, le sont si peu, qu'ils font honte à ceux qui leur donnent ce nom.' Marteilhe, *Mémoires d'un Protestant*, pp. 255–56; English translation by Goldsmith, *Memoirs of a Protestant*, II, 9–10.

[83] '[Robert Chasles] assez désintéressé pour rendre le plus souvent justice à toutes les Nations, et même à toutes les Communions, si l'on en excepte les Anglois et les Réformez, contre lesquels il est quelquefois d'un peu trop mauvaise Humeur. Tout Catholique-Romain qu'il étoit, il ne pouvoit souffrir la Persécution: il vouloit qu'on laissât à chacun la Liberté de suivre les Lumières de sa Conscience;

'As for myself, who have followed these priests and studied their comportment in Canada, I am thoroughly persuaded that it is only commerce and the pleasure of the senses which lure them so far, and not at all the zeal of propagating the faith, nor the desire to draw sheep into the fold of the Good Shepherd . . . the same experience shows me that those priests who die a violent, but well-deserved, death in those primitive lands and who are always made into saints in Europe, are in reality only martyrs to their lust and avarice.'[84]

'Indeed, it is certain that the salvation of the soul of a mere individual is as important before God as that of a great Lord: both are equal before Him; it is a truth which no one can doubt.'[85]

'Negroes, Blacks and Taunies are a real Part of Mankind, for whom Christ hath shed his precious Blood, and are capable of Salvation, as well as White Men.'[86]

'He [the Christian] knows . . . that men do not exist to be waited upon, that it is a misconception born of pride to think that some men are born to cater to the indolence and luxury of others; he knows that servitude has been established in contravention of natural equality, and that it is inhuman to abuse our power, which has as its basis only the indigence of others. Filled with these thoughts, he does not merely treat his servants with strict fairness. . . . The less education they have

---

et ce seul Point le fera sans doute regarder avec estime par les Honnêtes-Gens.' Editor's Preface to Chasles, *Journal d'un voyage*.

[84] 'Pour moi, qui ai suivi ces Pères, et examiné leur conduite dans le Canada, je suis absolument persuadé, que ce n'est que le Commerce, et le plaisir des sens, qui les mène si loin; et nullement le zèle de la Propagation de la Foi, ni l'envie d'attirer les ouailles dans le bercail du bon Pasteur . . . la même expèrience me montre, que ceux de leurs Pères, qui meurent dans ces Païs Sauvages d'une mort violente, mais pourtant bien méritée, et dont ils font toujours des Saints en Europe, ne sont véritablement Martirs que de leur lubricité et de leur avarice.' Chasles, *ibid.*, I, 390–91.

[85] 'En effet, il est certain que le salut de l'âme d'un simple particulier est aussi précieux devant Dieu, que celui d'un gros Seigneur : tous deux sont égaux devant lui ; c'est une vérité dont qui que se soit ne doute.' *Ibid.*, III, 39.

[86] George Keith, *An Exhortation and Caution to Friends Concerning buying or keeping of Negroes* (New York, 1693), 6 pp.

had, the more readily he pardons them. . . . [They] have almost always lacked instruction and good examples.'[87]

'Iglou [my slave] offered me all of his clothing in order to protect me at least from the excessive coolness of the night air; but I persisted in refusing them, by a feeling of humanity. I could not see that my status as master should cause him to lose his status as a man, nor that it should deprive him, consequently, of the natural right of protection which was as essential for him as it was for me.'[88]

'One of our sailors died last night; and I have already said that one fell into the sea from the flagship this morning. They work and wear themselves out all day and night at the risk of their lives; they are poorly fed in comparison to workers on land; they are poorly cared for and sometimes even whipped! Are they less men than others? How much those who are born with wealth have to be thankful for! *Non fecit taliter omni nationi.* I now look upon poverty with more compassion than ever – though I can say that I have always looked upon it without scorn.'[89]

'At the beginning of the world, there were only two brothers,

[87] 'Il sçait . . . que les hommes ne sont point faits pour être servis, que c'est une erreur enfantée par l'orgueil, de penser qu'il y en ait de nés pour flatter l'indolence et la mollesse des autres; que la servitude est établie contre le plan de l'égalité naturelle, et qu'il est inhumain d'abuser d'un pouvoir qui n'a de fondement que l'indigence d'autrui. Rempli de ces idées, il ne se borne pas à la justice rigoureuse avec ses Domestiques. . . . Moins ils ont eu d'éducation, plus il leur pardonne. . . . [Ils] ont presque toûjours manqué d'instruction et de bons exemples.' Quoted from Anon., *Les Charmes de la Société du Chrétien* (Paris, 1730), in *Journal des Sçavans*, February, 1731, pp. 274–75.

[88] 'Iglou m'offrit tous ses habits pour me garantir du moins de l'excessive fraîcheur de la nuit; mais je m'obstinai à les refuser par un sentiment d'humanité. Je ne voyois point que ma qualité de maître lui fît perdre celle d'homme, ni qu'elle pût lui ôter par conséquent le droit naturel qu'il avoit à des secours qui lui étoient aussi nécessaires qu'à moi.' Prévost, *Cleveland*, liv. 4, in *Œuvres*, V, 48–49.

[89] 'Il est mort un de nos Matelots cette nuit : je l'ai déjà dit : il en est tombé un ce matin de l'Amiral à la Mer. Ils travaillent et fatiguent beaucoup nuit et jour, au hazard de leur vie; ils sont mal nouris, en comparaison de ce que les ouvriers mangent à terre; peu soignez, et avec cela quelquefois bien battus! Sont-ils moins hommes que les autres? Que ceux qui sont nez avec des biens de fortune ont de grâces à rendre à Dieu! *Non fecit taliter omni Nationi.* Je regarde à présent la pauvreté, avec bien plus de compassion que jamais; quoi que je puisse dire, que je l'ai toujours regardé sans mépris.' Chasles, *Journal d'un voyage*, II, 118.

of whom one was perhaps scurvy and the other mangy: I do not think they had any other comb than their own fingers. All of the earth belonged to them: however, they could not live in peace: Cain killed Abel. The human race is descended from them and suffers the effects of its beginnings.'[90]

'Being alighted [at Bern] we were accosted by the Secretary of State, who there expected our Arrival. He received us with all the Politeness and Humanity in his Power. He was obliged, however, to let us know his Dignity, for we would otherwise never guess it from his Appearance; neither his dress nor Equipage testifying any thing above the common Rank. In this Country the Governors only differ from the Governed by superior Talents, and not by superior Fortune.'[91]

This section closes with two quotations which illustrate a more conservative, traditional point of view (which existed, after all, especially among those in power and their spokesmen), but these scarcely alter the fact that French writers of this period, including those who were not primarily concerned with social and political questions, found themselves, by and large, drawn toward attitudes which we regard as those of the Enlightenment.

'Let us pour out our hearts for Louis's piety. Let us shout our acclamations to Heaven, and let us say to this new Constantine, to this new Theodosius . . . "You have strengthened the faith, you have exterminated the heretics [by the revocation of the Edict of Nantes]: it is the worthy work of your reign, it represents its essence. Because of you, heresy exists no longer: God alone could perform this miracle." '[92]

[90] 'Dès le commencement du Monde, ils n'étoient que deux Frères, peut-être l'un teigneux, et l'autre galleux: je ne croi pas qu'ils eussent d'autre peigne que leurs doits. Toute la Terre étoit à eux: ils ne purent pourtant pas vivre en paix: Caïn assoma Abel. Le genre humain descend d'eux, et se ressent de son origine.' *Ibid*, I, 386.
[91] 'Étant descendus, nous y trouvâmes le secrétaire d'Etat, qui nous souhaita la bienvenue d'une manière aussi tendre que si nous eussions été ses propres enfants. Il nous dit, qu'il était le secrétaire d'Etat. Il fit bien de nous le dire, car nous ne l'aurions jamais connu pour tel, ni à ses habits ni à son équipage; tant il y a peu de différence dans ce pays-là entre les bourgeois et les seigneurs.' Marteilhe, *Mémoires d'un Protestant*, p. 410; English translation by Goldsmith, *Memoirs of a Protestant*, II, 159.
[92] '. . . épanchons nos cœurs sur la piété de Louis. Poussons jusqu'au ciel nos

N

In March, 1724, the King of France issued the 'Black Code', an edict to guide administrators and colonists in Louisiana – 'for the administration of justice, government, and discipline, and the Negro slave trade, in Louisiana'. The provisions of the code included the following:

'First Article: Banish all Jews from the aforementioned land . . . as declared enemies of Christianity . . . to leave in three months . . . under threat of seizure of life and property.

'Second Article: All slaves . . . will be instructed in the Apostolic Roman Catholic religion and will be baptized.

'Third Article: We forbid the practice of any religion other than the Roman Catholic.

'Sixth Article: We forbid our white subjects of either sex to marry Negroes . . . and all vicars, priests, and missionaries are forbidden to marry them.'[93]

EMERGENCE OF BOURGEOIS VALUES

Scientific progress, which steadily gained in importance in the eighteenth century, naturally had the ideal of utility as a concomitant. It is easy to find reflections of this in every aspect of French literature, and a few examples will suffice. Of greater interest than these, probably, is the position of Pierre Bayle, who with all his advanced views, including a

---

acclamations, et disons à ce nouveau Constantin, à ce nouveau Théodose . . . "Vous avez affermi la foi, vous avez exterminé les hérétiques : c'est le digne ouvrage de votre règne, c'en est le propre caractère. Par vous l'hérésie n'est plus : Dieu seul a pu faire cette merveille." ' Jacques-Bénigne Bossuet, 'Oraison funèbre de Michel le Tellier', January 25, 1686, in *Oraisons funèbres* (Paris : Hachette, 1906), p. 453.

[93] 'Article Premier : Chasser du dit Pays tous les Juifs . . . comme ennemis déclarez du nom chrestien . . . sortir dans trois mois . . . à peine de confiscation de corps et de biens.

'Article II : Tous les esclaves . . . seront instruits dans la Religion Catholique, Apostolique et Romaine, et baptisez.

'Article III : Interdisons tous exercices d'autres Religions que la Catholique, Apostolique et Romaine.

'Article VI : Deffendons à nos sujets blancs de l'un et de l'autre sexe de contracter Mariage avec les Noirs . . . et à tous Curez, Prestres ou Missionnaires de les marier.' Le Code Noir, ou Edit du Roy servant de Règlement pour le Gouvernement et l'Administration de la Justice, Police, Discipline et le commerce des Esclaves Nègres dans la Louisiane. Donné à Versailles au mois de mars 1724.

proper respect for science, refused to let practical utility steal
any of the ground traditionally occupied by the creative arts,
philosophy, and science. In discussing science, Bayle distin-
guished sharply between the men who are responsible for new
concepts and ways of looking at the world and those who make
practical inventions and applications. The first group is clearly
the one to which he pays the greater homage. We include the
passage from Bayle (our last excerpt) even though it antedates
our period by a few years. The warning which it expressed
was, as we now know in retrospect, frequently forgotten in the
eighteenth century, as well as in the nineteenth and even the
twentieth.

Scientific progress and utility are part of a complex of
bourgeois values which can be seen emerging in our period.
Certainly, preoccupation with science and utility, with the
rights of women or of Indians, with trade, productivity,
individual freedom, and material comfort is not limited to
the eighteenth century or to middle-class society. Yet these
values are so clearly in evidence, and so concentrated, in the
early eighteenth century that they must be regarded as
characteristic of the period; and, since this was a time of
growing power and influence of the bourgeoisie, the association
is one that cannot easily be dismissed.

'In reality, arbitrary taxes force a merchant to hide his
money and a farmer to leave his land fallow; because, if the
one wished to carry on trade and the other to till his ground,
they would both be overwhelmed with taxes levied by powerful
people who need pay nothing or next to nothing.'[94]

'. . . the almost universally established custom of keeping
women out of business, they [the men] attribute to their
weakness and ignorance. But I saw an example among the
Abaquis which destroys that unjust accusation. There the
women, living freely and receiving the same education as
men, were as energetic and as wise as their husbands; rather

[94] 'En effet, la Taille arbitraire contraint un Marchand de cacher son argent, et
un Laboureur de laisser sa Terre en friche ; parce que si l'un vouloit faire Commerce,
et l'autre labourer, ils seroient tous deux accablez de Taille par les personnes puis-
santes, qui sont en possession de ne rien payer, ou peu de chose.' Le Pesant de
Bois-Guilbert, *Le Détail de la France* (n.p., 1695), p. 214.

conclusive proof that if they are less capable in most other countries of the world, it is the effect of the injustice and the tyranny of men, who . . . soften them and thus usurp an authority over them which should by rights be shared.'[95]

'Aristocratic women [in France], above all, scorn that bashfulness, that rigid modesty. It appears to them something petty and forced, suitable to bourgeois women; and to avoid that extreme, they reject modesty itself. . . . Even in love affairs, toward which they naturally gravitate, they lose their femininity: it is not to love that they yield – which we could pardon in that weak, tender sex, exposed by the customs of the land to the machinations of men experienced and hardened in these matters; they are won, rather, by lavishness and by notoriety. In no way does notoriety daunt them: as men are fearless in war, women are in love; they are not turned aside by dangers or by the examples of indiscretion that they have before their eyes. . . .'[96]

' "When we came to this land," I said to him with a voice as proud as his own, "we claimed all the rights of the inhabitants, and especially the two principal ones, which are freedom and equality. If we recognize an authority above us,

[95] '. . . l'usage presque généralement établi d'éloigner les femmes des affaires ; ils l'attribuent à leur foiblesse et à leur ignorance. Mais j'avois un example chez les Abaquis qui détruit cette injuste accusation. Les femmes y vivant sans contrainte, et n'y recevant point une autre éducation que celle des hommes, y étoient aussi vigoureuses et aussi prudentes que leurs maris ; preuves assez fortes, que si elles le sont moins dans la plupart des autres pays du monde, c'est par un effet de l'injustice et de la tyrannie des hommes qui . . . les amollissent, et qui usurpent ainsi sur elles une autorité qu'elles devroient partager avec eux.' Prévost, *Cleveland*, liv. 4, in *Œuvres*, V, 134–35.
[96] Les Femmes de qualité, sur tout, dédaignent cette Timidité, cette Pudeur scrupuleuse. Elle leur paroit quelque chose de petit et de contraint, qui sied bien à des Bourgeoises, et pour s'éloigner de cette extrémité, elles s'éloignent de la Modestie. . . . Dans les Intrigues . . . vers lesquelles elles se trouvent portées plus naturellement, elles sortent encore du Caractère de Femmes : ce n'est pas à la Tendresse qu'elles se rendent, ce qui pourroit enfin mériter quelque indulgence à ce Sexe foible et tendre, exposé par les Mœurs du Païs aux entreprises des Hommes hardis et aguerris dans ce métier ; on les gagne avec de la Dépense et du bruit. En tout sens le Bruit ne les rebute point : comme les Hommes sont intrépides à la Guerre, les Femmes le sont en Amour ; elles bravent les Dangers, et tous les exemples d'Indiscretion qu'elles ont devant les yeux. . . .' Muralt, *Lettres sur les Anglois et les François*, p. 228.

it is not that of an individual who has no function but to recite prayers in the church; it is that of the general assembly of the colony." '97

'The next day we sent our jailor to the minister and to the principal elders, in order to let them know that we recognized no other tribunal than that of the entire body of the colony, and in order to urge them to call a general meeting promptly.'98

'Since sovereign authority resided in the colony as a whole, all the sentences of the consistory could be abrogated in a moment. If, with . . . our rights, we were unfortunate enough to obtain nothing, I was resolved to be the first to have recourse to arms. . . .'99

'As for the laws, I did not think it necessary to establish a great number of them. Nature's sufficed, and the most important of them was already included in the order that I established in family life. Live in unity; show the same considerations of tenderness and patience to others that you would like others to show you: such was the only political law that I tried to have the Abaquis appreciate.'100

'The French, like all nationalities, have merit as far as their

97 'Lorsque nous sommes venus dans cette île, lui dis-je d'un ton aussi fier que le sien, nous avons prétendu y entrer dans tous les droits des habitants, et sur-tout dans les deux principaux, qui sont la liberté et l'égalité. Si nous y reconnoissons une autorité supérieure à nous, ce n'est pas celle d'un particulier, qui n'a point ici d'autre emploi que de réciter les prières à l'église, c'est uniquement celle de l'assemblée générale de la colonie.' Prévost, *Cleveland*, liv. 3, in *Œuvres*, IV, 367.
98 'Le lendemain nous envoyâmes notre geolier chez le ministre et chez les principaux vieillards, pour leur signifier que nous ne reconnoissions point d'autre tribunal que celui du corps entier de la colonie, et pour les prier d'en hâter la convocation.' *Ibid.*, p. 385.
99 'L'autorité souveraine résidant dans le corps de la colonie, toutes les sentences du consistoire pouvoient être abrogées en un moment. Si avec . . . la justice de nos droits, nous étions assez malheureux pour ne rien obtenir, j'étois résolu d'être le premier à recourir aux armes. . . .' *Ibid.*, p. 401.
100 'Pour ce qui regardoit les loix, je ne crus pas devoir en établir un grand nombre. Celles de la nature suffisoient, et leur plus importante partie se trouvoit déjà comprise dans l'ordre que je mettois dans les familles. Vivez dans l'union; ayez les uns pour les autres les mêmes égards de douceur et de patience que chacun souhaite qu'on ait pour lui-même : telle fut la seule loi politique que je tâchai de faire goûter aux Abaquis. . . .' *Ibid.*, liv. 4, in *Œuvres*, V, 137.

general character is concerned, and they are, perhaps of all nationalities, the most humane; they deserve the friendship of others. However, in their uniformity they do not dare yield to their own personal qualities, and most often they reflect only the national traits. We owe less to the English, who like us less; however, in some areas the English deserve our attention and esteem; and even if the general character of their nation were not very worth while – which no one would dare maintain – the English would be worthy of distinction for the number of special characteristics that they have and the original men among them. We also owe them esteem for giving us an example of people who dare use their reason and who know how to live with themselves; they are more manly and more free by this ability than by the freedom they have succeeded in guarding *vis-à-vis* their government, which is moderate. . . . The Frenchman . . . is much concerned about what they [others] think of him and he seeks to give them a good opinion of himself, as well as to make others satisfied with themselves; wherefore there is so much courtesy and flattery in their conversation.'[101]

'But because among these professions there is one that serves as a link for the others, everyone has come to take great pains to preserve it. . . . This profession which is most essential and useful to the happiness of men is that of the merchant, whom

101 'Les François, comme toutes les Nations, dans leur Caractère general ont leur Mérite, et sont peut-être de toutes les Nations la plus humaine : ils méritent l'Amitié des autres. Mais dans leur Uniformité, ils n'osent pas se livrer à des Caractères propres et particuliers, et, le plus souvent, ils n'ont que celui de la Nation. Nous devons moins aux Anglois qui nous aiment moins ; mais, par d'autres endroits, les Anglois méritent notre Attention et notre Estime et quand le Caractère general de leur Nation ne vaudroit pas son prix, ce que personne n'oseroit soutenir, les Anglois vaudroient par le nombre des Caractères particuliers, par les Hommes originaux qui se trouvent parmi eux. Nous leur devons aussi de l'Estime, en ce qu'ils nous donnent l'Exemple de gens qui osent se servir de leur Raison, et qui sçavent vivre chacun avec soi-même ; plus Hommes encore et plus libres par là, que par la Liberté qu'ils ont sçû conserver à l'égard du Gouvernement moderé qui subsiste chés eux. . . . Le François . . . compte pour beaucoup l'Opinion qu'ils ont de lui, et il cherche de leur en donner une bonne de soi, aussi bien que de rendre les autres contens d'eux-mêmes; de là viennent tant de Douceurs, tant de choses flateuses qu'il dit dans la Conversation.' Muralt, *Lettres sur les Anglois et les François*, p. 230.

people look down upon today because they are unaware of his importance.'[102]

'. . . if I were to rid this forest of stags and roebuck, would my fame be increased? The wild boar ravage the countryside and ruin the farmer and the vine-grower; it is against those wild beasts that we ought to wage war.'[103]

'What contribution can astronomy and algebra make to the prosperity of a state? I go further: what need is there of architecture and sculpture? Can men not live in luxury without residing in a palace? . . . It is not, therefore, by the light of public benefit that one should judge the merit of an author. . . . I emphasize again: if the usefulness of a man's occupation were the basis of our praise, the inventor of the plough would be more deserving of praise as a great genius than Archimedes, Aristotle, Galileo, and Descartes.'[104]

[102] 'Mais parce qu'entre ces Professions, il s'en trouve une qui est la liaison des autres, tout le monde a interest de veiller principalement à sa conservation. . . . Cette Profession si utile et si nécessaire au bonheur des hommes est celle de Négociant, qu'on laisse aujourd'hui dans le mépris, parce qu'on en ignore la valeur.' Le Pelletier, *Mémoires pour le rétablissement du commerce en France* (Rouen ?, 1701), pp. 4–5.

[103] '. . . quand j'aurois dépeuplé cette forêt de Cerfs et de Chevreuils, ma gloire seroit-elle augmentée? Les Sangliers ravagent nos Campagnes, et détruisent l'espoir du Laboureur et du Vigneron; c'est à ces bêtes féroces que nous devons faire la guerre.' Du Castre d'Auvigny, *Les Avantures d'Aristée et de Telasie* (2 vols; Paris, 1731), quoted in review in *Journal des Sçavans*, May, 1731, p. 97.

[104] 'De quoi sert pour la prospérité d'un Etat que l'on sache l'Astronomie, et l'Algèbre? Je dis bien plus : quel besoin a-t-on de l'Architecture, et de la Sculpture? Ne sçauroit-on vivre dans l'abondance si l'on n'est logé dans un Palais? . . . Ce n'est donc point par rapport à l'utilité publique qu'il faut juger si un Auteur mérite des louanges. . . . Je le dis encore un coup : si l'utilité qui vient des occupations d'un homme étoit la règle de nos éloges, celui qui a inventé la Charrüe mériteroit mieux la loüange de grand esprit, qu'Archimède, qu'Aristote, que Galilée, que M. Descartes, etc.' Bayle, *Nouvelles de la République des Lettres*, August, 1684, Article IV.

Conclusion

THE material presented in this book was not intended by the late Geoffroy Atkinson to simplify but rather to complicate our conception of the interval between two well-known periods of French literature. For a long time now it has been rather unsophisticated to try to see events in history or literature as consistent and clear; for as we ascend the ladder of knowledge, it is complexity and contradiction which increasingly invade our consciousness. For these Atkinson had high regard, and though he was not against the efforts of great thinkers, who have passed from ignorance to the top rungs of knowledge, to formulate historical or artistic laws, he considered those efforts intellectual exercises rather than paths to understanding. He himself was not interested.

He never believed in the neat generalizations that used to be taught to students, generalizations which – to cite a familiar case – led Gustave Lanson, in his history of French literature, to relegate authors who failed to conform to his patterns to a brief section at the end of each major discussion, where they were called *retardés* (behind the times) or *égarés* (lost ones). Even now, it is difficult for a writer whose orientation is (or was) very different from that of his contemporaries to be accepted as a spokesman for his age, so tied down are we to trends and patterns. Atkinson rejected both the patterns themselves and the idea that a grasp of an epoch in the past depends on perceiving them. Better, he said, to become immersed in the variety and richness of life of a people, a goal which he achieved with signal success for the two centuries stretching from 1550 to 1750, thanks to tireless reading and an unshakeable faith in the revelatory powers of every literary production. It was his hope that, by providing a taste of what writers of all sorts were saying, he might help his readers too toward a 'feel' for the age. The issue in his mind was not between the intellectual and the emotional; the understanding that he sought was total, and his design of a three-volume survey of the transition from Classicism to Enlightenment will,

I hope, have contributed to the complicating process which
for some years has flourished in eighteenth-century studies
and which is the first step towards totality.

How up-to-date Atkinson was in this respect, in spite of
being a senior scholar, appears pointedly in Lester G. Crocker's
excellent survey of eighteenth-century studies over the last
forty or fifty years.[1] Crocker criticizes various scholars in our
field for failing to get at the 'living reality' surrounding the
literature (p. 429); he further points out the debilitating
effect of regarding the material which one is studying as
'steps leading to what was *really* significant' (in the case of
Cassirer, other writers merely paved the way for Kant, Lessing,
and Herder) (p. 432). In both of these respects Atkinson was
in the van; he devoured everything – politics, economics,
technology, agriculture – though prudence obviously taught
him as a writer to use restraint; his aim was the living reality.
As for the literature of this period being preparatory – in
this case leading to the literature of the Enlightenment and
the Revolution – Atkinson was too emotional to be able so
to regard any body of writing.

Once immersed in it, he could not avoid the lures and
appeals of every kind – for was not this age filled with human
beings and their problems? Did not the stories of poor people
sleeping in the cold bring tears to one's eyes? Were not the
financial manipulations of John Law in the eighteenth century
as exciting as, let us say, those of Samuel Insull in the twentieth?
Atkinson's modern point of view in these matters was perhaps
especially remarkable because earlier in his career, like other
scholars, he studied specific and limited aspects of an age
(Crocker cites his study of the 'extraordinary voyage'), rather
than the totality.

This collection did not start from any ready-made positions;
it therefore inevitably clashes at various points with generally
accepted opinions. Thus, there is an old idea that the common
people had no place in eighteenth-century literature. This

---

[1] Lester G. Crocker, 'Recent Interpretations of the French Enlightenment',
Journal of World History (also known as *Cahiers d'hist. mondiale* and *Cuadernos*), VIII
(1964), 426–56. Though Crocker's emphasis is on the second half of the century,
much of what he says applies to the first half as well.

notion, which comes in part from a limited reading among the authors of the time and has had a kind of official sanction from the fact that Condorcet criticized Voltaire for disregarding the masses in his otherwise admirable historical works, is contradicted by passages in both this volume and the preceding. The relationship between love and benevolence, usually disregarded in the past, appears in these volumes as a close one – not interdependence, as a recent book on love would have it,[2] but free-and-easy coexistence. Apparently the mood, or frame of mind, created by, or associated with, one of these sentiments facilitates accommodation of the other. Atkinson was not concerned with proving this, but the writings of the time point that way.[3] Indulgence in realistic detail, especially in passages taken from novels, may have come as a surprise to some readers of this and the preceding volume. Its appearance side by side with the wildest emotionalism – not merely in the same period or in the same author, but in the same book (by Prévost, for example) – is a phenomenon which it is well to recognize, just as we now accept reason and sentimentality as intertwining parts of the same movement later in the century.

The role of the emotions in the literature of our period, as compared to their place in the previous age, has been discussed by many critics and historians, often with too strong a penchant for dramatic differences. There was, to be sure, a premium on restraint in the seventeenth century and on emotional outbursts in the eighteenth. But, as some of the passages quoted in this volume have shown, the wall is far from solid. Thus Trahard, the great expert in this field, wrote that, in the seventeenth century, '*la sensibilité, on en jouit, mais on se refuse à en faire étalage*', and on the other hand, that for writers like Prévost and Rousseau feeling was not enough: it had to be accompanied by awareness, study, and analysis.[4]

[2] Robert G. Hazo, *The Idea of Love* (New York: Praeger, 1967), Pt II, Ch. viii.

[3] Varga has come to much the same conclusion. See A. K. Varga, 'La Désagrégation de l'idéal classique dans le roman français de la première moitié du XVIIIᵉ siècle', *Studies on Voltaire and the Eighteenth Century*, XXVI (1963), 965–98, esp. p. 986 for this point.

[4] Pierre Trahard, *Les Maîtres de la sensibilité* (2 vols; Paris: Boivin, 1931–32), I, 14, 18–19.

204 *Prelude to the Enlightenment*

But Atkinson's reading led him to sprinkle considerable salt on such statements, in so far as they claimed to present clear distinctions between the two periods.

It has long been fashionable to repeat that the literature of the eighteenth century was essentially a literature of ideas, of propaganda, to such a degree that, in the words of one critic, 'it is well nigh impossible to point to a single novel or even a poem which was not written with a definite social purpose'.[5] Atkinson could point to many. But most of them are not known or read and have not been reprinted (are not worth being, let me add); but they were known and read in their time, and some awareness of their existence helps us construct a more balanced picture. The idea of an age in which every play, novel, and poem is 'written with a definite social purpose' seems frightening. Fortunately, this has never happened in history, surely not in the early eighteenth century.

Atkinson was greatly impressed by the bourgeois nature of the literature of this period and concluded, with the help of considerable data about writers, publishers, and public acclaim or failure, that audiences were much larger and more bourgeois in their make-up than in the heyday of the reign of Louis XIV. This conclusion is part of an interesting history regarding public taste in the seventeenth and eighteenth centuries. If my own undergraduate studies were at all representative, as I think they were, and if my memory serves me even half well, it used to be emphasized by historians of French literature that Louis XIV, eager to gain control of the country at the time of his accession, brought large numbers of nobles to his court, where they would be too removed from their lands and too much occupied with social functions to meddle with politics or administration. For the latter Louis preferred competent bourgeois who would pose no threat such as the Fronde had done in the middle of the seventeenth century. The picture that was painted for us was one in which power, emanating from the king, was exercised by bourgeois, who thus played a very important part in the government of the realm. The importance of the bourgeoisie and the reduced influence of the nobility were further demonstrated, I recall,

[5] F. C. Green, *Eighteenth Century France* (New York: F. Ungar, 1964), p. 70.

by the large number of bourgeois among the famous writers of the time.

There followed a period in which the age of Louis XIV was usually characterized as predominantly aristocratic, and that, I think, is what most students and recent graduates now believe. Here, it seems to me, is where Geoffroy Atkinson's thinking on this subject belongs. More recently, however, there has been a new emphasis (Auerbach has had something to do with it) on the importance of the bourgeoisie in the seventeenth century, including literature; this, if true, might call into question Atkinson's conviction that much of the growing sentimentality and realism was associated with a new and rapid growth in the number and the power of the bourgeoisie in the early eighteenth century. In truth, unless all the historians are wrong, the bourgeoisie did grow in number, power, and influence in the years we are discussing, so that Atkinson was right. On the other hand, Auerbach was probably right in showing that the *theatre* audiences in the period of 1660–90 were already made up mostly of bourgeois. There may be no contradiction, but only a need for refinement. Perhaps the growth of bourgeois influence did not show itself as much in the theatre, where it was already strong, as in the novel.[6] This is my speculation; it is to be expected that the influence of a rising social class would manifest itself unevenly, that is to say, in different degrees in different areas of political and cultural life. Surely it would be as wrong to deny the bourgeoisie its role in the literature of the early eighteenth century as it would be to exaggerate it, which is perhaps what Atkinson was a little guilty of. Research certainly remains to be done on this point in order to arrive at a proper evaluation.

As I said above, few scholars now believe in sharp distinctions and abrupt changes between the classic age and the Enlightenment, and 1715 does not loom as a very important date any more. Louis XIV had really been 'fading away' over a period of years before his physical demise, and attitudes

---

[6] Moreover, the novel, being a newer and less rigid genre than tragedy and comedy, was more susceptible to influence from outside. On this point see Varga, 'La Désagrégation de l'idéal classique'.

toward him and his regime probably reflected this. Thus the
glorification of the monarch through works of art like Versailles, accepted as normal in the 1660s, would have been out
of the question even some years before Louis XIV's death.[7]
Similarly, there was hardly any difference in the degree of
police censorship of the press as between the last two or three
decades of Louis' reign and the 1740s[8] – so that here too the
end of the reign in 1715 is of small importance, and we are
left with a sense of continuity, not fissure, between the seventeenth and eighteenth centuries, between the *ancien régime* and
the Enlightenment, and even between the *ancien régime* as a
whole and the Revolution. Surely if any dates are to be found
for dramatic turns in the fortunes of the kingdom, 1715 is not
going to be one of them.

In spite of all this, and without trying to find patterns, trends,
or compartments, I think that the period that we have sampled
had a character of its own, as probably any sizeable chunk of
history does when we become acquainted with it. This is
scarcely altered by the fact that almost everything in our
period can be found before or after, for, understandably,
differences in degree and intensity often constitute special
qualities. Perhaps the most striking and consistent note that
rings through – surely what Atkinson thought paramount on
the basis of his wide knowledge – is the growing importance
of sentiment in literature and thought, and probably in life
generally. Unashamed display of emotion, though not unknown
to men of the seventeenth century, undoubtedly penetrated
in our period to new segments of society and achieved a greater
respectability. A corollary of this was that personal happiness
became steadily more prominent as the basis of conduct and
the foundation of morality. This is very obvious in the case
of Prévost but is not confined to him, or even to the novelists.
Virtue, in an absolute or predetermined sense, was to a
considerable extent replaced by happiness as the focus of
men's interest – as we might expect in this pre-Enlightenment

---

[7] See J. A. Leith, *The Idea of Art as Propaganda in France, 1750–1799* (Toronto:
University of Toronto Press, 1965), p. 158 and *passim*.

[8] See Ira O. Wade, *The Clandestine Organization and Diffusion of Philosophic Ideas in
France from 1700 to 1750* (Princeton, N.J.: Princeton University Press, 1938).

era. Old-time religion, which, as Muralt once wrote, is handed
down from God to man, gave way to a religion which started
with man and rose to God. In the new religion duties were
determined by men's happiness, so that virtue and happiness
tended to become identified (or, as some would have it,
confused) with each other.[9]

I think that, with sentiment becoming the accepted basis
for ethics – as well as for taste, it should be added – some
thinkers understood how fragile the whole structure of society
could become. Sentiment is personal and individual and
hardly subject to discussion or objective determination; it
does not provide the sure, unwavering base which is the hall-
mark of the old religion; if what is good, right, or beautiful
depends on how each man or woman feels about it, society
can become chaotic. Montesquieu understood this long before
Irving Babbitt. Happiness and pleasure, useful because they
were readily understood and fairly measurable as far as any
particular individual was concerned, were a welcome antidote
to the teachings of Bossuet and the Jansenists. There is no
doubt about the magnitude and importance of the shift,
whether, as Peter Gay has maintained, the identification of
pleasure with virtue is straight Epicureanism, adopted by men
who received much of their inspiration from antiquity, or
a simple reaction against excessive zeal in the recent past.

Atkinson's own convictions made him susceptible to the
lures of the Montesquieus, Marivaux, and the dozens of
unknown writers whom he unearthed, whose religion had
particularly large doses of idealism and rationalism. I think
that Atkinson's special rapport with the eighteenth century lay
here. But in two other respects he felt almost as much at home
there. The first of these, which I have already referred to,
was his emotionalism. I believe that his study of eighteenth-
century texts offered him just the balance that he needed
between an unbridled expression of personal emotions and a
rational understanding of their place in the world of men.
The other appeal of this period for Atkinson, which in the

---

[9] Speaking of the novel in our period, Varga has written : 'Le problème qui se
pose est donc de concilier vertu et passion, de rendre la vertu plus souriante et la
passion moins noire.' Varga, 'La Désagrégation de l'idéal classique', p. 985.

last analysis made it his favourite period of French literature, was its unprecedented exploratory approach toward the world. Although some writers, led by Voltaire, had strong streaks of dogmatism, the period as a whole seemed to Atkinson (and seems to me, after dipping into it for many months, though only fractionally) dominated by curiosity and the open mind. The desire to travel and see,[10] the eagerness to probe the secrets of nature, of the world, and of society, the intellectual capacity of men of the time to grasp and interpret a huge quantity of data for which their training had little prepared them, and the zeal to use all this for the improvement of life – all this was a new adventure for mankind and a moving experience for a man who lived close to it, even if it was in the libraries of Europe in the middle of the twentieth century. Never, Atkinson felt, had humanity shown so much power, both spiritual and cerebral; never had it been so nearly itself; all the new intellectual movements of our period showed enormous faith in human nature and in the conquest of truth.

In part this was because of the steadily broadening base on which human nature was set. Professor Roger Mercier[11] has demonstrated, with decent respect for the gradual processes of history, that 'natural', both word and concept, underwent a profound development in roughly the period we have been considering. Whereas the word had meant, and responsible thinkers had been interested in, the innate qualities of a being or the common denominators of a class, an enlargement, or externalization, took place and the emphasis came to be put upon conformity to the general laws of the universe. Reasons for this development are not difficult to find, principally the discovery of general laws of the universe into which 'human nature', for example, could fit. This was scarcely possible without a large context; no matter how much thinkers have always tried to picture man as part of the whole and subject to the same laws as the rest, anything resembling a unification which poets like Lucretius dreamed of had to await both actual discoveries and new conceptualizations for its realization; and in that development our period was crucial.

[10] Cf. Montesquieu : '. . . voyager pour voir des mœurs et des façons différentes, et non pas pour les critiquer'. *Voyages*, ed. Pléiade, I, 624, quoted by Roger Mercier, *La Réhabilitation de la nature humaine (1700–1750)* (Villemomble [Seine]: Edition La Balance, 1960), p. 176.

[11] Mercier, *La Réhabilitation de la nature humaine*, p. 17 and *passim*.

Bibliography

Aïssé, Charlotte-Elisabeth, *Lettres de Mademoiselle Aïssé à Madame C—— depuis l'année 1726 jusqu'en 1733*. Paris: La Grange, 1787.

Alègre, d', *Les Aventures, ou mémoires de la vie de Henriette Sylvie de Molière*. Paris et Bruxelles: J. van Vlaenderen, 1707.

Anon., *Les Mémoires du Chevalier de T——*. The Hague: Pierre Gosse, 1738.

——, *Relation d'un voyage du pôle arctique au pôle antarctique*. Paris: G. Amaulry, 1723.

Argens, Jean-Baptiste du Boyer, Marquis d', *Mémoires, nouvelle édition d'après l'édition de 1735*. Paris: F. Buisson, 1807.

——, *La Philosophie du bon sens*, 2 vols. The Hague: P. Paupie, 1740.

——, *Le Solitaire philosophe, ou Mémoires de Mr le Marquis de Mirmon*. Amsterdam: Wetstein et Smith, 1739.

Atkinson, Geoffroy, *Les Nouveaux horizons de la Renaissance française*. Paris: Droz, 1935.

——, *Le Sentiment de la nature et le retour à la vie simple (1690–1740)* (Vol. LXVI of Société de Publications romanes et françaises). Geneva: Droz; and Paris: Librairie Minard, 1960.

——, *The Sentimental Revolution: French Writers of 1690 to 1740* (ed. A. C. Keller). Seattle: University of Washington Press, 1965.

Aubin, Penelope, *The Life of Madam de Beaumont, a French Lady who Lived in a Cave in Wales Above Fourteen Years Undiscovered*. London: E. Bell, J. Darby, and A. Bettesworth, 1721.

——, *The Noble Slaves; or, the Lives and Adventures of Two Lords and Two Ladies who were Shipwreck'd*. London: E. Bell, 1722.

Aulnoy, Marie Catherine Comtesse d', *Histoire d'Hypolite, Comte de Duglas*. New edn. Brussels: G. de Backer, 1713.

Auvigny, Jean du Castre d', *Mémoires de Madame de Barneveldt*, 2 vols. Paris: Gandouin et Giffart, 1732.

——, *Mémoires du Comte de Comminville*. Paris: Josse, 1735.

Barber, Elinor G., *The Bourgeoisie in Eighteenth-century France*. Princeton, N.J.: Princeton University Press, 1955.

Bayle, Pierre, *et al.*, *Nouvelles de la République des Lettres*, 40 vols. Amsterdam: H. Desbordes, 1685–1718.

Biron, C., *Curiositez de la Nature et de l'Art, aportées dans deux voyages des Indes.* . . . Paris: J. Moreau, 1703.

Blanchard, A., *Secours spirituels*. Paris: Pralard, 1722.

Bois-Guilbert, Le Pesant de, *Le Détail de la France*. N.p., 1965.

Bonneval, Claude-Alexandre, Comte de, *Mémoires du Comte de Bonneval, Officier-Général au service de Louis XIV* (1737), ed. Guyot Desherbiers, 2 vols. Paris: Capelle et Renand, 1806.

Bossuet, Jacques-Bénigne, *Oraisons funèbres*, ed. Alfred Rébelliau, Paris: Hachette, 1906.

Boursault, Edme, *Lettres à Babet et de Babet*. Paris, 1697.

O

Buvat, Jean, *Journal de la Régence, 1715-23*, ed. Emile Campardon, 2 vols. Paris: Plon, 1865.

Charlevoix, R.P. François-Xavier, *Histoire de l'Isle Espagnole ou de S. Domingue*, 2 vols. Paris: Hippolyte-Louis Guerin, 1730.

Chasles, Robert, *Histoires françoises galantes et comiques*. Amsterdam, 1710.
———, *Les Illustres Françoises* (1713), ed. Frédéric Deloffre, 2 vols. Paris: Société d'édition 'Les belles lettres', 1959.
———, *Journal d'un voyage fait aux Indes orientales par une escadre . . . commandée par Mr Du Quesne*, 3 vols. Rouen: J.-B. Machuel le Jeune, 1721.

Châteillon, Sébastien, *Traité des hérétiques, à savoir si on les doit persécuter*. Rouen (but probably Lyon): Pierre Freneau, 1554. English trans. by Roland H. Bainton, *Concerning Heretics*. New York: Columbia University Press, 1935.

Chaulieu, Guillaume Amfrye Abbé de, *Œuvres*, new edn, 2 vols. Paris: David; Prault fils; Durand; 1757.

Crocker, Lester G., 'Recent Interpretations of the French Enlightenment', *Journal of World History* (also known as *Cahiers d'hist. mondiale* and *Cuadernos*), VIII (1964), 426-56.

Defoe, Daniel, *The History of Colonel Jack* (1721), Vols V-VI of *The Shakespeare Head Edition of the Novels and Selected Writings of Daniel Defoe*. Oxford: Basil Blackwell, 1927.

Duclos, Charles Pinot, *Considérations sur les mœurs* (1750), ed. F. C. Green. Cambridge: Cambridge University Press, 1939.

Ducros, Louis, *French Society in the Eighteenth Century*, trans. W. de Geyer. London: G. Bell and Sons, 1926.

Farquhar, George, *Beau-Stratagem*. London: B. Lintott, 1707.

Ferrand, Anne [?], *Lettres d'amour d'une religieuse portugaise . . . enrichies et augmentées de plusieurs nouvelles lettres, fort tendres et passionnées de la Présidente F. à Mr. le Baron de B——* (1669). The Hague: A. DeHondt, 1701.

Fontenelle, Bernard Le Bovier de, *Nouveaux Dialogues des Morts* (1683), ed. Donald Schier. University of North Carolina Studies in Romance Languages and Literatures, No. 55. Chapel Hill: University of North Carolina Press, 1965.
———, *Histoire des oracles* (1686), ed. L. Maigron. Paris: Droz, 1934.

Gentlemen's Magazine, London: F. Jeffries, 1731-34; E. Cave, 1735-53.

Glantzby (pseud.), *Les Voyages de Glantzby . . . avec les Avantures surprenantes des rois Loriman et Osmundar, princes orientaux*, trad. de *l'original danois*. Amsterdam: Aux dépens de la Compagnie, 1730.

Green, F. C., *Eighteenth-Century France*. New York: F. Ungar, 1964.

Gresset, Jean-Baptiste-Louis, *Œuvres*, 3 vols. Paris: L. de Bure, 1826.

Guilleragues, Gabriel-Joseph de Lavergne, Seigneur de, *Lettres portugaises, Valentins et autres œuvres* (1669), ed. F. Deloffre and J. Rougeot. Paris: Garnier Frères, 1962.

Hazo, Robert G., *The Idea of Love*. New York: Praeger, 1967.

Hachard, Marie Madeleine, *Relation de Voyage des dames religieuses Ursulines de Rouen à la Nouvelle Orléans*. Rouen: Antoine le Prévost, 1728.

Huber, Marie, *Sentimens différens de quelques théologiens*. Rouen: Prévost, 1728.

Jesuit Relations and Allied Documents: Travels and Explorations of the Jesuit Missionaries in New France, 1610–1791 . . . *with English Translations and Notes*, ed. Reuben Gold Thwaites, 73 vols. Cleveland: Burrows Brothers Co., 1896–1901.

Journal des Sçavans, 1st series, 1665–1753. Amsterdam: Chez Pierre le Grand; chez les Janssons à Waesberge (and other publishers for brief periods).

Journal littéraire, 1713–22, 1729–35. The Hague: G. J. s'Gravesande, T. Johnson, P. Marchand, J. van Effen, *et al.*, 1713–22; G. J. s'Gravesande, P. Marchand, D. de Superville, Gosse, Neaulme, *et al.*, 1729–32; Swart et Van Duren, 1733–35.

Keith, George, *An Exhortation and Caution to Friends concerning Buying or Keeping Negroes*. New York: n.p., 1693.

L. C. D., *Les Femmes militaires, relation historique d'une isle nouvellement découverte.* Paris: Claude Simon et Pierre de Batz, 1735.

La Chaussée, Nivelle de, 'Mélanide', in *Répertoire général du théâtre français, Comédies en vers*, Vol. IX, Paris: Veuve Dabo, 1822.

Lacroix, Paul, *France in the Eighteenth Century: Its Institutions, Customs and Costumes* (1876). New York: F. Ungar, 1963.

Lafeyette, Mme Marie-Madeleine de, *La Princesse de Clèves*. London: J. M. Dent and Sons; Paris: Georges Crès et Cie; n.d.

Lahontan, Louis-Armand, Baron de, *Dialogues curieux entre l'auteur et un sauvage de bon sens qui a voyagé* . . . (1703), ed. G. Chinard. Baltimore: Johns Hopkins Press and Oxford University Press, 1931.

La Loubère, Simon de, *Du Royaume de Siam*, 2 vols. Amsterdam: A. Wolfgang, 1691.

Lambert, Abbé Claude-François, *La Nouvelle Marianne, ou les Mémoires de la Baronne de —— écrits par elle-même*. The Hague: P. de Hondt, 1740.

Lambert, Anne-Thérèse de Marguenat de Courcelles, Marquise de, 'Avis d'une mère à sa fille' (1726), in *Œuvres morales de la M^{ise} de Lambert*. Paris: Bibliothèque des Bibliophiles, 1883.

——, 'Réflexions sur les femmes' (1730), in *Œuvres morales*.

Lamy, R. P. Bernard, *Entretiens sur les sciences* (1694), ed. F. Girbal and P. Clair. Paris: Presses universitaires de France, 1966.

——, *Del'Art de Parler*. Paris: André Pralard, 1676.

Latouche, Jacques Ignace de, *Le Militaire en solitude, ou le philosophe chrétien, entretiens militaires, édifians et instructifs*, 2 vols. The Hague: P. de Hondt, 1736.

Laufer, Roger, *Style rococo, style des 'lumières'*. Paris: José Corti, 1963.

Le Brun, Antoine-Louis, *Odes galantes et bacchiques*. Paris: G. Cavelier fils, 1719.

——, *Les Pensées ingénieuses, ou les Epigrammes d'Owen, traduits en vers françois*. Paris and Brussels: Jean Léonard, 1710.

Leith, J. A., *The Idea of Art as Propaganda in France, 1750–1799*. Toronto: University of Toronto Press, 1965.

Le Noble, Eustache, *L'Ecole du monde*, 4 vols. Paris: Jouvenel, 1700.

Lesage, Alain-René, *Aventures du chevalier de Beauchêne* (1732), Vol. IV of *Œuvres de Lesage*, 12 vols. Paris: A. A. Renouard, 1821.

Marivaux, Pierre Carlet de Chamblain de, *Romans*. Paris: Gallimard-Pléiade, 1949.

——, *Le Spectateur françois* (1725), ed. Paul Bonnefon. Paris: Editions Bossard, 1921.

Marteilhe, Jean, *Mémoires d'un Protestant, condamné aux galères de France pour cause de Religion . . . depuis 1700 jusqu'en 1713*. Paris: Société des Ecoles du dimanche, 1865. English trans. by Oliver Goldsmith, *The Memoirs of a Protestant condemned to the Galleys of France*, 2 vols. London: J. M. Dent, 1895.

Méheust, Mme, *Les Mémoires du Chevalier de* ——. Paris: Dupuis, 1734.

Mercier, Roger, *La Réhabilitation de la nature humaine (1700–1750)*. Villemomble (Seine): Edition La Balance, 1960.

Misson, Maximilien, *Nouveau voyage d'Italie*, 3 vols. The Hague: H. van Bulderen, 1702.

——, *Les Voyages et Avantures de François Leguat*, 2 vols. London: David Mortier, 1708.

Montesquieu, Charles-Louis de Secondat, Baron de la Brède et de, *Voyages de Montesquieu*, published by Baron Albert de Montesquieu, 2 vols. Bordeaux: G. Gounouilhou, 1894–96.

Muralt, Béat-Louis de, *Lettres fanatiques*, 2 vols. London: Aux dépens de la Compagnie, 1739.

——, *Lettres sur les Anglois et les François et sur les voiages* (1725), ed. Charles Gould and Charles Oldham. Paris: Honoré Champion, 1933.

Pecquet, Antoine, *Pensées diverses sur l'homme*. Paris: Nyon fils, 1738.

Le Pelletier, *Memoirs pour le rétablissement du commerce en France*. Rouen (?), 1701

Peregrine (pseud.), *The Compleat Mendicant*. London: E. Harris, 1699.

Pluche, Abbé Noël-Antoine, *Le Spectacle de la nature* (1732–33), 9 vols. Paris: Frères Etienne, 1764.

Prévost, Abbé Antoine-François, *Le Doyen de Killerine*, Vols. VIII–X of *Œuvres choisies* (39 vols). Paris: Hôtel Serpente, 1783–85.

——, *Le Philosophe anglois, ou Histoire de Monsieur Cleveland, fils naturel de Cromwell, écrite par lui-mesme, et traduite de l'anglois* (1731), Vols. IV–VII of *Œuvres choisies*.

——, *Manon Lescaut*, in Vol. III of *Œuvres choisies*.

——, *Mémoires et aventures d'un homme de qualité qui s'est retiré du monde*, Vols. I–III of *Œuvres choisies*.

—— (with the collaboration of Abbé Desfontaines and Lefebvre de Saint-Marc in Vols. II, XVII, and XVIII), *Le Pour et Contre, ouvrage périodique d'un goût nouveau, par l'auteur des 'Mémoires d'un homme de qualité'*, 20 vols. Paris: Didot, 1733–40.

Pure, Michel de, *La Prétieuse* (1666), ed. E. Magne. Paris: Droz, 1938.

Raveneau de Lussan, Sieur de, *Journal du voyage fait à la mer du Sud, avec les Flibustiers de l'Amérique en 1684 et années suivantes*. Paris: J.-B.Coignard, 1690.

Rollin, Charles, *De la manière d'enseigner et d'étudier les belles-lettres, par rapport à l'esprit et au cœur*. Paris: Vve Estienne, 1740.

[Roquelaure, Gaston-Jean-Baptiste, duc de], *Roger Bontemps en belle humeur*.

Donnant aux tristes et aux affligés le moyen de chasser leurs ennuis, et aux joyeux le secret de vivre tousjours contents (1670), new edn, 2 vols. Cologne: Pierre Marteau, gendre d'Antoine l'Enclume, 1730.

Rousseau, Jean-Baptiste, *Correspondance de J.-B. Rousseau et de Brossette*, ed. P. Bonnefon, 2 vols. Paris: Société des textes français modernes, 1910–11.

———, *Œuvres*, ed. Antoine de Latour. Paris: Garnier, 1869.

Saint-Evremond, Charles de, *Œuvres*, 7 vols. London, 1725.

———, *Œuvres de Saint-Evremond*, ed. René Planhol, 3 vols. Paris: Cité des Livres, 1927.

Saint-Pierre, Castel de, *Ouvrajes de politique*, 16 vols. Rotterdam: J. D. Beman; Paris: Briasson, 1733–41.

Saint-Simon, Louis de Rouvroy, duc de, *Mémoires*, 41 vols. Paris: Hachette, 1878–1930.

Sévigné, Marie de Rabutin-Chantal, Marquise de, *Lettres*, 3 vols. Gallimard-Pléiade, 1954–57.

Tencin, Claudine-Alexandrine Guérin de, *Mémoires du Comte de Comminge* (1735), ed. Henri Potez. Paris: Sansot, 1908.

———, *Mémoires du Comte de Comminge; Le Siège de Calais* (1739). Paris: A. Quantin, 1885. (Pp. 69–147, *Mém. de Comminge*; pp. 148–337, *Siège de Cal.*)

Trahard, Pierre, *Les Maîtres de la sensibilité française au XVIIIᵉ siècle*, 2 vols. Paris: Boivin, 1931–32.

Vallange, de, *Nouveaux systèmes ou nouveaux plans de méthodes . . . pour parvenir en peu de tems et facilement à la connoissance des langues et des sciences, des arts et des exercices du corps*, 3 vols. Paris: Jombert et Lamesle, 1719–20.

———, *Les Sciences dévoilées*. Paris: Jombert et Gandouin, 1729.

Varga, A. K., 'La Désagrégation de l'idéal classique dans le roman français de la première moitié du XVIIIᵉ siècle', *Studies on Voltaire and the Eighteenth Century*, XXVI (1963), 965–98.

Vauban, Sébastien Le Prestre, Marquis de, *Lettres intimes (inédites), adressées au marquis de Puyzieulx (1699–1705)*, ed. Hyrvoix de Landosle. Paris: Bossard, 1924.

Wade, Ira O., *The Clandestine Organization and Diffusion of Philosophic Ideas in France from 1700 to 1750*. Princeton, N.J.: Princeton University Press, 1938.

Index